S0-BYW-207

Nolo's Pocket Guide to

California

L A W

by Attorney Lisa Guerin & Nolo Press Editors

NOLO   PRESS   BERKELEY

YOUR RESPONSIBILITY WHEN USING A SELF-HELP LAW BOOK

We've done our best to give you useful and accurate information in this book. But laws and procedures change frequently and are subject to differing interpretations. If you want legal advice backed by a guarantee, see a lawyer. If you use this book, it's your responsibility to make sure that the facts and general advice contained in it are applicable to your situation.

KEEPING UP-TO-DATE

To keep its books up-to-date, Nolo Press issues new printings and new editions periodically. New printings reflect minor legal changes and technical corrections. New editions contain major legal changes, major text additions or major reorganizations. To find out if a later printing or edition of any Nolo book is available, call Nolo Press at (510) 549-1976 or check the catalog in the *Nolo News*, our quarterly newspaper.

To stay current, follow the "Update" service in the *Nolo News*. You can get a two-year subscription to the paper free by sending us the registration card in the back of the book. In another effort to help you use Nolo's latest materials, we offer a 25% discount off the purchase of any new Nolo book if you turn in any earlier printing or edition. (See the "Recycle Offer" in the back of the book.)

PRINTING HISTORY

Second Edition	JANUARY 1994
Editors	MARY RANDOLPH, PATRICIA GIMA AND RALPH WARNER
Design	JACKIE MANCUSO
Proofreading	ELY NEWMAN
Index	JANE MEYEHOFER
Printing	DELTA LITHOGRAPH

Guerin, Lisa, 1964-
   Nolo's pocket guide to California law / by Lisa Guerin & Nolo
Press editors . -- 2nd CA ed.
    p. cm.
  Includes index.
  ISBN 0-87337-244-1 : $10.95
  1. Law--California--Popular works. I. Nolo Press. II. Title.
KFC81.G83 1994
349.794--dc20
[347.94]
                                     94-2696
                                         CIP

ACKNOWLEDGMENTS

This book represents the hard work of many people. I owe special thanks to:

All the editors at Nolo, who not only wrote much of this book, but also edited, kibbitzed, researched and nurtured me through the writing process.

My editors Jake Warner and Mary Randolph, who had the idea for the book. Thank you for your tireless efforts to take the lawyer out of my writing, and for having confidence in me.

Barbara Kate Repa, who began my career at Nolo with the most cryptic response to a resume I've ever received, and has continued to delight and amuse me at work.

Stephanie Harolde, for her skillful handling of a messy manuscript and her many helpful comments.

Jackie Mancuso, for her wonderful book and cover design.

Deanne Loonin of Bet Tzedek Legal Services, for her patient explanations of government benefits and other legal intricacies, and for sitting next to me on that first day of law school—I can't imagine what it would have been like otherwise.

And to Arthur, Jamie and Jesse, my three significant others.

ABOUT THE AUTHOR

Lisa Guerin graduated from Boalt Hall School of Law in 1991 and has worked on several other Nolo books. She is currently working as a staff attorney in the federal courts.

Contents

ABOUT THIS BOOK

As citizens, we are presumed to know the law. Ignorance—as many of us learn the hard way—is no excuse. But how do we learn about the laws that affect our dealings with neighbors, family members, landlords, employers or creditors? Most schools and lawyers' organizations make little effort to teach us even the basics.

Trying to read up on our own is often a frustrating experience. Most books about law are written for lawyers and stay tucked away on law library shelves. Even if we do manage to get our hands on them, we find they are filled with nearly impenetrable jargon.

This book is Nolo's attempt to gather key legal rules into a readable, affordable little book that fits in your pocket, desk drawer or your car's glove compartment. When you have questions about the state laws that affect Californians on a day-to-day basis, you'll have the information you need at your fingertips.

WHAT THE BOOK COVERS

We have covered the legal topics likely to affect most people in the ordinary course of their lives: consumers' rights, divorce, traffic tickets, real estate, adoption and so on. Obviously, no one book—especially one intended to fit in your pocket—can cover all points of California law. So we opted not to discuss criminal law (except traffic violations), and such specialized topics as environmental regulations or banking laws. We also included a few basic topics covered by federal law, such as Social Security and bankruptcy.

HOW THE BOOK IS ORGANIZED

To make it easy to find the information you need, we have grouped laws into broad categories: Relationships, Landlords and Tenants, Real Estate, Wills and Inheritance, and Consumers' Rights, for example. The Table of Contents lists them all.

At the beginning of each section, you will find a list of the topics covered there (they're arranged alphabetically), plus a list of related topics covered elsewhere in the book. You may need to look at several entries to find the information you need, especially if your question doesn't fit neatly into any one category. Check the index for keywords you're interested in.

ADDITIONAL RESOURCES

Each section of the book also contains a list of additional resources. These include the names of books, pamphlets and organizations that can give you more information about a particular subject free or at a reasonable cost. For example, under "Children," we list several books and groups that help adoptive parents. Because Nolo is by far the state's largest publisher of self-help law materials, inevitably some of our referrals are to other Nolo publications. But we have done our best to include all helpful legal materials we know of, whether or not we publish them.

KEEPING UP-TO-DATE

The law changes constantly as the state legislature passes new bills and courts hand down their rulings. We will publish new, revised editions of this book periodically, but it will never be perfectly current. It's always your responsibility to be sure a law is current before you rely on it. For updates four times a year, check the "Updates" section of the *Nolo News*, our quarterly newspaper. You can get a free two-year subscription by sending in the registration card at the back of this book.

LEGAL CITATIONS

The Pocket Guide summarizes most laws of general interest; there may be times, however, when you will want to go further and read the full text of a statute. For this reason, citations to California and federal statutes (and occasionally, crucial court cases) appear throughout the book. The section on "Looking Up the Law" at the front of the book explains how to use these citations to look up the law.

LOOKING UP THE LAW

Nolo's Pocket Guide to California Law not only summarizes many laws, but serves as a way to find the text of any law you want to read word-for-word. And once you find the law, you will probably also find with it references to articles and court cases that discuss the law.

This brief discussion tells you how to use a reference from this book to look up a state or federal statute or court decision.

FINDING A LAW LIBRARY

To look up state or federal statutes or court decisions, go to your county law library (usually in the county courthouse) or the library of a law school funded by the state, such as the University of California at Berkeley, Davis or Los Angeles, or Hastings College of the Law in San Francisco. Some, but not all, large public libraries also have collections of state or federal statutes; call before you go.

If it's a local (city or county) ordinance you're curious about, you can probably find it at the main branch of your local public library. Or call the city or county attorney's office and ask for a copy.

FINDING STATUTES

When you go to look up a statute, try to use what is called an "annotated" version of the statutes. Annotated statutes include not only the text of the statutes themselves, but also brief summaries of court cases that have discussed each statute. After you look up a statute, you may well want to read the cases listed, too, to see how courts have construed the language of the statute.

Federal statutes. Federal statutes are organized by subject in a set of books called the United States Code (U.S.C.), which is available in virtually every law library. If you know the statute's common name or its citation, you should be able to find it easily.

EXAMPLE: *You want to read some of the provisions of the Fair Credit Reporting Act, 15 U.S.C. § 1681 and following. You would look in Title 15 of the United States Code (the numbers are on the spine of the books) and find section 1681. The statute begins with section 1681 and covers many sections.*

California statutes. California's statutes, which fill many volumes, are organized into "codes." Each code covers a separate area of law, such as Education or Health & Safety. If you have a citation from this book, you'll be able to look up the statute easily.

EXAMPLE: *You want to look up the law that's cited as Veh. Code § 541. Checking the table of abbreviations in the front of the book, you see that you want the Vehicle Code (the spine of each volume has the name of a code printed on it). Once you have the volume that contains the Vehicle Code, just look for section 451.*

MAKING SURE YOU HAVE THE MOST RECENT VERSION OF THE STATUTE

Every year, the California legislature and Congress pass hundreds of new laws and change (amend) lots of existing ones. When you look up a statute, it's crucial that you get the most recent version.

To do that, always look for a pamphlet that is inserted in the back of the hardcover volume of statutes. It's called a "pocket part," and it contains any changes made to the statutes in the hardcover book since the hardcover was printed. Pocket parts are updated and replaced every year—it's much cheaper than producing a whole new hardcover volume every year.

Look up the statutes again in the pocket part. If there's no entry, that means the statute hasn't been changed as of the date the pocket part was printed. If there is an entry, it will show you what language in the statute has been changed.

To check for changes that are even more recent—made since the pocket part was printed—you can check something called the Advance Legislative Service. It's a series of paperback pamphlets that contain the very latest statutory changes.

FINDING CASES

If you want to look up a case (court decision) and have the citation (either from this book or from an annotated code), all you need to do is decipher those strange numbers and abbreviations.

Let's take a hypothetical citation:

Smith v. Jones, 175 Cal. App. 3d 88 (1984).

The names at the beginning are the names of the parties to the lawsuit. The date at the end is the year the case was decided.

The "Cal. App." means that the case was decided by a California Court of Appeal. So in the law library, you need to locate the volumes (there will be hundreds, all in a row) that contain decisions written by the California Courts of Appeal.

In fact, there are so many that the publisher has started numbering over again (from 1) several times. Each new set of numbered volumes is called a series. The case we're looking for is in the third series; that's what the "3d" means in the citation. So look for volume 175, third series (the numbers are on the spines of the books). The case begins on page 88.

MAKING SURE THE CASE IS STILL GOOD LAW

Judges don't go back and change the words of their earlier decisions, like legislatures amend old statutes, but cases can still be profoundly affected by later court decisions. For example, the California Supreme Court has the power to overrule a decision of a California Court of Appeal. If it does, the Court of Appeal's written decision no longer has any legal effect.

There are several ways to check to make sure a case you're relying on still represents valid law. The most common is to use a collection of books called *Shepard's*, which lets you compile a list of all later cases that mention the case you're interested in. Unfortunately, the *Shepard's* system is too complicated to explain here. If it's important to you, consult one of the legal research tools mentioned below.

MORE LEGAL RESEARCH

Legal research is a subject that can (and does) easily fill a whole book of its own. Here are some good resources if you want to delve further into the subject:

- For a thorough, how-to approach to finding answers to your legal questions, see *Legal Research: How To Find and Understand the Law*, by Stephen Elias and Susan Levinkind (Nolo Press).
- For an entertaining and informative video presentation of the basics of legal research, take a look at *Legal Research Made Easy: A Roadmap Through the Law Library*, by Professor Robert Berring of the University of California-Berkeley (Nolo Press/LegalStar).

ABBREVIATIONS USED
IN THIS BOOK

CALIFORNIA CODES

Bus. & Prof.	Business & Professions
Civ.	Civil
Civ. Proc.	Civil Procedure
Comm.	Commercial
Corp.	Corporations
Educ.	Education
Elect.	Elections
Fam.	Family
Fin.	Financial
Gov't.	Government
Harb. & Nav.	Harbors & Navigation
Ins.	Insurance
Lab.	Labor
Mil. & Vet.	Military & Veterans
Pen.	Penal
Pub. Res.	Public Resources
Rev. & Tax.	Revenue & Taxation
Unemp. Ins.	Unemployment Insurance
Veh.	Vehicle
Welf. & Inst.	Welfare & Institutions

FEDERAL LAWS

C.F.R.	Code of Federal Regulations
I.R.C.	Internal Revenue Code
U.S.C.	United States Code

CASES

Cal. App.	California Court of Appeal
Cal.	California Supreme Court
F.2d	United States Court of Appeal
U.S.	United States Supreme Court

CHILDREN

Although the law usually lets parents decide how to raise their children, in certain circumstances the state gets involved in the relationship between parents and their children. The law regulates some methods of having a child, such as artificial insemination and adoption, as well as what happens to children when parents divorce or die. Children whose parents are unable to care for them may be removed from their home and put in alternative living arrangements. The law also grants children rights in school, in the courtroom and at home.

TOPICS
> **ADOPTION**
> **AGE OF MAJORITY**
> **ARTIFICIAL INSEMINATION**
> **BIRTH CERTIFICATES**
> **CHILD ABUSE AND NEGLECT**
> **CHILD SUPPORT**
> **CHILDREN BORN TO UNMARRIED PARENTS**
> **CUSTODY**
> **EDUCATION**
> **EMANCIPATED MINORS**
> **FOSTER CARE**
> **GAY AND LESBIAN PARENTS**
> **GRANDPARENTS' RIGHTS**
> **GUARDIANSHIPS**
> **HOUSING DISCRIMINATION**
> **JUVENILE COURT**
> **PARENTAL KIDNAPPING AND CUSTODIAL INTERFERENCE**
> **PARENTAL LIABILITY FOR THEIR CHILDREN'S ACTS**
> **SAFETY**
> **STUDENTS AND TEACHERS**
> **VISITATION**

RELATED TOPICS
> **EMPLOYEES' RIGHTS**
>> Child Labor
>> Parental Leave
> **GOVERNMENT BENEFITS**
>> Aid to Families with Dependent Children
> **INHERITANCE AND WILLS**
>> Inheritance by Minor Children

ADDITIONAL RESOURCES

The Adoption Resource Book, by Lois Gilman (Harper), explains independent, interstate and foreign adoptions.

How To Change Your Name, by David Ventura Loeb and David Brown (Nolo Press), includes information on birth certificates.

The Guardianship Book, by Lisa Goldoftas and David Brown (Nolo Press), contains all forms and instructions necessary to become a child's guardian.

Law in the School (California Dept. of Justice), Department of General Services, Publications Office, P.O. Box 1015, North Highlands, CA 95660, (916) 574-2200, gives detailed information about the rights of students and teachers in California schools.

How To Adopt Your Stepchild in California, by Frank Zagone and Mary Randolph (Nolo Press), contains forms and instructions for adopting stepchildren.

California Marriage and Divorce Law, by Ralph Warner, Toni Ihara and Stephen Elias (Nolo Press), explains state laws about marriage, divorce and child custody and support.

Adopting in California, by Randall Hicks and Linda Nunez (Wordslinger Press), explains all types of adoption procedures in California.

North American Council on Adoptable Children, 1821 University Ave. West, Suite N-498, St. Paul, MN 55104-2803, (612) 644-3036, is a coalition of adoptive parent support groups, with referrals to local organizations

Families Adopting Children Everywhere (FACE) National Helpline, (410) 488-2656, provides referrals to local specialist groups and conducts training courses for adoptive parents.

Legal Services for Children, Inc., 1254 Market St., 3rd Floor, San Francisco, CA 94102, (415) 863-3762, gives information, referrals and legal assistance to minors.

National Center for Lesbian Rights, 1663 Mission St., 5th Floor, San Francisco, CA 94103, (415) 621-0674, provides legal information, referrals and assistance to lesbian and gay parents. Publishes *Lesbians Choosing Motherhood: Legal Issues in Donor Insemination,* by Maria Gil de Lamadrid.

International Vital Records Handbook, by Thomas Jay Kemp (Genealogical Publishing Co., Inc.), gives information on how to get a birth certificate from any country. Order forms are included.

California Divorce Helpline, (800) 359-7004, gives legal information about child support for $2.50 a minute, and can also run the DISSOMASTER program to determine child support payments for about $75.

ADOPTION

Adoption is a court procedure by which an adult legally becomes the parent of someone who is not his or her natural child. Adopting parents assume legal responsibility for the child, including the duty to provide support, and the child inherits from the adoptive parents as if they were her birth parents. The birth parents' legal relationship to the child is terminated, unless there is a legal contract allowing them to retain or share some rights.

Consent of the Birth Parents

The rights of the child's natural parents to be notified of or object to a proposed adoption depend on the degree to which they have been involved in parenting the child.

A man who has taken any of the following steps to claim the child as his own is presumed to be the child's father, and is entitled to notice of any adoption proceedings regarding the child:

- he is married to the mother when the child is born, or within 300 days of the child's birth,
- he attempted to marry the mother, but the marriage was not valid for some technical reason,
- he married the child's mother after the child's birth, although the marriage could later be annulled, and he has acknowledged paternity in writing, been willingly named on the birth certificate as father, or has paid child support under a written promise or court order, or
- while the child is a minor, he welcomes the child into his home and openly holds the child out to be his natural child. (Civ. Code §§ 7000-7021.)

If a man is presumed to be the father under these rules but does not have custody, the adoption cannot go through without his consent, unless he has abandoned the child by willingly failing to communicate with the child or pay for the child's support for one year. This same rule applies to mothers without custody, but a woman does not have to take any special steps to be presumed the mother.

A custodial parent's consent to the adoption is necessary, unless he or she has deserted the child or has been deprived of custody through a legal abandonment proceeding.

Types of Adoption

- **Stepparent adoption** occurs when a parent with custody of a child marries, and the new spouse adopts the child. Consent of the child's other parent may be necessary. The natural parent and new spouse must file a petition in Superior Court, after which a social worker will write an investigation report for the judge. If the report is favorable, the judge is likely to grant the adoption.
- **Agency adoption** occurs when a licensed public or private adoption agency places a child in the home of adopting parents. The agency will make sure that the birth parent's rights have been terminated before the placement. The adopting parents must file a petition, receive a visit from a social worker and be approved by a judge.

  These agencies are usually extremely selective, because they have long waiting lists of prospective parents. Agencies charge between $1,000 and $6,000 for placing young children and up to $10,000 for placing newborns.
- **County adoption** occurs when the county has custody of a child because the parents have abused, neglected or abandoned the child, or the child has been declared beyond the parents' control. These children are usually placed in foster homes while efforts are made to reunite the family; typically, parents must agree to attend parenting classes or counseling and must meet other conditions

imposed by the judge. If, after 18 months, the parents have not met the conditions for reunification, the judge terminates their parental rights and frees the child for adoption. These children are often adopted by their foster parents.

- **Independent adoption** (also called private adoption) occurs when birth parents consent to place a child directly with the adoptive parents, without any agency or county participation. Although it is illegal in California for adoptive parents to advertise that they are looking for a baby to adopt (Fam. Code § 8609), few other state laws regulate independent adoption. In some counties—such as Los Angeles—local law requires that the birth mother and adoptive parents meet in person. The adoptive parents may pay the medical, legal and other necessary living expenses of the birth mother. However, if the birth mother decides not to go through with the adoption, the adoptive parents are not entitled to get their money back.

   As in other kinds of adoption, the adoptive parents must file a petition in Superior Court, be investigated by a county social worker and be approved by a judge. The adoption becomes final about six months after the birth parents agree to give up their parental rights.

- **Intercountry adoptions.** Anyone who adopts a child through an intercountry adoption that is finalized in a foreign country must readopt the child in this state if the U.S. Immigration and Naturalization Service requires it. Any state resident may choose to readopt a child whose adoption was finalized in a foreign country. (Civ. Code § 226.69.)

AGE OF MAJORITY

Every state designates children as minors until they reach a certain age—the age of majority. In California, that age is 18. (Fam. Code § 6502.)

A minor may not give legally binding consent in many situations. (Fam. Code §§ 6700, 6701, 6920, 6921, 6925.) Specifically, a minor may not:

- enter into a contract
- buy or sell property, including real estate and stock
- get married without the written consent of parents or guardian and a judge
- sue or be sued in his or her own name
- compromise, settle or arbitrate a claim
- make or revoke a will, or
- inherit property outright—it must be supervised by an adult.

   However, a minor in California may:

- donate blood if he or she is at least 17 years old, or if he or she is at least 15 years old and has the written consent of parents or guardian (Civ. Code § 25.5)
- consent to his or her own hospital, medical or surgical care if he or she is legally married or on active duty in the armed services (Fam. Code §§ 7002, 7050), and
- consent to his or her own mental health treatment or counseling on an outpatient basis or participate in a decision to consent to residential shelter services if he or she is at least 12 years old and is determined to be sufficiently mature to consent to residential shelter services. (Fam. Code §§ 6920, 6921, 6924.)

ARTIFICIAL INSEMINATION

Artificial insemination (also called donor insemination) is a procedure by which a woman is impregnated by a means other than sexual intercourse. If the semen came from her husband (called homologous artificial insemination), the father is treated the same as any other father of a child conceived during the marriage.

If a woman is married, and the semen came from a man other than her husband (called artificial insemination by donor or heterologous artificial insemination), the husband is treated as if he were the natural father of the child only if he consented in writing to the insemination, and the insemination was performed under the supervision of a licensed physician. (Fam. Code § 7613.) He has all the rights and responsibilities of fatherhood, including the duty to support the child. (Pen. Code § 270.)

If an unmarried woman is inseminated under the supervision of a physician, the semen donor is not considered the father of the child. Donors who provide semen to licensed physicians for use in artificial insemination of a woman other than the donor's wife have no parental rights. (Fam. Code § 7613.) However, if a woman is inseminated without a physician's help and the donor asserts his fatherhood, he is entitled to full parental rights and responsibilities. (*Jhordan C. v. Mary K.*, 179 Cal. App. 3d 386 (1986).)

BIRTH CERTIFICATES

A birth certificate is a document used to officially record the birth of a child. Birth certificates give the child's name and sex, the names of the child's parents and when and where the birth took place. Birth certificates are usually completed by hospital personnel or the person delivering the baby.

How To Get a Copy of a Birth Certificate

The State Registrar of Vital Statistics, 304 S St., Box 730241, Sacramento, CA 95814-0241, (916) 445-2684, provides official copies of California birth certificates for about $12 and provides application forms to amend or get a new birth certificate for about $19. The county recorder in the county where the birth took place also provides copies of birth certificates, as does the health department in the county where the birth took place, if the birth was within the last two years.

Birth certificates for a foreign country or a state outside of California can be obtained from the bureau of vital statistics for that state or country.

Amendments to a Birth Certificate

Birth certificates may be amended in certain situations. The amendment is attached to the birth certificate and becomes an official part of the birth record. Amendments are allowed only to:

- **Reflect a court-ordered name change.** If you obtained a name change from any court in the United States or territory, you may add this name to your birth certificate. (Health & Safety Code § 10470.)
- **Add a parent's new name to a child's birth certificate.** If a parent's name is changed by usage or court order, an attachment may be added showing the parent's new name. The attachment indicates that the parent is "AKA" (also known as) and gives the new name.
- **Correct minor typographical errors or omissions on the original birth certificate.** Minor errors or missing information may be corrected by amendment. There is no charge for correcting errors to a birth certificate if the change is made within one year of a child's birth. (Health & Safety Code § 10400.)
  If the incorrect sex is listed and the birth was recent, a hospital official should complete an affidavit (sworn statement) indicating the error. This affidavit should be sent with the application to amend.
  If the wrong father was listed on the birth certificate, an attachment cannot be used to correct either the certificate or the child's last name, regardless of the explanation.

How To Get a New Birth Certificate

When a new birth certificate is issued, the old one is sealed, and no one can look at it without a special court order. A new California birth certificate is issued only in these circumstances:

- **Acknowledgment of paternity.** If a birth certificate omits a child's father, or the father is listed but the child's last name is different from the father's, a new birth certificate is available. (Health & Safety Code § 10455.) The mother and father acknowledging paternity both must sign statements under penalty of perjury confirming that they are the natural parents and requesting changes to the birth certificate. The child's name may also be changed to reflect the father's last name.

- **Judicial decree of paternity.** If a court in the United States finds that a man is the father of a child and issues an order stating this fact—often referred to as a "judicial decree of paternity" or "adjudication of paternity"—a new birth certificate may be issued. Information about the father may be included on the birth certificate, and the child's last name may be changed to that of the father. (Health & Safety Code § 10450.)

- **Adoption** (court order required). A new birth certificate may be issued for the child in the name of the new parents (including same-sex adoptive parents). (Health & Safety Code § 10430.) The court clerk (or agency, if the adoption was outside of California) must send notice of the adoption to the State Registrar of Vital Statistics within five days after the adoption is finalized.

- **Sex change operation** (court order required). People born in California who have undergone a surgical sex change operation may obtain a new birth certificate using their new name and sex. They must first go to court and obtain an order that affirms both the sex and new name. (Health & Safety Code §§ 10475-10479.)

- **Offensive racial description.** A new birth certificate will be issued if the original contains a derogatory, demeaning or colloquial racial description and the person prefers a different racial description. (Health & Safety Code § 10406.)

CHILD ABUSE AND NEGLECT

Child abuse is any physical injury inflicted on a child by other than accidental means, or the willful infliction of unjustifiable physical pain or mental suffering on a child. Child abuse may be sexual in nature: touching a child's genitals or other private parts for sexual gratification, masturbating in front of a child, or filming or photographing a child participating in actual or simulated sex acts. Child abuse is a felony, punishable by up to six years in state prison for a first offense. (Pen. Code §§ 273(a), 273(d), 11165.1, 11165.6.)

Child neglect is the mistreatment or negligent (unreasonably careless) treatment of a child by a person responsible for the child's welfare, in circumstances that threaten or cause harm to the child. Failure to provide adequate food, clothing, shelter, supervision or medical care (except in the case of treatment by spiritual means) all constitute neglect. Neglect is a misdemeanor, punishable by up to one year in the county jail, a fine of up to $2,000, or both. (Pen. Code §§ 270, 11165.2.)

When a report of suspected child abuse or neglect is made, Child Protective Services (a branch of the California Department of Social Services) should immediately assess the child's safety. A child in serious danger will be removed from the home at once. Then a case plan will be developed, with the ultimate goal of reuniting the family safely. In some cases, the state may require counseling or parenting classes. If the child cannot return home safely, the child will stay in foster care and eventually be freed for adoption. (Welf. & Inst. Code § 16500 and following.)

Reporting Requirements

Teachers, administrators, camp counselors, foster parents and others whose job responsibilities include direct supervision of children have a duty to report suspected child abuse or neglect to a police or sheriff's department, a county probation department or a county welfare department. These people must report their suspicions immediately by phone and submit a written report within 36 hours. Similarly, any commercial film or photographic print processor who sees a depiction of a child under 14 engaged in sexual acts must make a report, and include a copy of the material in question, to the local law enforcement agency. (Pen. Code § 11166.)

If upon further investigation, it appears that the person making the child abuse report was mistaken, that person cannot be held liable for the mistake as long as it was honest; this helps to encourage reporting. However, someone who makes what he or she knows or should know to be a false report of child abuse is liable for any damages caused by that report. (Pen. Code § 11172.)

Lawsuits for Sexual Abuse

Many people who suffered sexual abuse as children don't remember the abuse until much later in their lives. When these memories surface, some want to sue their abuser. Formerly, these lawsuits were barred by statutes of limitation, which prevent personal injury suits that aren't brought within a certain time following the injury. However, in California, lawsuits based on sexual abuse suffered as a child can be brought until the person reaches age 26, or until three years have passed since the person discovers or reasonably should have discovered that their injuries were related to childhood sexual abuse. If suit is brought after the person turns 26, his or her attorney and a doctor must file statements with the court asserting that they believe the lawsuit has merit. (Code of Civ. Proc. § 340.1.)

CHILD SUPPORT

Parents are legally obligated to support their children until the children turn 18. The obligation may continue until age 19 if the children are attending high school full time and aren't self-supporting. Parents may have to support a child over 19 if the child is disabled and can't support himself or herself.

The actual amount of support owed a child is most often set in court orders issued in divorce or paternity actions. Typically, the non-custodial or "absent" parent is required to contribute his or her share of the support directly to the custodial parent, who uses it for the benefit of the children.

How the Amount Is Determined

The amount of child support owed by a parent is based on the net monthly income of each parent, the amount of time each spends with the children, and the number of children to whom support is owed. The actual figure is determined using an algebraic formula that is so complex that virtually all judges rely on computers to get it right.

Generally, the higher a non-custodial parent's income, the higher his or her support payments will be, especially if the custodial parent's income is significantly lower. Similarly, the more time a non-custodial parent spends with the children, the greater the amount the court will presume he or she spends on the children—so a non-custodial parent with very little visitation will have higher payments than a parent with equal custody. When the final figure is determined, it is adjusted to account for the number of children receiving support.

The child support obligation produced by the formula will usually be increased by:

- child care costs incurred by the custodial spouse (at least one-half but possibly more if the non-custodial spouse's income allows), and
- anticipated or actual uninsured health care costs incurred by the children.

In addition, the judge may increase the obligation if:

- the non-custodial spouse has remarried or has a live-in partner, and the new spouse or partner contributes enough to their joint living expenses to free up additional money for support (but only in extraordinary circumstances and not more than 20% of the new spouse or partner's income)
- the custodial spouse has or anticipates having uninsured health care costs for herself
- the custodial spouse suffers "extreme financial hardship" because of uninsured catastrophic losses
- the custodial spouse is also supporting either natural or adopted children from other marriages or relationships
- a child needs to attend private school or has other special needs that require additional support, or
- the custodial spouse has transportation expenses made necessary by the non-custodial spouse's visits with the child.

In addition, judges have authority to change the formula amount if they conclude, in writing, that its application would be unjust or inappropriate due to special circumstances in the particular case.

Finally, judges may depart from amounts produced by the formula in five specific instances:

- the parents agree to something else
- sale of the family home is postponed by the court, and the mother and children are allowed to stay there for some specified period of time to protect the emotional condition of the children
- either parent has remarried or has a new nonmarital partner who is helping with basic living expenses (mentioned earlier)
- the father has such an extraordinarily high income that the amount produced by the formula is more than the children need
- the father is not contributing to the needs of the children at a level commensurate with the parents' custodial time.

USING THE DISSOMASTER COMPUTER PROGRAM TO DETERMINE SUPPORT

Although the current formula for setting child support can be found at Section 4053 of the Family Code, we don't recommend calculating the amount owed yourself.

Most judges and divorce lawyers use one of the two computer programs published specifically for this purpose. These are DISSOMASTER (Stephen Adams) and Support Tax (Rutter Group). In fact, virtually all judges require such a computer determination to be made before they will set child support. To get a printout showing the support level in your situation, you can:

- call the Divorce Help Line, (800) 359-7004, which will run the program for $75,
- contact a divorce typing service or a community-based women's center, some of which offer this service for as little as $10, or
- ask the judge to make a computer run for you in the courtroom when the child support hearing is held; many will do so.

Modifying Child Support

Once child support is established, it can always be modified if circumstances change. For example, in July 1992, a new child support law (Senate Bill 370) mandated higher child support payments, allowing parents with child support orders to ask the court to increase their support consistent with the new levels. Similarly, a non-custodial parent who is laid off or becomes disabled and suffers a radical decrease in income can ask the court to lower support payments, at least temporarily. Payments may be lowered if a new spouse of partner's income was taken into consideration in setting the level of support and the circumstances were not extraordinary or the amount of income so considered was more than 20% of the new spouse or partner's income. Also, when a child support obligation that was set prior to July 1, 1992 is being modified upwards, the paying spouse's obligation will be phased in.

Enforcement of Child Support

Child support obligations can be enforced in many different ways. Usually, the most effective technique is to use a court order that automatically deducts money from the non-custodial parent's paycheck. Other enforcement techniques a judge can order include:

- intercepting federal and state tax refunds and lottery winnings
- suspending professional and business licenses
- requiring the non-custodial parent to deposit a year's worth of child support payments in a special security fund
- requiring the non-custodial parent to post sufficient assets with the court to cover two years of support, if a payment is missed
- requiring an unemployed or underemployed parent to prove he or she is looking for a job and to undergo job training if necessary, and
- filing an action against a non-paying spouse for contempt of court.

The State Bar of California will not issue or renew the license of any active or inactive attorney who is identified as someone who has not complied with a child support order. Child support obligations cannot be discharged in bankruptcy; once owed, they are owed for life, until paid in full.

CHILDREN BORN TO UNMARRIED PARENTS

Children whose parents are not married, or were not married at the time of the children's birth, have all the same rights as children of married parents, including the right to support from both parents. (Fam. Code § 7602.) These children are also entitled to Social Security or private insurance benefits if a parent becomes disabled or dies, provided that parentage can be proven.

Parental Rights

Sometimes the rights of the parents depend on whether or not they have treated the child as their own and supported the child. For example, a parent cannot inherit from a child born out of wedlock unless the parent has acknowledged that the child is his or hers and contributed to the child's support.

Inheritance

For purposes of inheritance, a child of unmarried parents is treated the same as a child whose parents are married. For example, if a parent dies without leaving a will, all children of that parent inherit equally under the state law that determines inheritance. And if a parent's will leaves property to "my children," this group includes all children, whether born within or outside of marriage. (Probate Code § 6408 (d).)

CUSTODY

One of the most important issues when couples split up is who gets custody of their minor children. Custody has two components. Legal custody is the right and responsibility of child-rearing, including the right to make decisions affecting the child's life. Physical custody is providing a home for the child, and having actual physical control over the child.

How Custody Is Determined

A judge ultimately decides who gets custody, although if the parents reach a custody agreement between themselves, the judge is likely to follow it. The judge's decision must be based on the child's best interests. California no longer has a statutory preference for joint custody (shared legal or physical custody), but shared custody is still presumed to be in the child's best interests if the parents choose it. (Fam. Code §§ 3002-3004, 3006, 3007, 3024, 3025, 3080-3089.) Even if joint custody is not appropriate, the judge will try to assure the child of frequent and continuing contact with both parents. A parent who is more likely to allow contact with the other parent is usually favored in custody disputes.

The court cannot consider the race or sex of the parent in determining custody, nor can the court award custody based on which parent has more money. If the child is old enough to have a reasonable preference about custody, the court must consider this preference.

In those rare situations when neither parent is fit for custody and the judge decides that parental custody would be harmful to the child, the judge should award custody to a person with whom the child has been living in a stable or wholesome environment. If the child has not been living with such a person, the judge can award custody to any person found suitable and able to provide proper care and guidance for the child.

Disputing Custody

If parents can't agree about custody, mediation is mandatory. (Fam. Code §§ 3155-3160, 3162, 3170-3176.) The court-appointed mediator tries to help the parents agree on custody after explaining possible arrangements that might make sense for the family. Mediation sessions are confidential and private, and are often conducted without lawyers. If there is any history of domestic violence, the mediator may meet with the parents separately. (Fam. Code § 3177.) The mediator will also meet with the children, if they are old enough.

If the parents still can't agree, the mediator makes a recommendation to the judge, based on what the mediator thinks is best for the children. Absent a history of abuse of the child, the mediator will suggest an arrangement that lets the child stay in a familiar school and neighborhood, continue to see relatives and maintain the closest possible relationship with both parents. Courts almost always adopt mediators' recommendations.

Modifying Custody Orders

The court can change custody at any time. A parent must request the change and show that there has been a significant change in circumstances since the previous order, or show that his or her right to custody or visitation has been interfered with. As with the original custody decision, the question is referred to mediation before a judge rules on it.

Taxes and Child Custody

Each year, only one parent can claim the child as a dependent on his or her income tax return. This is true even if parents have joint custody. If the custodial parent will not claim the exemption, he or she must sign a declaration waiving her right. Each parent can deduct the amount spent on a child's medical expenses, regardless of who takes the dependent deduction.

Interstate and International Child Custody Disputes

To avoid conflicting custody decrees—which arise if one parent is awarded custody in one state and the other parent is awarded custody in a different state—every state has adopted the Uniform Child Custody Jurisdiction Act. (Fam. Code § 3403 and following.) The Act requires that a state meet at least one of the tests below before its courts make or modify a custody award. These tests are listed in order of preference. If there is a conflict between the courts of two states, the state meeting the higher test is usually given priority.

1. The state is the child's home state. This means that the child has resided in the state for a least six consecutive months, or was residing there for six consecutive months but is now absent because a parent is outside the state, and a parent or person acting as a parent continues to live in the state.

2. The child and at least one parent have significant connections with the state, and there is substantial evidence in the state regarding the child's care, protection, training and personal relationships.

3. The child is physically present in the state and either has been abandoned or is in danger of being abused or neglected if returned to the other parent.

4. No other state can meet one of the above three tests, or another state that can meet at least one of the tests has declined to make a custody award when provided an opportunity to do so.

The Act also applies in international disputes. California courts will enforce properly made custody decrees from other countries and will refuse to make a custody award when a child has been snatched and brought to the U.S. unless the child is in danger. In addition, a parent who lives in the U.S. and has a valid custody order can deliver a copy of the order to the U.S. State Department's Passport Issuance Office. The State Department will either revoke any passport already issued for the child or make sure that no passport is issued for the child if one is requested by someone other than the custodial parent.

The U.S. signed an international treaty, the 1988 Hague Convention on Civil Aspects of International Child Abduction, to help parents involved in international custody battles. Countries that sign the treaty pledge to help each other when evidence of international child abductions are bought to the government.

EDUCATION

California law requires every child between the ages of six and eighteen to attend school or continuation school full-time unless he or she has graduated from high school or passed a basic skills proficiency test given by the State Department of Education. (Educ. Code §§ 48200, 48400 and following.) This used to be interpreted as requiring public school attendance by every child, but that is no longer the case. Private school, tutoring and independent study programs can all fulfill the mandatory education requirement.

Home Schooling

In a home school, parents teach their own children at home instead of sending them to school. Home schools used to be a relatively rare phenomenon; today, however, it is estimated that over one million children are being educated at home by their parents. In California, no specific law allows or prohibits home schools.

Parents who wish to educate their children at home typically choose one of the following options:

- **Tutoring.** A parent can be the child's private tutor. The parent must be qualified to teach under the state's guidelines. State certification is also required.

- **Independent study program.** A parent can teach the child using the same curriculum used by the public schools in that county or using a curriculum provided by a private school. This requires consultation with the principals of local public or private schools, but no special skills are required of instructors.
- **Private school.** A parent can form a private school at home, following the guidelines in the Education Code. This requires following some administrative procedures, such as keeping attendance records. Teachers must be "competent," but no test or certification is required.

Parents who wish to start a home school should talk to the principal of their local public school and other parents who have taught their children at home.

EMANCIPATED MINORS

An emancipated minor is a person under age 18 who has achieved legal adult status by demonstrating freedom from parental control. To be emancipated, the minor must either:

- **Marry.** Parental consent is required; court approval may also be required, and the court may require premarital counseling. (Fam. Code §§ 200, 301, 302, 304.)
- **Join the armed services.** Parental consent or a court order is required. (Fam. Code § 7002)
- **Get a court emancipation order.** Minors who are at least 14 years old, live apart from their parents and lawfully support themselves financially can ask the court for a declaration of emancipation. (Fam. Code §§ 212, 7120-7123 and 7140.)

Emancipated minors have most of the same rights as adults, such as the rights to:

- consent to medical treatment
- enter into binding contracts
- buy and sell real estate
- sue and be sued
- make a will or trust
- decide where to live
- apply for welfare, and
- apply for a work permit. (Educ. Code § 49110.)

If the law establishes an age different than 18 for certain activities (such as 16 to get a driver's license and 21 to drink), an emancipated minor must reach that age before legally engaging in that activity.

FOSTER CARE

Foster parents are licensed by the state to provide a temporary home for children who are abused or neglected by their parents. Foster care can consist of an emergency placement for a few days, or it can last for years.

If a child is abused, neglected or beyond parental control, the Child Protective Services of the California Department of Social Services usually tries to have the child removed from the home, but also tries to work out a plan for eventual reunification. If the parents don't agree to an arrangement, they will have a formal hearing before a juvenile court judge. If the judge orders the children removed from the home, the judge will also establish reunification conditions, such as parenting classes or drug treatment.

Children taken away from their parents are usually put into foster homes, though some are placed in juvenile centers. If the parents do not fulfill the court's conditions for reunification within about 18 months, the judge may order permanent foster care or guardianship, which gives the parents the right to stay in touch with the children. The court may, however, order the natural parents' rights terminated, freeing the child to be adopted by the foster parents or someone else.

Foster Parents

Foster homes must be licensed by state-operated or private agencies. Prospective foster parents must fill out an application and be interviewed by an employee of the agency. Single people as well as married couples can get foster parents' licenses, and openly gay households have been licensed in some large cities.

Prospective foster parents will also be visited in their homes by an agency social worker. The applicants should have a separate room for the child, and if they're asking for a young child, must show that they have time to care for the child or have arranged for child care. The agency will also require a medical exam and fingerprints; ex-felons and ex-sex offenders aren't eligible for foster care licenses.

The state pays foster parents a monthly amount for support of each foster child. The amount varies among counties, but in many urban areas the range is $200 to $275 per month.

GAY AND LESBIAN PARENTS

No laws prevent lesbians and gay men from becoming parents. Courts and government agencies may, however, try to discourage gay men and lesbians from adopting children or getting custody of their children.

Adoption

A gay or lesbian couple is not legally barred from adopting a child simply because of their sexual orientation. Nothing in the adoption statutes or the regulations put out by the state Department of Social Services prevents adoptions by same-sex parents, and several courts have allowed same-sex couples to adopt children, both through public agencies and private facilities.

As a practical matter, however, it may be more difficult for gay and lesbian couples to adopt than for married couples. Public and private agencies, as well as individuals putting their children up for private adoption, may see gay men and lesbians as less desirable parents and refuse to place children with them.

Second-Parent Adoption

Courts used to rule that a child could not legally have two parents of the same sex, so if a woman wanted to adopt a child, the child's legal mother would have to give up her rights to the child. Recently, however, several courts have granted the lesbian partner of a biological mother the right to adopt the child as a second parent, thus giving both women parental rights. This also means that if the couple splits up and can't agree on who will care for the children, a court will determine custody, visitation and child support.

Although second-parent adoption is more common (and has been tested in the courts) among lesbians, there is no legal obstacle to prevent gay men from adopting as second parents.

Because a child can never have more than two parents, second-parent adoption is an option only when the child has only one legal parent beforehand. If the child's other natural parent is still living and his parental rights have not been terminated, second-parent adoption is impossible.

Custody

Courts are required to award custody based on the best interests of the child, in all circumstances. California courts have ruled that a parent's gay or lesbian sexual orientation does not, in itself, go against the child's best interests. However, this standard is subject to the discretion of the judge. Where one judge sees a healthy, loving home, another may see a den of iniquity, particularly if the other parent is willing to fan the judge's prejudices in order to get custody.

GRANDPARENTS' RIGHTS

Grandparents have no rights to see grandchildren as long as the grandchildren's parents are still married and living. If the child's parents divorce or die, or a child is placed for adoption, however, the child's grandparents have certain rights.

Visitation

If the parents of a minor child divorce, the grandparents may seek visitation rights in Superior Court. The court will grant visitation if it would be in the child's best interest. If the parents disagree about grandparent visitation rights, the issue will be referred to mediation. (Fam. Code §§ 200, 3101, 3155-3160, 3180-3183, 3100.)

If a parent of a minor child dies, the grandparents may seek visitation rights in Superior Court. The court will grant visitation if it would be in the child's best interest. (Fam. Code §§ 200, 3102.)

Notice of Adoption

Before a court terminates parental rights to free a child for adoption, the agency seeking the termination (usually a public or private agency facilitating the adoption) must notify the parents that termination of their parental rights is being sought, give them the date and time of the hearing, and specify that they have the right to attend. If an address of a parent is unknown, the agency must give the same notification to the grandparents, adult siblings, adult aunts and uncles, and adult first cousins of the child. (Fam. Code §§ 7881, 7882.)

GUARDIANSHIPS

A guardian is an adult who is appointed by a court to be responsible for a minor (someone under age 18). A guardian isn't necessary unless a child's parents die or are unable or unfit to care for the child. Often, parents who die have named a guardian in their wills, and that person is confirmed by the court.

There are three categories of guardians:

- **A guardian of the person** has legal custody of the child and responsibility for the child's well-being. He or she provides food, shelter and health care, and may handle relatively small financial matters, such as government benefits, on behalf of the child.
- **A guardian of the estate** manages the child's money, real estate or other assets, provides accounts to the court and obtains court approval before handling anything but simple day-to-day financial matters. He or she uses the child's money to provide support, maintenance and education for the child. (Probate Code § 2420.)
- **A guardian of the person and estate** takes care of both the child's personal needs and financial assets.

To become a guardian, an adult must file documents with a court, notify the child's living parents and close relatives and attend a court hearing. If no one objects, the court will probably appoint the person petitioning to be guardian.

A guardian serves until released from his or her duties by the court or the minor reaches age 18, is adopted, marries or achieves legal adult status by court emancipation order. (Fam. Code § 7002.)

Alternatives to Guardianships

A legal guardianship isn't desirable in every situation when an adult cares for a child. Other options include:

- **Informal arrangements.** If the child's parents are alive but temporarily unable to take care of their child (because, for example, they are on a trip), a friend or relative can take care of the child without a guardianship. Parents should write a letter authorizing the arrangement that the caretaker can show to school officials, doctors and so on.

- **Adoption.** This court-ordered measure permanently changes the adult-child relationship; the adopting adult legally becomes the parent of the child. The natural parent (if living) loses all parental rights and obligations.
- **Foster care.** Foster parents are licensed to care for children who have been removed from their biological parents' home by a court. If foster parents want to become legal guardians, the local social services agency and county counsel handle the guardianship. (Welf. & Inst. Code §§ 366.25, 366.26.)
- **Mental health conservatorship.** This proceeding is used rather than a guardianship for children who are severely disabled because of a mental disorder or chronic alcoholism. A conservator of the person, who takes care of the personal needs of the child, assures that the child is given individualized mental health treatment and services. (Welf. & Inst. Code §§ 5000-5550.) These children are often hospitalized in mental health treatment facilities.
- **Conservatorship of the person.** For minors who are married or divorced, a conservator of the person, rather than a guardian, must be appointed. This is merely a technical difference.

HOUSING DISCRIMINATION

California law contains several provisions designed to ensure that all persons, regardless of their age or family status, have access to housing.

Families With Children

It is illegal to discriminate against families with children in the sale, lease or rental of real estate. The only exception is housing units that qualify as senior housing, which can legally be reserved for senior citizens, their family members and their health care assistants. (Civ. Code §§ 51-51.4; *Marina Point Ltd. v. Wolfson*, 30 Cal. 3d 721, 180 Cal. Rptr. 496 (1982).)

Some landlords try to avoid renting to families with children by enforcing space-to-people ratios, ostensibly to prevent crowding. However, if these limits are used only to prevent people with children from renting, or if they are too restrictive (for example, one person per bedroom), they may constitute illegal discrimination.

Seniors

Housing that is specially designed to meet the physical and social needs of senior citizens and is occupied by people 62 years of age or older, or consists of at least 150 units (35, in non-metropolitan areas) and is occupied by people 55 years of age and older, can be reserved especially for senior citizens.

Housing constructed before February 8, 1982, that was not specially designed or remodelled to meet the housing needs of seniors can still be reserved for seniors, but only if it meets two additional requirements:

- It must be in an area where it is not practicable to require that senior housing be specially designed to meet the specific meeds of seniors, and
- The housing units are necessary to provide important housing opportunities for seniors.

Even housing that is legally designated for seniors only cannot be too restrictive in its policies. All senior housing units must allow live-in health care providers of any age, if necessary. And certain people (spouses and unmarried companions, persons 45 years of age or older living with the senior citizen, or persons who are primary sources of support to the senior citizen) must be allowed to reside with the senior citizen, as long as they have or expect to have an ownership interest in the housing unit—that is, the unit is jointly owned, or the other resident is named as the inheritor of the unit in the senior citizen's will. (Civ. Code § 51.3.)

JUVENILE COURT

Juvenile Court is a special branch of the criminal justice system designated to deal with problems affecting children. Matters handled in juvenile court include:

- **Child neglect.** Parents who do not provide their children with adequate food, shelter, clothing or other necessities are guilty of child neglect. The children may be removed from their parents' care and temporarily placed in a foster home. They may also be put up for adoption through a dependency action in Juvenile Court. (Welf. & Inst. Code § 300.)

- **Status offenses.** Minors who won't obey their parents but haven't committed a crime are considered "incorrigible." Typically, they have run away from home, are chronically truant from school or are endangering their own or another's health or morals. (Welf. & Inst. Code § 601.) Sometimes these children are allowed to remain in their homes under the supervision of a probation officer; probation conditions may include regular school attendance, drug or alcohol rehabilitation or family counseling. Children may also be removed from the home and put into foster care or a state institution for minors.

- **Criminal offenses.** Minors who commit crimes typically face charges in Juvenile Court. Often, these children are given probation or sent to reform institutions. If the child is 16 or over when the crime was committed, and the judge decides that juvenile court proceeding aren't appropriate (such as for particularly violent crimes or frequent offenders), the minor can be charged as an adult. This means that he or she can be sent to county jail or state prison if found guilty of serious offenses. (Welf. & Inst. Code § 602.)

A number of agencies often participate in Juvenile Court cases, including the Department of Social Services or the Probation Department.

PARENTAL KIDNAPPING AND CUSTODIAL INTERFERENCE

A parent can be prosecuted for kidnapping his or her child or otherwise interfering with the custody or visitation rights of the other parent. It doesn't matter which parent has legal custody; if a parent conceals his or her child with the intent of depriving the other parent of custody or visitation rights, he or she can be prosecuted for a crime.

If there is not yet a court order determining custody and visitation rights—for example, during divorce proceedings or before formal divorce—a parent who conceals his or her child from the other parent can also be prosecuted. However, the parent can defend his or her action by showing that the child was in immediate danger of physical injury or emotional harm. (Pen. Code § 277.)

The kidnapping parent can be prosecuted for a misdemeanor (imprisonment in a county jail for up to one year, a fine of $1,000 or both) or a felony (imprisonment in a state prison for up to three years, a fine of up to $10,000 or both.) The penalties are the same, regardless of who has custody or when the kidnapping occurs.

PARENTS' LIABILITY FOR THEIR CHILDREN'S ACTS

Normally, parents aren't financially liable for the negligent or clumsy acts of their children. Courts seem to recognize that parents cannot prevent most accidents and mishaps of childhood. However, parents may be liable if the injured person can show that the parent's failure to supervise the child directly caused the injury.

In addition, state statutes make parents liable for:

- Willful misconduct—including defacement of property with paint or a similar substance—up to $10,000 for each incident. (Civ. Code § 1714.1.) If the child injures someone, liability is limited to medical, dental and hospital expenses, up to $10,000.

- Any injury inflicted with a gun that a parent let the child have or left where she could get it, up to $30,000 for the death or injury of one person or his property, or $60,000 for the deaths of or injuries to more than one person. (Civ. Code § 1714.3.)

- Willful misconduct that results in injury to school employees or other pupils, damage to school property or damage to personal property belonging to school employees. Parents must pay up to $10,000 in damages. (Educ. Code § 48904.)

- Stealing merchandise from merchants, or books or materials from libraries. Parents are liable to a merchant or a library facility for damages of $50 to $500, plus the retail value of the merchandise or fair market value of the books or materials, plus costs. The total damages may not exceed $500. (Pen. Code § 490.5.)

Suing Children

People who have been harmed by the carelessness of a child usually sue the child's parents because the child has no money. However, children can be sued for their own careless acts in a personal injury lawsuit. A child will be held liable for his or her action only if the court determines that he or she was capable of knowing that it was wrong at the time. Also, the court will take the child's age into account when determining liability; what may be unreasonable carelessness for a teenager may be acceptable behavior for a preschooler.

SAFETY

Children are subject to several safety requirements not imposed on adults.

Bicycle Helmets for Children

All bicycle riders under the age of 18 must wear a bicycle helmet. (Veh. Code § 21204.)

Life Jackets for Children in Boats

Children under the age of six must wear a life jacket if they are on boat decks under 26 feet long. (Harb. & Nav. Code § 6583.)

Child Restraint Requirements for Motor Vehicles

See Traffic and Vehicle Laws, Seatbelt and Child Restraint Requirements.

STUDENTS AND TEACHERS

Schools are allowed a good measure of control over pupils, in order to provide a safe learning environment. In addition, teachers are responsible for ensuring the safety of students during school hours. However, students have certain rights.

Student Rights

Students don't leave all their constitutional rights at the school door. Getting their rights enforced, however, may be difficult.

- **Prayers and pledges.** Public schools must maintain the same separation of church and state that is required of the government. Prayers cannot be recited in public schools, even if students are not required to attend. Similarly, moments of silence intended for religious contemplation are prohibited.
  A student cannot be required to salute the flag or recite the pledge of allegiance, and cannot be disciplined for failure to do so.

- **Dress codes.** A school can impose a dress code to prevent disruption or ensure student safety. Some schools prohibit gang colors for this reason. However, if a school prohibits clothing bearing only certain slogans, this may violate the students' right to free speech.

- **Free speech.** Students' right to freedom of speech is guaranteed by Educ. Code § 48907. School officials cannot censor the content of student speech—in a

17

school paper, for example—unless the statements are obscene, libelous or slanderous, or will cause an immediate danger of inciting students to break the law or a school rule, or otherwise substantially disrupt the school's operations. Clearly, this gives schools considerable discretion in banning controversial speech.

In addition, school officials may regulate the time, place and manner of student statements, as long as the regulations are reasonable, apply equally to all kinds of speech, and are not intended merely to prohibit speech. For example, a school can require that students not distribute written materials during class, or that students give their speeches during recess.

- **Discrimination.** School officials cannot discriminate on the basis of a student's race, national origin, sex, religion or physical disability. However, this does not require that all students participate in the same activities. Some examples:

  — **Athletic teams.** Schools must provide equal opportunity for both boys and girls to participate in team sports and use athletic facilities, which includes parity of coaching pay, scheduling game and practice times, and locker rooms. This does not require schools to allow competition between boys and girls. If the school does not offer a girls' team in a non-contact sport, girls may try out for the boys' team, but schools are free to prohibit girls from trying out for boys' teams in contact sports.

  — **Bilingual education.** The U.S. Supreme Court has ruled that students who cannot benefit from instruction solely in English are entitled to transitional bilingual education, designed to increase their mastery of the English language. California law also requires bilingual education for students whose primary language is not English, as well as limited instruction in other subjects in the student's primary language until English fluency is achieved. (Educ. Code § 52160 and following.)

Discipline and Student Safety

School officials have a responsibility to provide safe schools. However, officials' efforts to discipline students are subject to these rules:

- **Corporal punishment** is prohibited in California. (Educ. Code § 49001.)
- **Suspension** is to be used only as a last resort. A student can be suspended from school only for the following behavior:
  — threatening or causing physical injury to another, or trying to injure another
  — possessing, selling or using a dangerous weapon
  — possessing, selling or using alcohol or drugs, or selling anything that the student claims is alcohol or drugs
  — possessing or selling drug paraphernalia
  — committing or attempting to commit robbery or extortion
  — smoking cigarettes or possessing or using other tobacco products
  — damaging or attempting to damage school or private property
  — habitually using profanity or engaging in obscene acts
  — disrupting school activities or deliberately defying school authorities, or
  — knowingly receiving stolen property. (Educ. Code § 48900.)

Only the first five of these behaviors are grounds for suspension following a first offense, unless the principal determines that the student poses a danger to other students or property, or will disrupt the educational process. In addition, suspension (and expulsion) can be imposed only for actions that are related to school activity or attendance, including events that happen at school, while the student is going to or coming from school, during recess or lunch periods, or during school-sponsored activities.

- **Expulsion** must be recommended by a school principal for any student who commits the following acts, unless the circumstances render expulsion inappropriate:
  - causing serious physical injury to another, except in self-defense
  - possessing a firearm, knife or explosive at school
  - selling a controlled substance, except for a first offense of selling less than an ounce of marijuana
  - robbery or extortion.

  In addition, a student can be expelled for committing any of the acts for which suspension would be appropriate, if other means of correction are not feasible or have failed, and if the presence of the student poses a danger to the safety of other students. Students are usually entitled to a hearing, where they can defend their actions. (Educ. Code §§ 48900, 48915.)

Searches, Detentions and Arrests

Schools cannot search or detain students freely; they must follow state rules destined to protect students' rights.

- **Searches.** A school official who wants to search a student must have a reasonable suspicion that the search will turn up evidence that the student has engaged in prohibited acts. This suspicion must be based on reasonably reliable facts, and must be directed specifically at the students involved; searching the whole student body is probably not allowed. In addition, the scope of the search must be reasonably related to the object of the search, and cannot be overly intrusive. Body cavity searches ("strip searches") are never allowed. (Educ. Code § 49050.)

- **Detentions and arrests.** School officials have the right to detain students for their safety, or to wait for police to arrive if there has been some wrongdoing. School officials can also make citizen's arrests, just as anyone else can, but they have no special power to arrest students.

  School officials can call in police to help them conduct searches, quell disturbances or provide other assistance. School officials are required to notify police if a student:

- menaces or attacks a school employee
- commits an assault with a deadly weapon
- possesses a weapon at school, or
- possesses or sells a controlled substance at school.

  Police can enter school grounds at any time to perform their duties. They do not have to be invited by school officials, nor can the school prevent the police from coming on campus.

Teacher Liability

The state constitution guarantees all students the right to safe schools, and teachers have a duty to use reasonable care to protect students from reasonably foreseeable injuries. This doesn't mean that a teacher must constantly supervise students or prevent all but the safest activities. Teachers must act reasonably to protect students, in light of the students' ages, how dangerous the activity is, the skill level of the students, the number of other supervisors and so on. If a teacher fails to fulfill this duty, and a student is injured as a result, the teacher and the school district may be liable for the injury.

VISITATION

When one parent is awarded physical custody of a child, the other parent is usually given the right to visit the child, unless visitation would not be in the child's best interests. (Fam. Code § 3100.) Courts want both parents to have as much contact with their children as possible and sometimes award custody to the parent more likely to allow the other frequent contact with the child.

Visitation Disputes

Mediation is mandatory whenever custody or visitation are disputed. (Fam. Code §§ 3155-3160, 3162, 3170-3176.) (For a discussion of the mediation process, see "Custody.")

Modifying Visitation Orders

The court can change visitation rights at any time. A parent must request the change and show that there has been a significant change in circumstances since the previous visitation order, or show that his or her visitation rights have been frustrated by the custodial parent. A parent whose visitation rights have been violated by the other parent may also be entitled to payment from the custodial parent, to make up for time lost with his or her children. As with original visitation decisions, the question is referred to mediation before a judge rules on it.

Limited, Supervised and Denied Visitation

Normally, a judge denies visitation only if a parent has a history of dangerous or illicit conduct, such as drug or alcohol abuse, prostitution or domestic violence. Instead of denying visitation altogether, the court may order supervised visitation, which requires that an adult acceptable to the court be present when the dangerous parent sees the child. A court may not order unsupervised visitation to a parent convicted of abusing the child, unless the court finds no significant risk to the child. (Fam. Code § 3044.) But even if a parent is obviously unfit to take care of children over a long period, courts usually try to allow some limited contact.

Religious differences between parents are not ordinarily a sufficient reason to deny or limit visitation, unless the tension created is clearly harmful to the child.

Visitation and Child Support

A parent cannot refuse to pay child support even if the custodial parent interferes with his or her visitation rights. The parent must continue to make the payments regardless of the custodial parent's behavior. (Fam. Code §§ 3556, 3028.) However, if a custodial parent deliberately conceals a child from the non-custodial parent, and then many years later reveals the child's location and tries to collect the child support unpaid all those years, a court may agree that the non-custodial parent need not pay.

CITIZENS' RIGHTS

State and federal laws try to make the government accountable to citizens, by guaranteeing that all adults can vote on public officials and ballot measures and can attend the meetings of their elected officials, except in a few narrowly defined circumstances. This section discusses citizenship and the basic rights and responsibilities it confers.

TOPICS

RELATED TOPICS

ADDITIONAL RESOURCES

How To Get a Green Card, by Loida Lewis with Len T. Madlansacay (Nolo Press), gives easy-to-grasp information on how to get a green card.

CALIFORNIA CITIZENSHIP AND RESIDENCY
You are a California citizen if:

- you were born in California and reside in the state, unless your parents were not citizens of the United States, or
- you were born out of state, but are a U.S. citizen and California resident.
(Gov't. Code § 241.)

Residency
Your residence is the state in which you live when not called elsewhere for work or some other temporary purpose. The state statute quaintly defines it as the place where "a person returns in seasons of repose." You can be a resident of only one state at a time. You must not only live there, but also intend for that state to be your residence. (Gov't. Code § 244.)

Many state benefits, such as most welfare payments, are conditioned on California residency. In addition, residents may receive other benefits, such as lower tuition at state universities. To receive these services, you must not only be a resident, but also be able to prove your residency.

PROVING CALIFORNIA RESIDENCY

To prove you are a California resident, take the following steps:
- Register to vote in California.
- Get a California driver's license and California license plates for your car.
- Establish a permanent home mailing address in California.
- Open bank accounts, take out memberships and get a local library card or any other tangible evidence that you live in the state and intend to stay here.

IMMIGRATING TO THE UNITED STATES
There are two ways that a non-citizen can live in the United States legally: get a green card, which gives permanent resident status, or get a visa, which allows a limited stay in the U.S. for a specified purpose, such as doing business, attending school or traveling.

Green Cards
A green card—more formally known as an Alien Registration Receipt Card—is a means of identifying yourself as a permanent legal resident. It gives you the right to work and live in the U.S.

Only people who fit into one of the categories of eligible people established by the Immigration and Naturalization Service (INS) can get a green card. Most of these categories are limited by quotas, which restrict both the number of people that can be admitted in any one category, and the number of people that can be admitted from any given country.

Generally, the categories of people who are eligible for green cards include:
- family members of U.S. citizens and permanent residents
- those who have been offered jobs in the U.S. for which they are qualified
- those who invest large amounts of capital in U.S. companies

- people who have been granted refuge or asylum in the U.S.
- a number of specially recognized immigrants—such as religious workers, former employees of the Panama Canal Zone, and former employees of the U.S. consulate in Hong Kong.

There are numerous technical requirements for each category, and restrictions on who qualifies as, for example, a relative or an investor. (8 U.S.C. § 1151.)

Non-Immigrant Visas

A non-immigrant visa gives its holder the right to stay temporarily in the United States to pursue a specific activity. The visa authorizes only that activity—so, for example, a student visa authorizes studying at a university, but does not authorize full-time employment. Non-immigrant visas may be valid for varying lengths of time, depending on the purpose for which they are issued.

Among the non-immigrant visa categories are:
- ambassadors, diplomats and representatives of foreign governments
- business visitors
- tourists
- students
- registered nurses
- fiancés and fiancées of U.S. citizens who are coming to America to get married
- artists, entertainers and athletes coming to the U.S. to perform, and
- religious workers. (8 U.S.C. § 1184.)

LOCAL GOVERNMENT MEETINGS

Most local governments in California are required by law to hold open meetings, except under very limited circumstances. (Gov't. Code § 54950 and following.) An open meeting means that any member of the public can attend, and there is an opportunity for public comment on specific issues before or during the time the agency is taking action on those issues. However, the agency can limit overall speaking time and the time allotted for each speaker.

People who wish to attend cannot be forced to do anything—such as identify themselves or sign something—as a condition of attending the meeting. Open meetings can be tape-recorded by members of the public, unless taping would be disruptive.

What Meetings Must Be Open

All meetings of the legislative body of a local agency—such as a county board of supervisors, city or town council, school board or municipal corporation board of directors—must be open and public, unless an exception applies.

Notice and Agendas

If the meeting is one that is regularly scheduled, the legislative body must publicly post an agenda for the meeting at least 72 hours before it is to be held. Items not on the agenda can be discussed only if an emergency arises, if the need to discuss the item arose after the agenda was posted, or if the item was continued from a prior meeting held not more than five days before. For special meetings (that is, meetings that are not regularly scheduled), a notice must be posted at least 24 hours in advance and in a location that is freely accessible to the public, stating the time and place of the meeting and the specific business to be discussed.

Emergency meetings can be called to deal with threatened or actual disruption of public facilities, such as work stoppages or disasters. Although no notice to the public is required, the legislative body must make an effort to notify local newspapers that have requested mailed notice of meetings.

People who file a written request are entitled to receive mailed notice of every regular meeting and of every special meeting that is called more than one week in advance.

What Meetings Can Be Closed to the Public
Legislative bodies can hold closed sessions for the following reasons:
- To determine whether or not a person with a criminal record who is applying to have a license renewed is sufficiently rehabilitated to be granted the renewal.
- To meet with a negotiator before the purchase, sale or lease of real property, regarding the price and terms of payment for the property.
- To confer with or receive advice from legal counsel regarding pending lawsuits, if an open session would be harmful.
- To consider hiring, evaluation, complaints about or firing of a public employee, or to discuss the security of public facilities.
- To discuss employee compensation and benefits.

Violations of the Law
If any legislative body holds a closed meeting that should have been open, all of its members who knew that the meeting should have been open are guilty of a misdemeanor—a minor criminal offense punishable by a fine or short sentence in county jail. In addition, any person can sue for an injunction or declaration requiring meetings to be open in the future.

Any person can sue to invalidate an action taken during an improperly closed meeting. First, the person must ask the legislative body to cure its action (by rescinding the decision and holding an open meeting) within 30 days of the violation. If an additional 30 days go by without legislative action, a lawsuit can be brought within 15 days. However, the results of the closed meeting will not be invalidated if any of the following is true:
- the legislative body substantially complied with these rules, although there was a technical violation
- the decision regarded the sale or issuance of notes, bonds or debts
- the decision gave rise to a contractual agreement, and the other party to the agreement relied on the decision
- the decision involved tax collection.

If the lawsuit is successful, the legislative body must pay attorney fees and court costs.

UNITED STATES CITIZENSHIP
There are several ways to become a U.S. citizen. If you were born in the U.S., you are automatically a citizen, as long as *one* of your parents was in this country legally, either as a citizen or as a legal resident. Children of U.S. citizens are automatically U.S. citizens, even if they were born in a foreign country and have never been to the U.S. This means that if one of your grandparents was a U.S. citizen, so is your parent, and so are you. However, if none of your grandparents or parents was a United States citizen, you must become a citizen through naturalization.

Naturalization
Naturalization is a process by which immigrants can become U.S. citizens. You must meet six requirements to be naturalized:
- You must be at least 18 years old.
- You must have a green card (giving you permanent legal resident status).
- You must have lived continuously in the U.S. for five years (occasional short trips outside the U.S. don't count) and in the state where you will apply for citizenship for three months. These time requirements are shorter for spouses of U.S. citizens.

- You must have good moral character, as determined by the Immigration and Naturalization Service (INS).
- You must not have been a member of the Communist Party for ten years before applying for citizenship.
- You must not have broken any immigration laws or been asked to leave the U.S. at any time.

If you meet these requirements, you can apply to the INS for naturalization. You will be interviewed, which serves three purposes: to verify the information on your application, to test your ability to speak, read and write basic English, and to test your knowledge of American government and history. You must pass these tests to be approved for citizenship.

When your application is approved, you will be sworn in at a ceremony. You must take an oath to defend the U.S. and to relinquish your allegiance to your former country.

Rights of Citizenship

Once you become a citizen through naturalization, you have almost all the same rights as native-born citizens, including the right to register to vote, the right to get a U.S. passport and the right to run for most public offices. However, you may not run for president or vice president of the United States.

You can stop reporting your status to the INS, and you can no longer be deported if, for example, you are convicted of a crime or lose your job.

VOTING

You can vote in California if you have first registered and you are:
- a United States citizen
- a resident of California
- at least 18 years old, and
- not in prison or on parole for a felony conviction. (Elect. Code § 300.5.)

Registration

To register to vote, you must submit a signed application to the county clerk at least 29 days before the election in which you want to vote. Clerks cannot accept applications during the 28 days immediately before an election, unless the application was signed more than 28 days before the election and the clerk receives it at least 25 days before the election. (Elect. Code § 305.)

Absentee Voting

Any registered voter can request, in writing, an absentee ballot between the 29th and 7th day before the election. The clerk mails the ballot to the voter; there is no fee for the service. The voter must return the ballot, in person or by mail, before the close of the polls on election day. It may be returned to the official who sent it or dropped off at any polling place. (Elect. Code § 1000 and following.)

Voters who have certain serious disabilities may apply for permanent absent voter status. (Elect. Code § 1450 and following.)

CONSUMERS' RIGHTS

When you purchase a product or a service, both California and federal law protect you not only from outright rip-offs, but also from misleading advertisements, overbearing salespeople who come to your home and products that don't work as promised.

TOPICS
> ADVERTISING
> CANCELLING CONTRACTS
> CAR RENTALS
> CAR REPAIRS
> CAR SALES
> CONTRACTORS
> DELIVERIES AND SERVICE CALLS
> HEALTH INSURANCE
> LAYAWAY PURCHASES
> MAIL ORDER MERCHANDISE
> REFUNDS AND EXCHANGES
> SALES TAX
> WARRANTIES

RELATED TOPICS
> DEBTS, LOANS AND CREDIT
> DOGS
>> Pet Stores
> REAL ESTATE
>> Buying and Selling a House
> TRAFFIC AND VEHICLE LAWS
>> Car Insurance Requirements
>> Registration and Smog Checks

ADDITIONAL RESOURCES
> *Nolo's Pocket Guide to Consumer Rights: A Resource for All Californians*, by Barbara Kaufman (Nolo Press), is a guide for California consumers.

> *Consumers' Guide to the California Lemon Law*, by Joseph J. Caro (J. Caro & Associates, P.O. Box 7486, Long Beach, CA 90807), focuses on California's new car lemon law.

> *The Lemon Book*, by Ralph Nader and Clarence Ditlow (Center for Auto Safety), explains each state's lemon law.

Consumer Law Sourcebook Volume 2: Consumer Law (Consumer Affairs) gives detailed information about California laws that protect consumers.

Department of Consumer Affairs, Bureau of Automotive Repair (BAR), (800) 952-5210, can help resolve customers resolve disputes with mechanics.

New Motor Vehicle Board, 1507 21st St., Suite 330, Sacramento, CA 95814, (916) 445-1888, takes complaints about cars that are lemons, helps customers deal with car dealers and manufacturers and makes sure that customers follow the proper procedures to get a refund.

National Highway Traffic Safety Administration Auto Safety Hotline, (800) 424-9393, tells consumers which cars are currently being recalled or investigated for safety problems.

Contractor's State Licensing Board, P.O. Box 26000, Sacramento, CA 95826, (916) 255-3900, can give information about a contractor's license and any complaints filed against a contractor. The Board also takes complaints about licensed contractors.

The Federal Trade Commission, 6th and Pennsylvania Ave., NW, Washington, DC 20580, publishes a number of free pamphlets on consumer issues, including *Door-to-Door Sales, Layaway Purchase Plans, Shopping By Mail, Shopping By Phone and Mail, Warranties, A Businessperson's Guide to Federal Warranty Law* and *Facts for Consumers—Service Contracts.*

ADVERTISING

To protect consumers from deceptive advertising, California law prohibits advertisers from making false or misleading statements about products or services. An advertiser who makes such statements knowing that they are false, or without taking reasonable steps to make sure that they are true, can be fined up to $2,500, sentenced to up to six months in the county jail, or both. (Bus. & Prof. Code § 17500.)

Price

An advertisement cannot compare its prices with a "former price" unless that former price was actually the prevailing market price within three months before the ad ran, or the ad clearly and conspicuously specifies when the former price was in effect. (Bus. & Prof. Code § 17501.)

If a company sells its product or service in multiple units only, it must advertise the price of the minimum number of units in which the product or service is offered. For example, a company that sells razor blades in packages of twelve cannot advertise the price per blade. As long as the company advertises the package price, it can also advertise a single unit price, but the single unit price must not be larger or more conspicuous than the multiple unit price. (Bus. & Prof. Code § 17504.)

If a manufacturer's cash rebate requires the buyer to send in a coupon, the merchant's advertisements must state the price the buyer must actually pay the merchant for the product. The merchant may not simply advertise the price of the product after the rebate. (Bus. & Prof. Code § 17701.5.)

Availability

If an advertisement doesn't state a limit on how many of an advertised item a customer can buy (for example, two per customer), the customer is entitled to buy as many as she wants. If the store refuses to sell this amount, the customer can sue for any losses suffered as a result, plus a $50 penalty. (Bus. & Prof. Code § 17500.5.)

Unless an advertisement indicates that quantities of advertised products are limited, the store must stock an amount large enough to meet the reasonably expected demand for the product.

"Bait and switch" advertising is illegal. That means a store cannot advertise a product that it has no intention of selling. For example, a store may not advertise a low-priced product—which turns out to be unavailable or defective—simply to lure customers into the store to sell a higher priced product. (Bus. & Prof. Code § 17500; Civ. Code § 1770.)

Quality of Goods

An advertisement cannot state that goods are original or new if they are in fact used, previously owned, altered or deteriorated. (Bus. & Prof. Code § 17531.) In addition, an advertisement can't claim that goods are of a particular standard, grade or style if they are not, and can't falsely claim that a product has been endorsed or sponsored by a person or group if it has not. (Civ. Code § 1770.)

A product cannot be advertised as "ozone friendly," "biodegradable" or any other environmental term that has a specific meaning unless the product meets the statutory definition of that term. (Bus. & Prof. Code § 17508.5.) Similarly, a product cannot be marked "Made in USA" if the product or any part of it is partially or substantially manufactured or produced outside the United States. (Bus. & Prof. Code § 17533.7.)

Any person or company that violates these laws is subject to a civil penalty of up to $2,500; this penalty is paid to the state of California, not the victims of the ads. (Bus. & Prof. Code §§ 17206, 17536.) Victims can sue the manufacturer or merchant for their actual losses and, in some cases, for an additional amount intended to punish the wrongdoer, called punitive damages.

CANCELLING CONTRACTS

Even after you sign on the dotted line, the law gives you a chance to back out of certain kinds of contracts if you have second thoughts.

The Three Day Cooling-Off Rule

Federal law (16 C.F.R. § 429.1) gives consumers the right to cancel the following kinds of contracts until midnight of the third business day after the contract was signed:

- door-to-door sales of personal, family or household goods or services for more than $25 and
- sales made anywhere other than the seller's normal place of business—for instance, at a hotel or restaurant, outdoor exhibit, computer show or trade show.

In addition, the federal Truth in Lending Act (15 U.S.C. § 1637A) lets consumers cancel home improvement loans, second mortgages or other loans where you pledge your home as security (except a first mortgage or first deed of trust) until midnight of the third business day after the contract was signed.

The seller must give you written notice of the right to cancel and a cancellation form when you sign the contract. If you are not given a form, ask to be sent one. Your cancellation right extends until the seller sends it to you, even if it takes months. The notice of cancellation and contract must be written in the same language as the salesperson's pitch. (Civ. Code § 1689.7.)

Other Contracts You Can Cancel Under State Law

California law gives you the right to cancel these contracts, within the time limits indicated:

- dance lessons, within 180 days (but you must pay for lessons received) (Civ. Code § 1812.54)
- dating service contracts, within three days (Civ. Code § 1694.1)
- purchase contracts for houses sold immediately before a foreclosure sale, within five days or until 8 am of the day of the sale, whichever is first (Civ. Code § 1695.4)
- contracts with prepaid job listing service firms, within three days (Civ. Code § 1812.516(6))
- contracts for seller-assisted marketing plans, within three days (Civ. Code § 1812.208-209)
- seminar sales, within three days (Civ. Code § 1689.20)
- contracts for weight loss, within three days. (Civ. Code § 1694.6)
- home solicitation contract for a personal emergency response unit, within seven days (Civ. Code § 1689.6)

How To Cancel

To cancel a contract, call the seller and say you want to cancel. Then sign and date the cancellation form or, if you were not given a form, write your own letter. It must be postmarked (or fax-marked) by midnight of the third business day after your purchase. You may send your written cancellation notice by certified mail, telegram or delivery. (Civ. Code § 1694.1.) If you hand deliver it, get a signed, dated receipt from the business. The seller must refund your money within 10 days, and then either pick up the items purchased or reimburse you within 20 days for the cost of mailing the goods back. If the seller doesn't come for the goods or make an arrangement for you to mail them back, you can keep them. (Civ. Code § 1689.6.)

CAR RENTALS

The driver of a rental car, not the owner, is responsible for having current registration tags. A California Highway Patrol officer who stops you for expired registration will issue the citation to you unless you have the name of the rental agency manager, so you should always write the manager's name on the rental contract.

The driver is responsible for all collision damage to a rented vehicle, even if someone else caused the damage (although if the other person pays, the driver should be reimbursed) or the cause is unknown. The driver is liable for the cost of repair up to the value of the vehicle, as well as loss of use, and towing, storage and impound fees. However, the rental company may not try to recover for damage or loss by charging, debiting or blocking the driver's credit card without approval. The cost may be paid:

- by the driver's own auto insurance policy
- through certain automatic credit card coverage (Visa Gold and American Express). These companies have been cutting back coverage, so call first before assuming your card will protect you.
- by any collision damage waiver (CDW) coverage the driver purchased from the car rental company.

Collision Damage Waivers

A collision damage waiver is a form of liability protection offered by most car rental companies. The law regulates industry practices regarding CDWs, and other optional goods or services, as follows:

- A rental company cannot require the purchase of optional insurance (such as CDW), goods or services.
- A rental company cannot charge more than $9 a day for CDW.
- A rental company cannot engage in any unfair, deceptive or coercive conduct to induce a renter to purchase optional features such as CDW.
- A rental company cannot debit or block the renter's credit card account as a deposit if the renter declines to purchase optional services such as CDW.

CAR REPAIRS

Mechanics must give a written estimate of the cost of proposed repair work before they start work on a car. If they find that more work is necessary, they must get the customer's consent, in writing or over the phone, before proceeding. Mechanics must provide an invoice itemizing the work done and the parts supplied. The customer is also entitled to all replaced parts, if he or she asks for them when bringing the car in for service.

If Your Car Is a Lemon

California's "lemon law" covers new cars with serious problems that can't be fixed. (Civ. Code § 1793.2.) It applies to new vehicles purchased or leased for more than four months for personal or family use only. It does not apply to motor homes, motorcycles or off-road vehicles.

The lemon law applies during the first 12 months or first 12,000 miles of the car's warranty period, whichever ends sooner. It applies to defects covered by the warranty that substantially reduce the use, value or safety of the car. The law entitles you to a new car or refund if you get stuck with a lemon—a car that cannot be repaired after at least three tries by the dealer and one by the manufacturer, or is out of service for any combination of defects for more than 30 days during the 12 year/12,000 mile period, not counting delays beyond the control of the dealer and manufacturer.

To get a new vehicle or a refund, you must give the dealer or manufacturer the opportunity to fix the vehicle. If they can't, you can select arbitration, where you can ask for either a refund or replacement. The arbitration proceeding may not get you either one, but at least you should finally get the car fixed right. The manufacturer is bound by the arbitrator's decision, but you still have the right to sue the manufacturer if you are dissatisfied with the outcome.

CAR SALES

California law includes several provisions intended to protect consumers when they buy new or used cars.

New Cars

When you buy a new car, you have no right to cancel the contract later. The sales contract for both new and used cars must contain a notice informing you that California law does not provide a "cooling off" or other cancellation period for vehicle sales. (Civ. Code § 2982.) However, if the dealer knows of any "material" (significant) damage to a new or previously unregistered vehicle that's been repaired, he must tell you in writing before you sign a contract. If the car suffers any damage that is unknown at the time the contract is signed, the dealer must tell you about it before you take delivery, unless the car is repaired. Material damage means damage that:

- exceeds 3% of the manufacturer's suggested price or $500, whichever is greater
- occurred in connection with the theft of the vehicle
- is to the frame or drive train
- is to the suspension, requiring repairs other than wheel balancing or alignment.

Damage to components that are bolted or attached to the vehicle, such as bumpers, tires and glass, are exempt from this disclosure requirement only if replaced with identical new, original manufacturer's components—unless the repairs exceed 10% of the manufacturer's suggested price. (Veh. Code § 9990 and following.)

New car dealers' demonstrator cars are legally considered used cars, so these disclosure laws don't apply—even if the dealer gives a new car warranty. (Veh. Code § 665; 13 Cal. Regulatory Code § 404.20(c).)

Used Cars

All dealers selling used cars must post a large sticker in the car window stating whether or not the car is being sold "as is" or with a warranty. Most used car dealers sell vehicles "as is." If you get any written warranty, you automatically also get an implied warranty that the car is fit for driving. (Fed. Trade Commission Used Car Rule, 16 C.F.R. 455.)

Private sellers do not have to post these stickers. Normally, the law simply assumes the car is being sold "as is" with no warranty. Nevertheless, if the buyer relies on the seller's positive statements about the car and then discovers they were lies, the buyer may be successful in suing the seller in Small Claims Court for the cost of repairs or cancellation of the contract.

As with new cars, there is no right to cancel the purchase contract. The purchase contract must, however, contain a notice informing you that California law does not provide a "cooling off" or other cancellation period for vehicle sales. (Civ. Code § 2982.) Certain safety features must be working on the car: horn, lights, windshield wipers, tires and brakes. Also, the smog equipment must be intact. It is illegal to sell a car with smog equipment that has been disconnected or tampered with.

Service Contracts

All new cars come with a written warranty covering repairs and adjustments for specific lengths of time or mileage. When you buy a new car, dealers will also try to sell you a service contract (extended warranty), which are high-profit items for the dealership. Service contracts cannot merely duplicate coverage offered by the manufacturer's express warranty (Civ. Code § 1794.41), although a service contract may run concurrently with or overlap an express warranty.

If you change your mind after you buy a service contract, you can cancel it. The dealer must notify you, in writing, of your right to cancel and receive a refund. Your cancellation must be in writing and sent to the person specified in the contract. (Civ. Code § 1794.41.) The amount of your refund depends on when you cancel.

Financing

If you have taken possession of an automobile but the dealer cannot get financing for you, the contract is void. You must return the car, but you are entitled to get your deposit back as well as any trade-in. If the trade-in has been sold, you are entitled to its fair market value or the price listed in the contract, whichever is higher. You are not required to sign another contract, no matter how long you have been driving the car. (Civ. Code § 2982.)

In addition, sellers cannot change the financing or payment terms after you take possession of the vehicle. (Civ. Code § 2982.05.)

CONTRACTORS

The legal definition of a contractor is anyone who makes alterations or additions to a structure that become part of the real estate—for example, fixing a roof, building an extra room or strengthening a house's ability to withstand an earthquake.

Licensing Requirements

Any contractor who does home improvement work worth more than $300 (labor and materials), or who advertises as a contractor, must be licensed by the California Contractor's State License Board (CSLB). The license number must be included in all advertisements, bids and contracts. However, you need not be licensed to work on your own home as long as the work is done by you or your employees, the employees receive wages as their sole compensation, and the work is not intended for sale. If you buy a house solely to fix it up and sell it, you will probably have to be licensed.

There are various license classifications, depending on the contractor's specialty, such as roofing or plumbing. A general building contractor is one licensed in several types of work.

Unlicensed contractors:
- may be fined up to $15,000 and prosecuted by the local district attorney
- can't get local building permits, which are required for jobs involving structural work or remodeling
- can't sue to get paid for work requiring a license.

(Bus. & Prof. Code §§ 7000-7173.)

Complaints About Licensed Contractors

The CSLB handles complaints about licensed contractors—such as shoddy or incomplete work on a home remodeling project—and may mediate or arbitrate some cases. However, the CSLB has a large backlog of complaints, and may take quite a while to address a problem.

Contractors who are at fault may be fined up to $2,000, be required to make repairs or restitution, or have their licenses suspended or revoked.

Checking a Contractor's Record and Insurance

The CSLB will verify that an individual contractor's license is current and valid and will disclose whether or not any legal action has been taken against a contractor for inadequate or unfinished work. However, the CSLB will not disclose the number or specifics of any complaints filed.

Contractors must be insured against claims covering workers' compensation and meet the other legal obligations of independent contractors, such as contributing to state and federal benefit programs like unemployment and Social Security and withholding state and federal income taxes.

Deposits

By state law, a contractor cannot require an advance payment larger than $200 or 2% of the contract price for swimming pools or $1,000 or 10% of the contract price for other home improvements (excluding finance charges), whichever is less. (Bus. & Prof. Code § 7159(d).)

Mechanics' Liens

California law allows anyone who furnishes labor or materials to your home to place a "mechanic's lien" against your home if you do not pay them. (Civ. Code § 3109 and following.) A mechanic's lien is a legal claim for money owed.

Even if you paid the general contractor, if he did not pay the subcontractors or material suppliers, they can also place a lien on your home by recording it at the County Recorder's office. This means you might have to pay a bill twice to remove the lien.

To enforce a mechanic's lien, the contractor must file a lawsuit to foreclose on your home within 90 days of the date the lien was recorded.

DELIVERIES AND SERVICE CALLS

Finally responding to consumers irked by deliveries and repair people who never come, the legislature has put limits on businesses' freedom to make promises.

Merchandise Deliveries

Retailers employing 25 or more people must specify a four-hour time period within which any delivery will be made, if you must be home to receive the delivery.

Home Services

Utility and cable TV companies are also covered by the four-hour requirement. These companies must inform you of your right to have service begin during a four-hour connection or repair period (if your presence is required) before the date of service or repair.

Late Deliveries and Service Calls

If the merchandise or covered service is not delivered or begun within the specified four-hour period, you can sue in Small Claims Court for lost wages, expenses actually incurred or other actual damages up to $500. However, the retailer, utility or cable company is not liable if the delay was caused by unforeseen or unavoidable events beyond its control. (Civ. Code § 1722.)

HEALTH INSURANCE

Health insurance pays some or all of the costs of treating specified medical problems. If you pay your premiums, you are entitled to coverage under the terms of your policy.

Very few laws regulate health insurance. You are not required to have health insurance, nor is your employer required to provide it to you. There are no rules regarding what injuries or illnesses must be insured, but the policy must clearly spell out what is covered and what is excluded.

California law gives you the right to cancel a health insurance policy for 30 days after you receive the policy or insurance certificate. This gives you a chance to peruse the policy without obligation.

California law also provides that your insurer must pay any covered bill within 30 days. However, since there is no penalty against insurance companies that don't meet the deadline, the law has no real teeth.

LAYAWAY PURCHASES

A layaway agreement is a contract in which you make a deposit on retail goods, and then the retailer holds the goods for you until you finish making the payments. If you decide before you finish paying that you no longer want the item, you may be able to get a refund of what you have already paid. Your written layaway agreement will indicate whether or not you are entitled to a refund. If you do receive a refund, the seller may be able to keep a portion of your payments as a service fee. However, this fee should not be more than the cost of storing your goods.

If you complete the layaway payments, you are entitled to a refund if the goods aren't available in the same condition as when you first bought them. (Civ. Code § 1749.)

MAIL ORDER MERCHANDISE

The federal government puts strict requirements on how mail order companies conduct business.

Delayed Goods

If you order goods by mail (except photo-finishing orders, magazine subscriptions other than the first shipment, COD orders, or seeds or plants), the seller must ship within the time promised or, if no time was stated, within 30 days. (Fed. Trade Commission Mail Order Rule, 16 C.F.R. 435.) If the seller cannot ship within that time, it must notify you of a new shipping date and offer you the option of cancelling your order and getting a refund.

If you opt for the second deadline and the seller can't meet it, you must be sent a notice requesting your signature to agree to a third date. If you don't return the second notice, your order must be cancelled and your money refunded. The seller must issue the refund within seven days if you paid by check or money order, or within one billing cycle if you charged your purchase.

Mail Fraud

If you receive a mailing that you suspect contains false or fraudulent representations, notify the Fraud Complaints section of the Inspection Service Operations Support Group, U.S. Postal Inspection Service, 433 West Van Buren St., 7th Floor, Chicago, IL 60607-5401. An inspector who agrees it's fraudulent will get a court order to intercept the company's mail. The inspector will investigate the company and try to get back any money you sent.

REFUNDS AND EXCHANGES

Merchants are not required to give a cash refund or even a store credit for returned merchandise, although many do. However, merchants who do not allow a full cash or credit refund, or equal exchange, within seven days of purchase must post the store's refund-credit-exchange policy at each cash register and sales counter, at each public entrance, on tags attached to each item or on the retailer's order forms. If the merchant doesn't post the policy, you may return the goods, for a full refund, for up to 30 days after the purchase. (Civ. Code § 1723.)

A merchant is not required to post a no-return policy for, or accept returns of, the following items: food, plants, flowers, perishable goods, merchandise marked "as is," "no returns accepted" or "all sales final," goods used or damaged after purchase, special order goods received as ordered, goods not returned with their original package, and goods that can't be resold due to health considerations.

SALES TAX
Sales tax is assessed on products and services purchased in California, as well as products bought out of state for use in California, in certain circumstances. The amount of tax charged varies by county, from 6% to 8 ¼%.

What Can Be Taxed
Almost all products sold are subject to sales tax. Periodicals (which were formerly not taxed) are subject to sales tax, and only the following foods are not taxed:
- candy and other confections
- food and non-alcoholic drinks sold by nonprofit groups (such as the Boy Scouts or the 4-H Club) at occasional events like fairs and parades
- cookies or other snack foods sold by nonprofit youth groups (Girl Scout cookies, for example). (Rev. and Tax. Code §§ 6359, 6359.5, 6361.)
  Prescription medicines are not subject to sales tax. (Rev. and Tax. Code § 6369.)

Products Bought Out of State
If you purchase products from a mail-order company based out of state, you may have to pay sales tax. California law requires companies that have a physical presence in California (a store, warehouse or sales personnel, for example) to pay sales tax to the state. Some businesses meet this requirement by simply incorporating the tax into their pricing; others include a separate sales tax charge on your bill. If the company has no physical presence in the state, it does not have to pay sales tax to California.

If you purchase a car in another state, you will have to pay California sales tax (called a "use tax"), or the difference between the tax that you paid in the state where you bought the car and the California state tax, when you register the car in California. You may not be subject to this tax if you can show that the person who sold you the car is a close relative who isn't in the automobile business, or that you purchased the car intending to use it in another state, and then moved to California unexpectedly.

If you buy something in a foreign country, you must pay a use tax on all items brought into the state that are normally subject to sales tax in California. The first $400 worth of purchases are exempt, however.

WARRANTIES
A warranty is a guarantee about the quality of goods or services. Warranties can be express or implied. An express warranty is a statement made by the merchant or manufacturer about the quality of its goods or services. It may be written or oral. An implied warranty is one that the law automatically entitles you to because it would be unjust for you to be without the protection.

Express Warranties
A federal law (the Magnuson-Moss Warranty Act) governs express warranties. This act does not require manufacturers to give written warranties. If one is given, however, the following rules apply:
- It must be written in ordinary language that is easy to read and understand.
- The seller must show you a copy of warranty before you make a purchase of more than $15 and provide you with a copy when you buy.

- It must be labeled either "full" or "limited."
  A full warranty must have these features:
- The product must be repaired or replaced for free during the warranty period.
- The product must be repaired within a reasonable time.
- You don't have to do anything unreasonable—such as return a heavy item—to get warranty service.
- You do not have to return a warranty card for the warranty to be valid.
- Implied warranties cannot be disclaimed, denied or limited to a specific length of time.

A limited warranty offers less protection. You still don't have to return the owner registration card to be eligible for the warranty, regardless of what the warranty says. However, you may have to pay for labor or reinstallation, or bring a heavy item in for service. In addition, your implied warranty may expire when your written warranty expires, and you may be entitled to only pro-rata refunds or credits, which means you have to pay for the time you used the product.

Implied Warranties

California's Song-Beverly Consumer Warranty Act (Civ. Code § 1790 and following) provides an "implied warranty of merchantability" on almost every new product. This means that the manufacturer and seller automatically promise that the product is fit for its ordinary purpose. The Act also provides an "implied warranty of fitness for a specific purpose" when a product is sold or marketed in a context where the specific need or intent of the consumer is known. For instance, if you buy a sleeping bag after telling the sporting goods salesperson that you plan to camp in sub-zero weather, the sleeping bag must be suitable for very cold temperatures. If the product comes with a written warranty, the implied warranty lasts as long as the written one. If there is no written warranty, the implied warranty lasts one year.

Sales of the following items are not covered by the implied warranty:

- food, personal care or cleaning products
- clothing, including under and outer garments, shoes and accessories made of woven material, yarn, fiber, leather or similar fabrics (unless a written warranty is provided)
- "as is" sales that have a disclaimer conspicuously attached to the product. A seller who gives a written warranty, however, can't legally get out of an implied warranty.

Implied warranties apply to used products only when a written warranty is given, and then last only as long as the written warranty, but no shorter than 30 days or longer than 90 days. Implied warranties on used goods imply that the item will work, given its age and condition.

Servicing a Product Under Warranty

The Song-Beverly Act requires manufacturers who give a written warranty to maintain service facilities in California reasonably close to all areas where their products are sold. The manufacturer can use retailers or independent repair shops. Repairs must be completed within 30 days, unless a delay is beyond the control of the manufacturer or its representative. While a product that costs more than $50 is being repaired, your written warranty is extended by the amount of time the item is in the shop.

If the product's size and weight or installation make it impossible or very hard for you to return the product, the manufacturer must provide warranty service at your home or arrange to have the malfunctioning product picked up without additional charges for transportation.

Some retailers, particularly those who sell consumer electronics, sell extended warranties on their products. These warranties usually offer service, repair or replacement of the product for a period of time beyond the regular warranty. The value of these extended warranties is variable, depending on the product, coverage under the regular warranty, and the likelihood of malfunction. The only legal rule governing these warranties is that they cannot merely duplicate coverage offered by the manufacturer's express warranty. (Civ. Code § 1794.41.)

COPYRIGHTS AND PATENTS

The law of copyright, patent and trademarks (called intellectual property law) allows people to protect their creations from unauthorized use by others.

Most of the laws and agencies regulating intellectual property are federal. All patent and copyright lawsuits must be brought in federal court.

TOPICS
> **COPYRIGHTS**
> **PATENTS**

RELATED TOPICS
> **COURTS AND LAWSUITS**
>> Federal Court System
> **SMALL BUSINESSES**
>> Trademarks and Service Marks

ADDITIONAL RESOURCES
> *Patent It Yourself,* by David Pressman (Nolo Press), takes you step-by-step through the process of getting a patent without a patent lawyer. *Patent It Yourself* software for Windows will be available January 1994.
>
> *The Inventor's Notebook,* by David Pressman and Fred Grissom (Nolo Press), shows inventors how to document the invention process to ensure they are entitled to the greatest legal protection available.
>
> *The Copyright Handbook: How To Protect and Use Written Works,* by Stephen Fishman (Nolo Press), is a complete guide to the law of copyright and includes forms for registering a copyright.
>
> *Circular 2: Publications on Copyright* is a list of government pamphlets about copyright law. To order a copy, write to Information and Publication Section LM-455, Copyright Office, Library of Congress, Washington, DC 20599 or call (202) 707-2100.

COPYRIGHTS

Federal copyright law gives someone who creates an original work of expression—a play, song, painting or book, for example—the right to control how that work is used. A copyright grants a number of specific rights regarding the expression, including the exclusive right to:

- make copies or authorize others to make copies
- make derivative expressions, such as translations or updates
- sell the expression
- perform or display the expression, and
- sue others who violate these rights.

A copyright automatically comes into existence when expression takes a tangible form—when words are written on a page, for example. Copyrights last a long time: for works made after 1977, a copyright lasts for 50 years after the death of the creator. For works created by employees for an employer, a copyright lasts for 75 years from the date of publication (which includes any form of dissemination), or 100 years from the date of creation, whichever ends first. (17 U.S.C. § 100 and following.)

The Fair Use Rule

Under the "fair use" rule of copyright law, an author may make limited use of another author's work without asking permission. The fair use privilege is perhaps the most significant limitation on a copyright owner's exclusive rights.

Subject to some general limitations, the following types of uses are usually deemed fair uses:

- Criticism and comment—for example, quoting or excerpting a work in a review or criticism for purposes of illustration or comment
- News reporting—for example, summarizing an address or article, with brief quotations, in a news report
- Research and scholarship—for example, quoting a short passage in a scholarly, scientific or technical work for illustration or clarification of the author's observations
- Nonprofit educational uses—for example, photocopying of limited portions of written works by teachers for classroom use.

In most other situations, copying is not legally a fair use. Without an author's permission, such a use violates the author's copyright.

Violations often occur when the use is motivated primarily by a desire for commercial gain. The fact that a work is published primarily for private commercial gain weighs heavily against a finding of fair use.

What Can Be Copyrighted

Literary works, computer software, musical arrangements, graphic works, audiovisual works, or compilations of these and other works are all covered by copyright. The work must be in some way original. A copyright does not protect merely clerical work, such as a blank form or the phone book. The facts or ideas expressed are not themselves protected by copyright—only the way the creator has expressed those facts or ideas. Anyone, for example, is free to write a book about a subject that other books have already covered. But the author of a new book cannot legally copy language from an earlier book.

Notice of Copyright (©)

A copyright notice tells the world that the creator of the work is claiming a copyright. A complete notice consists of the © symbol or the word "copyright" or "copr.," the year of publication, and the name of the copyright owner. Works published before March 1, 1989 must have a copyright notice to maintain the copyright in the work. For works published after that date, a notice is not required. Even if no notice is required, however, putting a copyright notice on your work serves to warn others that your work is protected, and will help you enforce your copyright in court if necessary.

Registration of Copyrights

You can register your copyright with the Federal Register of Copyrights at the Library of Congress in Washington, D.C. To get the full benefits of registration, you must register within three months of the date of publication, or before the infringement began. For unpublished works, you must register before the infringement begins. Those benefits make it easier to prove and win an infringement action in federal court. Also, you must register before you can bring a lawsuit for infringement of copyright.

PATENTS

A patent is the legal right, granted by the U.S. Patent and Trademark Office, to exclude others from making, using or selling an invention for up to 17 years. The certificate that grants the patent and describes the invention is called a patent deed. If someone infringes on your patent by marketing your invention, you may sue in federal court for the economic loss you suffer as a result.

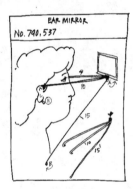

Types of Patents

There are three types of patents:

- **Utility patents** cover inventions that work in a unique manner to produce a "utilitarian result." Most gadgets that perform a function fall under this category. A utility patent lasts for 17 years.
- **Design patents** cover unique, ornamental or visible shapes or designs of objects. Inventions that are aesthetic rather than functional—such as a computer screen icon—fall into this category. A design patent lasts for 14 years.
- **Plant patents** cover new strains of plants. These patents last for 17 years.

Patent Requirements

Not everything can be patented. For example, you can't patent an abstract idea, a purely mental process or a process that can be simply performed using a pencil and paper. Nor can you patent naturally occurring things. To be patentable, an invention must be a process, a machine, a manufacture, a composition or an improvement on one of these. Each of these categories includes a wide variety of items, from computer software to genetically engineered bacteria.

An invention must satisfy three additional requirements to be patentable:

- **Novelty.** The invention must be a new idea, physically different in at least some small way from what already exists (known in inventors' circles as the "prior art").
- **Nonobviousness.** The invention must be a new or unexpected development, something that, at the time of its invention, would not be obvious to a person skilled in the technology of that particular field.
- **Usefulness.** The invention must have some positive use, or in the case of a design patent, must be ornamental. This requirement precludes, for example, inventions that have only illegal uses, or drugs that have only unsafe uses.

How To Get a Patent

To get a patent, you must submit a detailed application to the federal Patent and Trademark Office. You must file your application within one year of the first commercialization of your invention or the first publication of the details of your invention. It generally takes 18 months to two years to get a patent.

COURTS AND LAWSUITS

Many people, when faced with a seemingly unresolvable dispute, consider taking legal action. Almost as many are brought into court unwillingly to defend themselves. But for most people, the court system is unfamiliar and intimidating—and there may be easier, faster and cheaper alternatives to lawsuits.

TOPICS

    ALTERNATIVES TO COURT
    APPEALS
    CALIFORNIA COURT SYSTEM
    FEDERAL COURT SYSTEM
    GOOD SAMARITANS
    JURY DUTY
    LAWSUITS OVER CONTRACTS
    LAWYERS' FEES
    PERSONAL INJURY LAWSUITS
    SETTLING A LAWSUIT OUT OF COURT
    SMALL CLAIMS COURT
    STATUTES OF LIMITATION
    VICTIMS OF CRIME

RELATED TOPICS

    CHILDREN
        Juvenile Court
    TRAFFIC OFFENSES AND VEHICLE LAWS

ADDITIONAL RESOURCES

    Represent Yourself in Court: How to Prepare and Try a Winning Case, by Paul Bergman and Sara Berman-Barrett (Nolo Press), explains how to conduct a civil trial without an attorney.

    How To Win Your Personal Injury Claim, by Joseph Matthews (Nolo Press), takes the reader through the process of negotiating with an insurance company over a personal injury claim.

    Everybody's Guide to Small Claims Court (California Edition), by Ralph Warner (Nolo Press), explains how to evaluate your case, prepare for court and convince a judge you're right.

Everybody's Guide to Municipal Court, by Roderic Duncan (Nolo Press), explains how to handle a lawsuit for up to $25,000 in California Municipal Court without a lawyer.

California Crime Victims Handbook, by Benvenuti and Villmoare (McGeorge School of Law, University of the Pacific), explains how crime victims can participate in the California criminal justice system.

ALTERNATIVES TO COURT

A lawsuit is not usually the best or only way to resolve a dispute. Non-adversarial approaches can provide a fair, mutual solution without the typical delay, expense and hostility of a formal court proceeding.

Because of the expense of lawsuits, many companies (banks, for example) now put a standard clause in their contracts requiring dissatisfied customers to submit their disputes to mediation or arbitration.

Mediation

Mediation is a process in which a neutral third party meets with the people having the disagreement to help them find a mutually agreeable solution. The mediator is chosen by the parties. The goal of mediation is to allow the disputing parties to reach their own agreement; the mediator has no authority to impose a solution on anyone. In California, all disputes about child custody or visitation must go to a mediator before a court makes a ruling.

You can select a mutual acquaintance as a mediator, or call your local neighborhood mediation or conciliation service. Many cities and counties offer free or low-cost mediation services. Or look under "Alternative Dispute Resolution" in the yellow pages.

Arbitration

Arbitration is a more formal proceeding in which the disputing parties agree to submit their problem to a third person and be bound by the arbitrator's decision. The arbitrator is a neutral outsider chosen by the parties to judge their dispute. In arbitration, both sides can give evidence and have witnesses testify, and both sides can have a lawyer, if they wish. Often, parties to a contract agree in advance to submit any dispute arising under the contract to arbitration.

You can find an arbitrator and rules for arbitration through the American Arbitration Association (AAA), a nonprofit organization. The AAA can give you the names of arbitrators in your area; expect to pay from $300 to $1,200 for arbitration, depending on how much is in dispute and how complicated the problem is.

APPEALS

An appeal is a rehearing of a case that has already been decided. When you appeal a case, you are asking a higher court to change the decision of the trial court. Appeals are not like initial trials, where witnesses can be heard and evidence about the facts in dispute is presented (except Small Claims Court appeals). The sole role of the Appeals Court is to decide whether the trial court made an error in interpreting the law. It accepts the factual findings of the trial court (for example, the disputed work was not done according to specifications or the light was green when the plaintiff entered the intersection).

IMPORTANT TERMS

Appellant. The person who brings the appeal, who may have been either the plaintiff or defendant in the original case.
Respondent. The person opposing the appeal.

Where To Appeal

If you are appealing a case originally brought in small claims court, you must appeal to the Superior Court. If you are appealing a case originally brought in municipal or justice court, you must appeal to the Superior Court, Appellate Division. Appeals from the Superior Court go to the Court of Appeal. The highest state court, where Court of Appeal rulings are appealed, is the California Supreme Court.

How To Appeal

To bring an appeal, the losing party must first file a notice of appeal with the clerk of the trial court. The appeal must be filed within 30 days after the clerk mails the losing party a notice of entry of the judgment. In Municipal or Justice Court, the court may not send a notice of entry of judgment; in that case, an appeal can be brought within 90 days after the judgment is actually entered.

The fee for filing a notice of appeal is currently about $30 to $60.

Someone who appeals from Municipal or Justice Court must file additional papers within ten days of filing the notice of appeal.

CALIFORNIA COURT SYSTEM

California state courts are organized in a three-tier system. On the first level are the trial courts, which hear disputes for the first time. On the second level are the appellate courts, which decide appeals from the trial courts. And on the third level is the California Supreme Court, which rules on appeals only in certain, select cases.

Trial Courts

There are three kinds of trial courts in California, and each is empowered to hear different cases.

- **Small Claims Courts** can hear disputes only if the amount at stake is $5,000 or less. Eviction lawsuits cannot be brought in Small Claims Court.
- **Municipal and Justice Courts** can hear disputes in which the amount in controversy is $25,000 or less, including cases that could also be brought in small claims court. They also decide all residential eviction cases and misdemeanor and infraction criminal cases. Municipal and Justice Courts are essentially the same; the name of the court simply depends on the population of the county or city where the court is located.
- **Superior Courts** hear all other cases, including divorces, adoptions and guardianships. They also hear appeals from Small Claims Court.

Appellate Courts

- **Superior Court, Appellate Division** hears appeals from Municipal and Justice Court.
- **California Courts of Appeal** hear appeals from the Superior Court, except cases involving the death penalty.

Supreme Court

The California Supreme Court hears death penalty appeals from the Superior Court, and hears appeals in cases of its choosing from the Courts of Appeal. The Supreme Court is free to decide what appeals to hear. The court is more likely to hear an appeal if:

- different Courts of Appeal are in disagreement over an issue presented in the case, and a Supreme Court decision could provide uniformity in the law
- the case presents important legal questions that the Supreme Court wants to address, or
- the Court of Appeal didn't have the authority to decide the case.

Where To Bring Your Case

You must not only bring a case in the proper court, but also in the proper location. There are many Small Claims, Municipal and Superior courts in California. The rules of "venue" determine which location is proper for a particular lawsuit.

The state is divided into judicial districts. In any dispute, suit can be filed in the following judicial districts:

- where the defendant resides
- where the defendant does business, if the defendant is a corporation
- where damage to property or personal injury occurred
- where the real estate that is the subject of the suit is located.

In certain cases, additional judicial districts are also appropriate.

Contract cases (other than an auto sale or retail installment contract) can also be brought in the district:

- where the contract was entered into or signed
- where the contract was to be performed
- where the defendant resided at the commencement of the action.

Automobile sale or retail installment contracts can also be brought in the district:

- where the buyer signed the contract
- where the buyer lived when the contract was signed
- where the buyer resides when suit is brought
- where the car is permanently garaged or the goods are attached to real estate (for example, a heating unit or portable storage shed).

FEDERAL COURT SYSTEM

The federal court system has three tiers, like the California state court system. Federal district courts, the trial courts of the federal system, hear cases for the first time. On the second level are the federal Courts of Appeal, which hear appeals from the district courts. And on the top level is the United States Supreme Court, which hears appeals in a few select cases of its choosing.

In addition, certain cases are heard in specialized federal courts, such as bankruptcy court or tax court.

Which Cases Can Be Heard in Federal Court

Only certain cases can be brought in a federal court. They are:

- **Cases involving a question of federal law.** Cases that arise under the U.S. Constitution, U.S. statutes or treaties can be brought in federal court. Examples include free speech and civil rights cases alleging a violation of federal (rather than state) rights.

- **Cases where jurisdiction is granted by statute.** Certain types of cases can be brought in federal court because a statute specifically allows it. Examples include bankruptcy, patent, copyright and federal antitrust lawsuits.
- **Cases where there is "diversity of parties."** Cases where there is more than $10,000 in controversy can be heard in federal court if all the parties are from different states, citizens from one state are suing citizens of a foreign country or a foreign country is suing citizens of a state.

Which Federal Court Is Appropriate

The country is divided up into a number of federal judicial districts. The district in which suit should be brought depends on what kind of suit it is.

- **Federal question.** A suit based on a federal question can be brought in the district where all the defendants reside or in the district where the claim arose.
- **Bankruptcy.** A bankruptcy case must be filed in the judicial district where the person declaring bankruptcy has lived for the last six months.
- **Diversity.** A suit based on the diversity of the parties can be brought in the district where all the plaintiffs reside, where all the defendants reside or where the claim arose.

GOOD SAMARITANS

The law wants to encourage people to give whatever assistance they can in emergencies. To that end, California law protects people from lawsuits over injury they may inadvertently cause while trying to help someone in an emergency. The law provides that anyone who, in good faith and not for compensation, gives emergency care is not liable for any losses that result from an act or omission. (Health & Safety Code § 1799.102.)

Anyone who is hurt trying to prevent a crime, catch a criminal or rescue a person in immediate danger of injury or death, may make a claim to the state for his or her losses. If such a good Samaritan is killed, his or her surviving spouse or dependents may make a claim. (Gov't. Code § 13970.)

JURY DUTY

Jury service is an obligation of citizenship, and it can be an onerous one. Potential jurors spend most of their time waiting to be questioned, and most never get called to sit on a jury.

Potential jurors are randomly selected from lists of names provided by voter registration rolls and the Department of Motor Vehicles' list of licensed drivers. In many California counties, once someone is summoned to appear as a juror, that person is "on duty" for 10 week days—although the specifics of service vary considerably from courtroom to courtroom.

Being Excused From Serving

If you are summoned for jury duty, you must attend as directed or respond promptly to court officials and explain why you cannot attend. If you don't, you may be held in contempt of court and fined or incarcerated, or both. (Code of Civ. Proc. § 209.)

A judge may excuse a potential juror for health reasons or for extreme hardship, such as possible foreclosure on your home if you are without income. (Code of Civ. Proc. § 204.) California National Guard members on active duty are excused from jury duty, as are people who don't have a sufficient knowledge of English or have been convicted of a felony. (Mil. & Vet. Code §§ 391, 560; Code of Civ. Proc. § 203.) And it is possible to have jury service postponed for vacations and other valid reasons. But once you are seated as a juror in a trial, you must serve until the trial is over—no matter how long it lasts.

Employers' Responsibilities

Employees may not be fired or otherwise punished for serving on a jury, but they must give the employer reasonable notice that they will need time off work for jury duty. (Lab. Code § 230.) Employers are not required to pay employees for time away from work. The court pays most jurors a small sum for each day they serve and reimburses them for some expenses incurred in getting to the courtroom; jurors are not paid for the trip back home. (Code of Civ. Proc. § 215.)

LAWSUITS OVER CONTRACTS

A contract is an agreement between two people in which each promises to do something for the other. The key to a contract is that each side must promise or do something of value. A promise to make a gift does not form a contract, because the person to whom the gift is promised has not done or promised anything in return.

Many everyday transactions are contracts, such as opening a checking account, purchasing goods or services, arranging for utility services or buying an insurance policy. Common types of contracts include:

- **Promissory notes.** Agreements to lend money to be paid back later.
- **Bills of sale.** Receipts or other documents that record the terms of a sale.
- **Warranties.** Guarantees about the quality and performance of a product or service.
- **Service contracts.** Arrangements for everything from fixing your TV to remodeling your kitchen.
- **Leases and rental agreements.** Contracts to rent property.

Contracts That Must Be in Writing

In most situations, an oral contract is legally valid and binding. But if one party wants to sue over the contract, it can be very difficult to prove that the contract was ever made or what its terms were.

Certain contracts, however, must be in writing before a court will enforce them. The goal is to protect both sides from fraud and failing memories. They are:

- Contracts that cannot be completed within one year. If there is any possible way a contract could be completed within a year, even if it's highly unlikely or actually takes longer than one year to perform, it can be oral
- Contracts that by their terms are not to be performed during the lifetime of the promisor
- Contracts for the sale of more than $500 worth of goods
- Contracts for the sale of real estate
- Contracts of employment with real estate agents
- Contingency fee contracts with a lawyer. (Civ. Code § 1624.)

When a Contract Is Broken

If one person doesn't keep her promise, the contract has been broken ("breached"). The other person can try to negotiate, seek mediation or arbitration to settle the dispute, or take the breaching party to court. The usual legal remedy for a broken contract is for the person who broke the contract to pay an amount equal to what the other person expected to get from the contract. However, the person who is suing must also show that he took steps to mitigate (minimize) his losses. For example, a landlord whose tenant breaks a lease cannot simply sue for all the rent owed under the contract; she must try to find a new tenant as soon as possible, and will be able to collect only the money she actually lost when the place was not rented.

In some situations, such as when the contract involves a unique item (usually real estate), a court may order both sides to actually go through with the deal.

What Contracts Are Not Enforceable

Courts won't enforce some contracts because they violate public policy or because enforcement is impossible. These contracts include:

- an agreement to do something illegal
- an agreement that is unconscionable—very unfair to one person because of the other person's superior bargaining power.
- a contract that is extremely vague. If a court cannot determine what the actual agreement was, it cannot order enforcement of the contract.

LAWYERS' FEES

Most disagreements between lawyers and clients involve fees.

Hourly Fees

Many lawyers do not charge for an initial half-hour or hour consultation. But they do charge for everything else—usually between $75 and $250 an hour.

If it is reasonably foreseeable that a client will end up paying more than $1,000 for legal fees and costs, the agreement between lawyer and client must be in writing. (This law doesn't apply if the client is a corporation or has hired the lawyer for similar services before.) The contract must state the hourly rate and other standard fees that may apply, the general nature of the services to be provided and the responsibilities of both attorney and client (for example, the client may be responsible for paying out-of-pocket court fees as the case progresses). (Bus. & Prof. Code § 6148(a).)

Bills sent by the attorney can't contain just a bare amount due; they must state the rate or other method of arriving at the total. If the client is billed for costs and expenses, the bill must clearly identify them. A client who hasn't gotten a bill in a month may ask for one, and the lawyer must provide it within 10 days. (Bus. & Prof. Code § 6148(b).)

Contingency Fees

Under a contingent fee, a lawyer agrees to handle a case for a fixed percentage of the amount finally recovered in a lawsuit. If the client wins the case, the lawyer's fee comes out of the money awarded. If the client loses, neither the client nor the lawyer gets any money. Although there is no set percentage for contingency fees in most types of cases, the standard amount demanded by lawyers is about 35% if the case is settled before a lawsuit is filed with the courts, and 40% if a case goes to trial.

Contingency fee agreements (unless the client is seeking workers' compensation benefits) must be in writing, and the client must receive a signed copy of the contract. The contract must include the contingency fee rate, explain how incidental costs will be paid, and state to what extent, if any, the client might have to pay the lawyer for related matters that aren't covered by the contingency fee contract. The contract must state that the fee is not set by law, but is negotiable. The contract must also disclose whether the attorney maintains errors and omissions insurance coverage applicable to the services to be rendered and the policy limits of that coverage if less than $100,00 per occurrence and up to a maximum of $300,000 per policy term. If the lawyer doesn't comply with these requirements, the client can declare the agreement void at any time. In that case, the lawyer is entitled to collect a "reasonable" fee. (Bus. & Prof. Code § 6147.)

In medical malpractice suits, state law limits the amount of contingency fees to 40% of the first $50,000 recovered, 33 $\frac{1}{3}$% of the next $50,000, 25% of the next $500,000, and 15% of any amount over $600,000. (Bus. & Prof. Code § 6146.)

Clients are always free to change lawyers if the relationship between lawyer and client turns sour.

HOW TO FILE A COMPLAINT ABOUT A LAWYER

To complain about any behavior by a lawyer that appears to be deceptive, unethical or otherwise illegal, call the State Bar of California's toll-free number (800) 843-9053. Or contact the Bar at 555 Franklin Street; San Francisco, CA 94102, (415) 561-8200. It can tell you what types of behavior are prohibited and how to file a complaint.

PERSONAL INJURY LAWSUITS

There are as many different kinds of personal injury lawsuits as there are accidents: car crashes, injuries caused by a dangerous or defective product, dog bites or a fall on someone's property are all potential grounds for a lawsuit. However, not everyone who suffers an accident and is injured can sue; they must show that the person they are suing is responsible for the injury.

Liability

Legal responsibility (liability) for an accident is based on a few common sense rules. Most accidents happen because someone was unreasonably careless (negligent). In most cases, the law requires the person who was negligent to compensate the injured person for his or her injuries.

The injured person can collect even if he or she was also negligent, but the injured person can only collect the percentage of the loss caused by the other person. For example, if you are in a car accident in which you were speeding and another car made an illegal turn and hit you, a court might decide that you were 30% at fault and deduct this amount from the other driver's liability. (This is referred to as "comparative negligence.")

Depending on the circumstances there may be additional legal twists on the rules of liability:

- If the injured person was someplace he or she was not supposed to be (for example, breaking into someone's home), or should have expected the kind of activity that caused the accident (for example, getting hit by a baseball at a baseball game), the person who caused the accident may not be liable.
- If an employee causes an accident while working, the employer may also be legally responsible for the accident.
- If an accident happens because property is poorly built or maintained (for example, a poorly lit parking lot or a broken elevator), the owner of the property is probably liable, even if the owner did not create the dangerous condition.
- If an accident is caused by a defective product, the manufacturer and the seller of the product are liable even if the injured person cannot show how the defect happened or which one was careless. The law presumes liability in these cases—this is referred to as "strict" liability.

Joint Liability

Many accidents involve the carelessness of more than one person. For example, an automobile accident may involve several careless drivers. In these cases, all of those who were negligent are responsible for compensating the injured person. If the injured person sues only one person, that person must pay the full amount. The person who was sued can sue the other negligent people and make them pay their share. However, the law does not allow the injured person to collect more than once.

When To Consult a Lawyer

In most cases, an injured person does not have to sue to be compensated for his or her injuries. If the person who caused the accident has insurance, the injured person can usually make a claim against that policy. Although this is taxing at times, it can usually be done without the assistance of a lawyer.

In certain cases, however, an injured person will need the help of an attorney. These cases include:

- accidents that cause long-term, severe or disabling injuries
- medical malpractice cases, and
- cases involving toxic exposure.

SETTLING A LAWSUIT OUT OF COURT

A settlement is an agreement between two people to end a dispute. Typically, one person agrees to pay money or provide services in exchange for the other person's promise to drop (or not bring) a lawsuit. Both sides agree to drop any claim they may have against each other. A settlement can be entered into at any time, even in the midst of a lawsuit. In fact, most lawsuits are settled without ever going to trial.

SETTLEMENT TIPS

Remember that a settlement is a compromise; you should be willing to accept less than what you might have been able to win in court to avoid the delay, uncertainty and expense of trial.

To negotiate a settlement, first determine how much it would cost to reimburse you for the damage done by the other person. Consider medical bills, property damage, time taken off work, pain and suffering, lost business, money you spent to repair poor work or materials, and so on. Then scale this figure back to reflect the possibility that you might lose the lawsuit or be found partially at fault, the likelihood that the other person will be difficult to collect a judgment from, even if you win, and the time and money you will save by avoiding a lawsuit. Once you figure out how much you're willing to settle for, ask for a bit more to give yourself room to maneuver, and begin negotiating.

Be sure that you get all settlement agreements in writing, signed by everyone involved. This will protect you in case you and your opponent later disagree on what was decided, or your opponent suddenly tries to back out of the bargain.

If you have suffered physical injuries, do not settle until you know the full extent of your problem. Often injuries are more serious than they first appear to be, and you should not accept a settlement that does not compensate you adequately.

If your dispute involves substantial personal injury or property damage, you may want to have a lawyer look over your settlement agreement.

If two people settle after a lawsuit has begun, the one who initially brought the lawsuit has two options: ask the court to enter a judgment based on the settlement or ask the court to dismiss the case.

Both sides can agree (stipulate) to a judgment that is the same as the settlement. Then, if one person doesn't fulfill those specific legal obligations, the other person can use collection methods that otherwise would require going to court and winning a lawsuit.

The plaintiff—or person who originally filed a case—can also dismiss the case. This is done by filing a form called a Request for Dismissal. The plaintiff should indicate on the form that the suit is being dismissed "with prejudice"—that is, the dispute has been resolved and the plaintiff has agreed not to sue. However, the case should not be dismissed until the settlement agreement has been fulfilled. Once the case is dismissed with prejudice, it cannot be reinstituted.

SMALL CLAIMS COURT

Small Claims Court is designed to resolve relatively minor disputes quickly, without lawyers or legal formalities.

Monetary Limit

You may sue for any amount up to $5,000. However, you may file only two actions in any 12-month period for amounts of $2,501 to $5,000. Up to $2,500, there is no limit on the number of suits you may bring, with one exception: suits against guarantors (companies that write insurance bonds) based on the default or actions or omissions of the person taking out the bond (often a contractor or someone else who must be bonded) can't exceed $1,500.

Who Can Sue?

With a few exceptions, any mentally competent person at least 18 years of age and any business can sue or be sued in Small Claims Court. There are, however, some exceptions and special rules:

- Although attorneys can sue or be sued on their own behalf, no one may be represented by an attorney.
- Collection agencies and other assignees (persons who are not the original creditor) cannot sue in Small Claims Court.
- Minors (children under 18) must have a parent or guardian sue for them.
- Contractors must be licensed, and car and TV repair dealers and pest control operators registered, with the appropriate state agency.
- Prisoners and military personnel transferred out of state can submit testimony in writing or authorize someone to appear on their behalf.

Where Suits Can Be Filed (Venue)

Small claims suits must be filed in the local Small Claims Court district where the defendant lives or, if a business is being sued, where it is located. In addition, you can sue:

- where an injury to persons or property occurred
- where a contract was signed or, for non-consumer (business to business) transactions, where the parties agreed in writing it was to be performed
- for consumer transactions, where the buyer resided at the time the contract was signed and where the goods or vehicle in question is permanently installed or kept.

A defendant who has been sued in the wrong place can write to the court, explain the situation and ask for a change to the correct court. (Code of Civ. Proc. § 116.370.)

Small Claims Court Procedures

Someone who wants to bring a suit in Small Claims Court must first contact the other party and request payment. This demand should be in writing.

The small claims clerk will help you complete a Plaintiff's Claim and Order to Defendant form. Businesses using a fictitious name must state that they have properly registered their name. The filing fee is $15 if you file 12 or fewer claims in any 12 month period and $30 for more frequent filers. Plaintiffs who win can recover these fees from the defendant.

Every person or business sued must receive a copy of the plaintiff's court papers. Usually this must be accomplished at least 10 days before the court hearing (15 days if it's in a county other than where the defendant lives or does business). There are several ways to serve court papers:

- **Certified mail.** The court clerk does the mailing. Service is complete if the defendant signs for the mail.

- **Personal service.** Any person age 18 or older, including a sheriff, marshal, constable or private process service, except the person bringing suit, may hand the papers to the defendant.

- **Substituted service.** Where service is difficult, a copy of the papers may be left with a competent member of the defendant's household (or in the case of a business, with someone apparently in charge) and another copy mailed to the defendant.

The cost of serving papers is recoverable if the plaintiff wins. Some counties may require the plaintiff to try the least costly method first in order to collect.

Defending a Small Claims Lawsuit

Defendants need only show up on the appointed day ready to present their side of the story. There are no forms to file or fees to pay unless they want to sue the plaintiff, in which case they must promptly file a Defendant's Claim with the Small Claims Court clerk and pay a $15 filing fee ($30 for frequent filers). If the defendant's claim is for more than $5,000, the entire lawsuit may be transferred to Municipal Court (up to $25,000) or Superior Court (over $25,000) if the defendant has filed in another court.

PRESENTING YOUR CASE IN COURT

Be prepared to stand and politely tell the judge what happened, when and where. Bring witnesses and evidence (pictures, letters, etc.) to court to back up your story and the amount of your loss. Don't argue with the other party, but be prepared to refute all likely claims.

Appeal Rights

A plaintiff who loses in Small Claims Court has no right to appeal the judge's decision. However, the party defending a claim (this could be the plaintiff, if a Defendant's Claim is filed) can appeal within 30 days after the mailing or delivery of the Notice of Entry of the Small Claims Judgment. The appeal results in a completely new trial, in Superior Court, of all claims of all parties. Both sides may have a lawyer on appeal, but this is often considered unnecessary, because rules are still informal. A judge can award up to $150 for attorney fees, as well as up to $150 for actual loss of earnings and transportation and lodging costs for the appeal. If the judge finds that an appeal was not in good faith, but was intended to delay or harass the plaintiff, the court may penalize the defendant up to $1,000. (Code of Civ. Proc. §§ 116.110-116.950.)

STATUTES OF LIMITATION

A statute of limitation is the deadline for filing a lawsuit. Here are the time limits for some common kinds of disputes:

- **Personal injury.** One year from the injury, or one year from the date it was discovered if it wasn't immediately discovered.
- **Breach of a written contract.** Four years from the day the contract is broken.
- **Breach of an oral contract.** Two years from the date the contract is broken.
- **Damage to real or personal property.** Three years from the date the damage occurs.
- **Claims against government agencies.** You must file a claim with the agency within six months of the incident. If this claim is denied, you are then free to bring a lawsuit.
- **Collecting a debt with a court judgment.** Ten years from the date of the judgment.

Other statutes of limitations can be found in the Code of Civ. Proc. §§ 312-363.

"Tolling" the Statute

In certain situations, the statute of limitations is suspended (tolled) for a period of time, then begins to run again. If the defendant is out of the state, in prison, insane or a minor, the statute does not run as long as this condition continues. When the condition ends, the clock starts running again.

Death of a Party to the Lawsuit

Some legal claims survive even the death of the person with the right to sue, or the person who can be sued. In these cases, the statute of limitations is extended. If the person who has the right to sue dies before the statute of limitations has run, that person's representatives can sue after the deadline has passed, as long as they bring suit within six months of death or within the limitations period that would have applied if the person had not died, whichever date comes later. (Code of Civ. Proc. § 366.1.) Similarly, if the person who is going to be sued dies before the statute of limitations has run, the person with the right to sue can bring suit after the deadline has passed, as long as suit is brought within one year of death. (Code of Civ. Proc. § 366.2.)

When the Statute Runs Out

Once the deadline passes, no lawsuit can be brought. Sometimes, however, an old legal claim will give rise to a new legal claim that starts a new statute of limitations. For example, if one person owes a debt to another, and the creditor doesn't bring suit within the deadline, the creditor loses the right to sue. But if the debtor promises again to pay the debt and begins payments after the original deadline passes, these actions create a new legal claim for the debt, with a new statute of limitations.

VICTIMS OF CRIME

Crime victims have certain rights to be notified of important events and to make statements to the judge or parole board. In addition, they may be eligible for compensation for their injuries.

Notice and Statements. As a crime victim, you have a right to be notified of the time, date and place of all felony sentencing proceedings. In addition, you will be notified of the following events, if you request such notice in writing beforehand, from the prison where the inmate is incarcerated:

- escape of the inmate
- placement of the inmate in a re-entry facility
- release of the inmate on parole.

You can also be notified of parole suitability hearings for life term inmates, if you request such notice by writing to Executive Officer, Board of Prison Terms, 428 J Street, Sacramento, CA 95814.

You also have the right to make certain statements, including:

- a victim impact statement to the parole board, indicating the effect the crime has had on your life
- a statement made before sentencing, indicating any factors the court should consider in deciding what sentence to impose
- an oral statement at the sentencing hearing
- a statement before the parole board, when it considers parole for a life term inmate.

BEFORE THE TRIAL

Before the trial, you should tell the prosecutor any special concerns you have about the proceedings, including the amount of bail, the possibility of plea bargaining or the defendant's eligibility for a diversion program. The prosecutor isn't required to follow your recommendations, but may try to do so.

Compensation. You may be able to recover for your financial losses that resulted from the crime, using one of the following methods:

- Victims of Crime Program, which can provide up to $46,000 in compensation for monetary losses, including medical bills, lost wages and funeral expenses. There are certain eligibility requirements, and you must have filed a criminal complaint. Family members and dependents of crime victims can also seek compensation. For more information, contact the Board of Control, P.O. Box 3036, Sacramento, CA 95812, (916) 322-4426.
- Restitution ordered by the court as part of a sentence, parole requirement or plea bargain. If restitution is ordered, be sure to get a certified copy of the criminal minute order or sentencing order from the court clerk. You will need this order to collect your restitution award, which you can do using standard collection techniques such as garnishing the wages or bank account of the defendant. If you would like the court to order restitution, talk to the prosecutor.
- Civil Lawsuits. Some victims sue their assailants in civil court to recover for property damage or personal injury, but it's usually not worth the effort.

Further Information. Contact your local victim assistance center, or call the Victims Resource Center at 1 (800) VICTIMS for more information on your legal rights.

DEBTS, LOANS AND CREDIT

It's not a crime to fail to pay debts—there is no longer any such thing as debtor's prison. However, creditors can use a number of legal tools to collect debts. This section discusses these debt collection methods, as well as legal options for debtors.

Consumer laws regarding credit and other forms of payment are also covered in this section.

TOPICS
>ATM AND DEBIT CARDS
>BANKRUPTCY
>CHECKS
>COSIGNERS' RIGHTS
>CREDIT AND CHARGE CARDS
>CREDIT BUREAUS
>CREDIT DISCRIMINATION
>DEBT COLLECTION
>LIENS
>LOANS
>REPOSSESSING PROPERTY
>STUDENT LOANS

RELATED TOPICS
>CONSUMERS' RIGHTS
>COURTS AND LAWSUITS
>>Federal Court System
>LANDLORDS AND TENANTS
>>Cosigning Leases and Rental Agreements
>REAL ESTATE
>>Homesteads
>RELATIONSHIPS
>>Marital Debts
>SMALL BUSINESSES

ADDITIONAL RESOURCES
>*Money Troubles: Legal Strategies To Cope With Your Debts,* by Robin Leonard (Nolo Press), explains your legal rights and offers practical strategies for dealing with debts.

>*Nolo's Law Form Kit: Rebuild Your Credit,* by Robin Leonard (Nolo Press) provides over a dozen strategies for cleaning up your credit file.

How To File for Bankruptcy, by Stephen Elias, Albin Renauer and Robin Leonard (Nolo Press), is a complete guide to choosing and filing for Chapter 7 bankruptcy, including all the forms you need.

Nolo's Law Form Kit: Personal Bankruptcy (Nolo Press) contains all the bankruptcy forms and instructions needed for filing a Chapter 7 bankruptcy.

Homestead Your House, by Ralph Warner, Charles Sherman and Toni Ihara (Nolo Press), contains a tear-out California homestead form so owners can protect the equity in their homes from creditors.

Collect Your Court Judgment, by Gini Graham Scott, Stephen Elias and Lisa Goldoftas (Nolo Press), explains 19 ways to collect after you win a lawsuit in California.

A Personal and Small Business Guide: Surviving Bankruptcy, by Dan Goss Anderson and M.J. Wardell (Prentice Hall), is filled with practical strategies for getting back on your feet after bankruptcy.

How To Get Out of Debt, Stay Out of Debt, & Live Prosperously, by Jerrold Mundia (Bantam) explains how to live—happily—without credit.

The Federal Trade Commission, at (310) 575-7575 in Los Angeles and (415) 744-7920 in San Francisco, takes complaints about credit bureaus and collection agencies.

The Federal Trade Commission, 6th & Pennsylvania Ave., NW, Washington, DC 20580, publishes a number of free pamphlets on debts and credit, including *Building a Better Credit Record, Buying and Borrowing: Cash in on the Facts, Cosigning a Loan, Credit and Older Americans, Credit Billing Errors, Credit Practices Rule, Equal Credit Opportunity, Fair Credit Billing, Fair Credit Reporting, Fix Your Own Credit Problems and Save Money, Getting a Loan: Your Home as Security, Lost or Stolen Credit and ATM Cards, Solving Credit Problems* and *Women and Credit Histories.*

The Federal Deposit Insurance Corporation, 550 17th St., NW, Washington, DC 20429 publishes free pamphlets about credit, including *Equal Credit Opportunity and Age, Fair Credit Billing, Fair Credit Reporting Act* and *How the Equal Credit Opportunity Act Affects You.*

AUTOMATED TELLER MACHINE (ATM) AND DEBIT CARDS

ATM cards are issued by banks to allow customers to make most of their banking transactions at a terminal, whenever they wish. Debit cards, also issued by banks, are used as a form of payment at stores. Although a few banks issue separate ATM and debit cards, in most instances an ATM card serves as a debit card. When you pay with a debit card, the money is automatically deducted from your checking account.

Statement or Receipt Errors

If your bank statement or receipt for an ATM or debit transaction includes an error, you have 60 days from the date of the statement or receipt to notify the bank. (15 U.S.C. § 1693f.) If you don't notify the bank within 60 days, it has no obligation to investigate the error.

The bank has 10 business days from the date of your notification to investigate the problem and tell you the result. If the bank needs more time, it can take up to 45 days, but only if it deposits the amount of money in dispute into your account. If the bank later determines that there was no error, it can take the money back, but it first must send you a written explanation.

Lost or Stolen ATM or Debit Cards

If your ATM or debit card is lost or stolen, you are not liable for any money taken out of your account without authorization after you report the card missing. Otherwise, your liability is limited to:

- up to $50, if you notify the bank within two business days of realizing the card is missing
- up to $500, if you fail to notify the bank within two business days (unless you were on extended travel or in the hospital) of realizing the card is missing but do notify the bank within 60 days of receiving your bank statement
- unlimited, if you fail to notify the bank within 60 days of receiving your bank statement (15 U.S.C. § 1693g.)

If a bank violates these rules, you can sue to recover your actual loss, twice the amount of any finance charge (not less than $100 nor more than $1,000), attorney fees and court costs. (15 U.S.C. § 1640.)

ATM Fees

Banks must disclose any fees for using an ATM card before the transaction is completed. (Fin. Code § 13080.)

BANKRUPTCY

Bankruptcy is a legal proceeding that wipes out some or all of your debts. After you file in federal bankruptcy court, your creditors can't collect from you, except that secured creditors (businesses that made auto, furniture or house loans, for example) are entitled to have the secured item (auto, furniture, house) returned as a condition of wiping out the debt. When the bankruptcy is over, your debts are erased (discharged), and creditors are barred forever from trying to collect, unless a particular debt is not discharged during your bankruptcy case.

Kinds of Bankruptcy

There are several kinds of bankruptcy, all of them creatures of federal law.

- **Chapter 7 bankruptcy**, also called straight or personal bankruptcy, is the most common kind. Debtors, both individual and business, ask the court to erase their debts. In exchange, debtors must give up certain kinds of property, which are used to pay creditors on a pro-rata basis.

The Chapter 7 bankruptcy process takes about three to six months, currently costs $150 in filing and administrative fees and commonly requires only one trip to the courthouse. To begin it, you must fill out forms describing your property and income, your debts and monthly living expenses, the property the law entitles you to keep (exempt property) and your property transactions of the prior two years.

The court appoints a trustee to oversee your bankruptcy case. The trustee collects your non-exempt property to sell to pay your creditors. At the end of your bankruptcy case, your "dischargeable" debts are wiped out.

- **Chapter 11 bankruptcy** allows businesses and individuals with an enormous amount of debt to reorganize so they can pay off their debts. The debtor does not have to give up any property during the case.

- **Chapter 12 bankruptcy** is only for family farmers. It lets them reorganize their farm businesses and pay off their debts under the supervision of the bankruptcy court.

- **Chapter 13 bankruptcy** allows you to keep your property and partially pay off creditors over three to five years. You make monthly payments to the bankruptcy court; the court in turn pays your creditors. Your creditors must receive at least as much as they would have had you filed for Chapter 7 bankruptcy—that is, the value of your non-exempt property. You must also dedicate all of your disposable monthly income to repaying your debts for three to five years. Some creditors must receive 100% of what you owe. Others may receive as little as 5%. To begin a Chapter 13 bankruptcy, you fill out forms listing your income, property, expenses and debts, and file them with the bankruptcy court. It currently costs $150 in filing and administrative fees and usually requires only one or two trips to the courthouse. In addition, you must file a workable plan to repay your debts, given your income and expenses.

If you cannot finish a Chapter 13 plan, the trustee can give you a grace period, reduce your total monthly payments or extend the repayment period. Or the court may let you convert your case to a Chapter 7 bankruptcy. If you won't be able to complete the plan because of circumstances beyond your control, the court might let you discharge the remainder of your debts on the basis of hardship.

After You File for Bankruptcy

When you file for bankruptcy, a protection called the "automatic stay" immediately stops any action (including a lawsuit or eviction) against you by a creditor, collection agency or government entity. The automatic stay may be lifted by the bankruptcy court if a creditor convinces the court that the stay will not serve its purpose—that is, to freeze your account so the bankruptcy court can deal with it.

How Often Can You File?

You cannot file for Chapter 7 bankruptcy if you received a Chapter 7 discharge in the past six years. Nor can you file for Chapter 7 bankruptcy if a previous Chapter 7 case was dismissed within the past 180 days because you violated a court order, the court ruled that your filing was fraudulent or an abuse of the bankruptcy system, or you requested the dismissal after a creditor asked the court to lift the automatic stay.

Chapter 13 bankruptcy has no restrictions; you can file for it at any time.

Property You Can Keep

When you file for Chapter 7 bankruptcy, you may claim certain assets as exempt—property that can't be taken and sold by the trustee. In California, you must choose between two different exemption systems. System One includes a much larger homestead exemption, and System Two includes a "wildcard" category that allows you to choose some of your otherwise non-exempt property to keep.

Debts That Survive Bankruptcy

You are not allowed to discharge these debts in bankruptcy:

- debts you forget to list in your bankruptcy papers and that the creditor doesn't otherwise learn of your bankruptcy
- some federal, state and local taxes
- child support and alimony
- personal injury debts caused by your intoxicated driving
- recent student loans
- fines and penalties imposed for violating the law, such as traffic tickets, criminal court penalties and criminal restitution.

Debts that couldn't be discharged in a previous bankruptcy may be dischargeable in a later Chapter 13, but are not dischargeable in a subsequent Chapter 7. In addition, the following debts are not dischargeable in Chapter 7, if a court so rules:

- debts incurred by fraud, such as lying on a credit application
- credit purchases of $500 or more for luxury goods or services within 40 days of the bankruptcy filing
- loans or cash advances of $1,000 or more within 20 days of the bankruptcy filing
- debts from willful or malicious injury to another or another's property, including assault, battery, false imprisonment, libel and slander
- debts from embezzlement, larceny or breach of trust.

CHECKS

You may have more rights than you know when it comes to dealing with your bank about checks you write or receive.

Check Holds

Banks used to make a lot of money by holding onto deposits for a few days before letting the depositor withdraw the funds. Now, state and federal laws restrict this practice. You can withdraw the money from government checks, cashier's checks and money orders the day after you deposit them. Local checks (for Northern Californians, checks drawn on financial institutions in Northern California and parts of Nevada; for Southern Californians, checks drawn on financial institutions in Southern California, Arizona and the Las Vegas area) cannot be held more than two business days. Other checks cannot be held more than five business days. A bank can, however, hold a local check for seven business days and a non-local check for 11 business days if the check is for over $5,000 or is a redeposited bounced check, or if the bank has reason to believe the check will be uncollectible.

These check hold rules do not apply to money market funds.

Stopping Payment

You may legally stop payment on a check if you don't do it to defraud a creditor. The stop payment order must be in writing. (Comm. Code § 4493.)

Stale and Postdated Checks

Banks are not obligated to honor a stale check—one older than six months or 180 days. (Comm. Code § 4404.) Most do, however, unless the check says "void after six months."

A postdated check is one dated later than the date it was actually written. If you receive a postdated check and present it to a bank for cashing before its date, a bank may legally cash the check, although many refuse to do so. A business may not request a postdated check. (Bus. & Prof. Code § 17538.6.)

Proper Identification

A merchant cannot refuse your check solely because you won't show a credit card or allow the merchant to write your credit card number on your check. Merchants can ask you to show a credit card and can record the type of card, the issuer of the card and expiration date. Merchants can also ask to see reasonable forms of identification, such as your driver's license, and may record that number on your check. (Civ. Code § 1725.)

Checks for Payment in Full

If a check says "cashing this check constitutes payment in full," the recipient can cross out the "full payment" language, deposit the check and sue for the balance owed. A debtor who wants to avoid this must take three steps:

- Send a letter to the creditor stating that she intends to send a full payment check.
- Wait at least 15 days, but not more than 90 days, to give the creditor time to object.
- Send a second letter and the check. Write on both items the following: "This check is tendered in accordance with my letter of (date). If you cash this check you agree that my debt is satisfied in full." (Civ. Code § 1526.)

Bad Checks

If a check bounces, the recipient may be entitled to collect up to three times the amount of the check. He must demand, by certified mail, that the person who wrote the check make payment within 30 days. If the person who bounced the check does not make it good within 30 days, and does not have a good faith dispute with the recipient, the recipient has two options:

- Sue for the original amount of the bounced check plus three times that amount— with a minimum of $100 and a maximum of $500—as a penalty. (Civ. Code § 1719.) The recipient may also sue for the costs of sending the notice by certified mail, plus costs of filing the lawsuit.
- Turn the matter over to the county district attorney's office. If that office has a check diversion program, writers of bad checks may be able to avoid criminal prosecution if they make the check good and comply with other rules. A recipient who enlists the help of the district attorney cannot sue.

Someone who willfully writes a bad check, knowing the account has insufficient funds to pay it, with the intent of defrauding the recipient of the check, can be sentenced to up to one year in county jail or state prison. (Pen. Code § 476(a).)

COSIGNERS' RIGHTS

A cosigner on a credit or loan application promises to pay if the primary borrower does not. If the primary borrower defaults, the cosigner's credit report may be affected. For this reason, the Federal Trade Commission requires that the cosigner be given a disclosure statement pointing out the obligations and risks. California requires that the notification shown below be given, in both English and Spanish, in 10-point type. (Civ. Code § 1799.91.)

NOTICE TO COSIGNER

You are being asked to guarantee this debt. Think carefully before you do so. If the borrower doesn't pay the debt, you will have to. Be sure you can afford to pay if you have to, and that you want to accept this responsibility. You may have to pay up to the full amount of the debt if the borrower does not pay. You may also have to pay late fees or collection costs, which increase this amount.

The creditor can collect this debt from you without first trying to collect from the borrower. The creditor can use the same collection methods against you that can be used against the borrower, such as suing you, garnishing your wages, etc. If this debt is ever in default, that fact may become part of *your* credit record.

This notice is not the contract that makes you liable for the debt.

CREDIT AND CHARGE CARDS

Credit cards and charge cards both allow you to buy goods on credit and pay later, but charge cards (such as American Express) don't allow you to carry an unpaid balance from month to month. Credit or charge cards are governed by your agreement with the bank, merchant or other creditor who issued the card, and several laws: the California Beverly-Song Credit Card Act (Civ. Code § 1747 and following), the Federal Fair Credit Billing Act (15 U.S.C. § 1666 and following) and the Federal Truth in Lending Act (15 U.S.C. § 1638 and following).

Interest

Credit card companies are free to charge as much interest as they want. State laws prohibiting usury (exorbitantly high interest) don't apply.

Unrequested Credit and Charge Cards

A company that issues credit or charge cards cannot legally send you one except in response to your request or application. However, there are no penalties against companies that send unrequested cards. If you "accept" the card—that is, if you use it, sign it or notify the card issuer in writing that you plan to keep it—you become liable for all charges made after your acceptance. But if you do not accept the card and it is used—for example, by a thief—the company is responsible.

Disclosures

When a credit or charge card company sends you an application or pre-approval letter, it must fully disclose the terms of your agreement, including finance charges, interest rates, membership fees and how interests rates and daily balances are calculated. (15 U.S.C. § 1637.) If the card issuer doesn't disclose this information or gives you the wrong information, you can sue for any loss you suffered as a result, including attorney fees, court costs and twice the amount of interest you were wrongfully charged (from $100 to $1,000). However, if the card issuer notifies you of the error within 60 days of discovering it, makes the necessary corrections, and does not improperly charge you interest, or if the error was unintentional and resulted from a clerical or calculation error, the card issuer is not liable.

Lost, Stolen and Borrowed Cards

Your liability for unauthorized charges made on your credit or charge card after it has been lost or stolen is limited by federal law. (15 U.S.C. § 1643.) If you notify the card issuer within a reasonable time, usually 30 days, after you discover the loss or theft, you're not responsible for any charges made after the notification, and are liable only for the first $50 of charges made before you notified the card issuer. If you don't notify the card issuer within a reasonable time, you could be liable for all charges made on your card before the notification.

If a friend or relative borrows your card, you are not liable for the charges incurred if you didn't know the person was using your card or you didn't authorize the person to use the card in the way in which it was used. But if you give someone your card and don't put a limit on charges, anything charged—until you say to stop—is your responsibility.

Disputes Over Credit or Charge Card Purchases

If you buy a defective item or service with a credit or charge card, you may refuse to pay if the seller won't replace or repair the item or otherwise correct the problem. Explain to the credit or charge card company in writing why you are withholding payment. (15 U.S.C. § 1666i.)

Before refusing to pay, you must attempt in good faith to resolve the dispute with the merchant. In addition, if you used a card not issued by the seller—such as a Visa, MasterCard, American Express or Discover card—you can refuse to pay only if the purchase was for more than $50 and was made within the state you live in or within 100 miles of your home. The law is unclear on whether or not telephone orders are considered made at your home—and therefore subject to this law—or made at the place where the merchant is located.

If you used a card issued by the seller—such as a department store or gas company card—or the seller obtained your order by mailing you an ad where the card issuer participated and urged you to use the credit card in question, you can withhold payment even if the purchase wasn't for more than $50 or made within your state or 100 miles of your home.

Billing Errors

If you find an error in your statement, you must send a letter to the company that issued the card within 60 days after it mailed the bill to you. The company must acknowledge receipt of your letter within 30 days unless it corrects the bill within that time. The card issuer must correct the error or explain why it believes the amount to be correct within two billing cycles (but in no event more than 90 days). If the card company does not comply with this limit, you don't have to pay any portion of the disputed balance. (Civ. Code § 1747.50.)

During the two-billing-cycle/90-day period, the company cannot report the amount to a credit bureau as delinquent or threaten or actually take any collection action against you. It can send you periodic statements, apply the amount in dispute to your credit limit (which lowers the amount available for you to charge) or charge you interest on the amount in dispute (to be dropped if you're later proven correct). (15 U.S.C. § 1666a.)

If the company violates these rules, you can sue to recover your actual losses, such as costs you incur in trying to remove erroneous information from a credit bureau file, twice the amount of any interest (but not less than $100 nor more than $1,000), attorney fees and court costs. (15 U.S.C. § 1640.)

Credit Card Surcharges

Retailers cannot charge consumers a surcharge for using a credit card. (Civ. Code § 1748.1.) Retailers can, however, offer a discount on the established price if you pay cash—which amounts to the same thing.

Personal Information on Credit Card Slips

Merchants cannot ask customers to write their phone number on a credit card slip. (Civ. Code § 1747.8.) The rule doesn't apply if you are having merchandise shipped, delivered or installed or for special orders.

Debiting Bank Accounts to Pay Credit Card Bills (Setoffs)

A bank cannot take money out of a deposit account to cover a missed credit card payment. (15 U.S.C. § 1666h, Regulation Z of the Truth-In-Lending Act, 12 C.F.R. § 226.12(d).)

CREDIT BUREAUS

Credit bureaus (officially called "consumer credit reporting agencies") are companies that make money by gathering and selling information about a person's credit history. The three major credit bureaus are TRW, TransUnion and Equifax. Credit bureaus are regulated by the Federal Fair Credit Reporting Act (15 U.S.C. § 1681 and following) and by California law. Here are the major rules:

- Bureaus may gather information about your credit-worthiness, credit standing, credit capacity, character, general reputation, personal characteristics or mode of living as it relates to your eligibility for credit or insurance, or for employment purposes.
- Bureaus cannot report an arrest unless it resulted in a conviction. (Civ. Code § 1785.13.)
- Bureaus can report bankruptcies for no more than ten years and can report any other adverse information for no more than seven years.

Bureaus may provide this information to anyone who intends to use it in a credit transaction, for employment purposes, to determine your eligibility for government benefits or for any other legitimate business need that relates to you.

Seeing Your File

Bureaus must show you your credit file if you present proper identification. You have a right to see your file as often as you want. If you are denied credit because of adverse information in a credit file, you have the right to a free copy, but must request it within 60 days. If you haven't been denied credit, the bureau can charge you a "reasonable fee." California caps the fee at $8. (Civ. Code § 1785.17.) TRW now provides one free copy a year.

Mistakes in a Credit File

If you complain to a bureau about a mistake or inaccuracy in your file, it must investigate within 30 days. If you are right, or if the creditor who provided the information can no longer verify the information, the bureau must remove it from your file. If the creditor later re-reports the information and the bureau intends to re-add it to your file, the bureau first must notify you.

If the credit bureau includes information in your file that you disagree with, you have the right to place a 100-word statement in your file describing your version of the dispute. A credit bureau employee will help you write the statement if you request it. The credit bureau must give a summary of your statement to anyone who requests your file. If you request it, the bureau must also give the summary to anyone who received a copy of your file within the past six months—two years if your file was given out for employment purposes.

Suing a Credit Bureau

You can sue a credit bureau for negligent (unreasonably careless) or willful noncompliance with the law within two years after the bureau's harmful behavior first occurred. You can sue for actual financial loss, such as court costs, attorney fees and lost wages and, if applicable, intentional infliction of emotional distress. In the case of truly outrageous behavior, you can recover from $100 to $5,000 in punitive damages—damages meant to punish for malicious or willful conduct. (Civ. Code § 1785.31.)

CREDIT DISCRIMINATION

The Equal Credit Opportunity Act prohibits a creditor from refusing to grant credit because of race, color, religion, national origin, sex, marital status or age, or because you receive public assistance. A creditor can ask about age or public assistance, but only to determine your credit history and the likelihood of your continued income. (15 U.S.C. § 1691.)

Race Discrimination

In general, lenders are prohibited from asking your race on a credit application or to ascertain it from any other means (such as a credit file) other than by personal observation. A mortgage lender, however, must ask your race for the purpose of monitoring home mortgage applications. Lenders are accused of getting around race discrimination prohibitions by "redlining"—denying credit to residents of predominantly black or hispanic neighborhoods.

Three laws prohibit redlining.

- The federal Home Mortgage Disclosure Act requires that mortgage lenders maintain and disclose their lending practices for certain areas. (2 U.S.C. § 2801 and following)
- The federal Community Reinvestment Act requires that bank mortgage lenders demonstrate that they serve the needs of the communities in which they are chartered to serve. If the bank fails to do so, bank regulators can deny the bank the right to establish branches or other activity requiring regulatory approval. (12 U.S.C. § 2901 and following)
- Redlining is also barred by the Fair Housing Act of the Federal Civil Rights Act. (42 U.S.C. § 3601 and following)

Sex Discrimination

A creditor may ask you to designate a title (Mr., Ms., etc.), but must make clear that selecting one is optional. A creditor may also ask your sex when you apply for a real estate loan; this information is collected by the federal government for statistical purposes.

Marital Status Discrimination

A married person may apply for credit in his or her name alone—a creditor cannot require an applicant's spouse to cosign an application. In California, the creditor may ask about marital status but can't deny credit based on the answer. (Civ. Code § 1812.30.)

If an unmarried couple applies for a joint loan, the creditor must consider their combined income, just as it would for a married couple. (*Markham v. Colonial Mortgage Service Co.*, 605 F.2d 566 (D.C. Cir. 1979).)

DEBT COLLECTION

The law prohibits creditors from using abusive or deceptive tactics to collect a debt. The law, however, also grants powerful collection tools to creditors once they have won a lawsuit over the debt.

IMPORTANT TERMS

Judgment creditor. A person who has sued and won a judgment against someone else. This person is a creditor because the loser of the lawsuit owes him or her money.

Judgment debtor. The person who lost the lawsuit and owes money to the judgment creditor.

Prohibited Debt Collection Practices

Debt collection practices are governed by the Federal Fair Debt Collection Practices Act (15 U.S.C. § 1692 and following) and California's Fair Debt Collection Practices Act (Civ. Code § 1788.4 and following). The federal law governs only collection agencies. The state law covers any debt collector, including a collection agency, who collects debts regularly in his own behalf or for others. Under both laws, a debt collector may not:

- **Communicate with a debtor** by:
  - calling, writing or talking with the debtor directly, if the bill collector knows the debtor has an attorney
  - calling repeatedly or at an unusual or inconvenient place or time
  - reaching the debtor at work, if the collector knows that the debtor is prohibited from receiving collections calls at work
  - sending a document that misleadingly appears to be from a court, government agency or attorney.
- **Harass or abuse a debtor** by:
  - harming or threatening the debtor or another person, or the reputation or property of the debtor or another person
  - using obscene or profane language
  - publishing the debtor's name as a person who doesn't pay bills.
- **Communicate with third parties about the debtor**, including:
  - giving false credit information about the debtor, or failing to disclose that the debtor disputes a debt, if true
  - contacting a third party (other than the debtor's attorney or a credit bureau) for any purpose except locating the debtor, verifying the debtor's employment, or finding out if the debtor has medical insurance (for medical debts only)
  - failing to reveal the debt collector's company name to any third party contacted, if asked.
- **Make false or misleading statements**, including:
  - falsely claiming to be an attorney, police officer or government agent
  - threatening to take action that isn't intended or can't be taken, such as stating that welfare benefits will be cut off, the debtor will be jailed or the debtor's property will be taken
  - falsely claiming that the debtor has committed a crime
  - falsely claiming to be taking a survey, casting a movie or TV show, or promising money or a valuable gift if the debtor discloses certain information. (16 C.F.R. § 237.1.)

- **Use unfair or outrageous debt collection methods,** such as:
  - adding interest, fees or charges not authorized in the original agreement or by state law
  - accepting a check postdated by more than five days, unless the collector notifies the debtor between three and ten days in advance of when he will deposit it
  - calling the debtor collect or otherwise causing the debtor to incur communications charges
  - sending the debtor a postcard or envelope with words or symbols on the outside that indicate the collector is trying to collect a debt.

CALLING OFF A DEBT COLLECTOR

If you've been contacted by a collection agency, the Federal Fair Debt Collection Practices Act gives you the right to tell the bill collector to cease all communications with you. Begin over the phone; follow up with a letter. If the collection agency contacts you again (other than to say collection efforts are ending or that it is going to take a specific action—such as suing you), it has violated the law.

How Judgment Creditors Can Collect Debts

Once the creditor has won a lawsuit affirming the debt, the creditor can use any of the following collection techniques.

Wage Garnishment. A wage garnishment orders the debtor's employer to withhold a portion of the debtor's wages from each paycheck and pay that money directly to the judgment creditor. For most judgments, the employer will withhold 25% of each paycheck; the creditor can ask that less be withheld. As much as 50% can be withheld if the debt is for spousal or child support. Garnishment lasts until the creditor collects the entire judgment or until a wage garnishment of higher priority (for spousal or child support or taxes) is instituted.

- To garnish a debtor's wages, the judgment creditor must prepare a few fill-in-the-blanks forms available free from the court clerk and send them to a local levying officer, usually a sheriff or marshal. The levying officer will serve these papers on the debtor's employer.
- A debtor who wants to protest a wage garnishment may file a claim of exemption. The debtor must show that his entire paycheck is needed to support himself and his family. If the creditor opposes this claim, the court will decide whether or not garnishment is appropriate, and if so, in what amount.

Seizing the Debtor's Property. When a creditor gets the court's permission to have certain items of the debtor's property seized or sold, it's called levying on the judgment. A creditor can take a portion of the debtor's wages (wage garnishment), the debtor's bank account or safe deposit box, money owed to the debtor by a third person or the contents of a business debtor's cash register. In addition, a creditor can seize the debtor's real estate or personal property, have it sold and collect the proceeds.

To use a levy, the judgment creditor must prepare a form (called a Writ of Execution), and send it, along with instructions and fees, to a local levying officer. The levying officer will serve these papers on the person or business who has the debtor's assets, such as a bank, and will seize or sell the debtor's property.

Some kinds of property are exempt from collection, which means the creditor can't take them or force the debtor to sell them. Whenever a creditor seeks to take a debtor's property, the debtor is given a form explaining how to file a claim of exemption. Using this form, the debtor can request a hearing to argue that the property is exempt or that it will be a financial hardship if the property is taken.

The debtor's homestead (a certain amount of the equity in his residence) and a portion of the debtor's wages are exempt from collection in California. In addition, the debtor can keep:

- insurance policies, including disability or health benefits, life insurance proceeds and unmatured life insurance of up to $4,000 loan value
- pensions
- personal property, including appliances, furnishings, necessary food and clothing, bank deposits from Social Security, burial plots, health aids, motor vehicles worth up to $1,200, and jewelry, heirlooms and art worth up to $2,500
- public benefits, such as AFDC, Social Security, workers' compensation and unemployment benefits
- tools of trade, such as materials, uniforms, books, equipment and a motor vehicle worth up to $2,500, if used for the debtor's work.

Creditors can also place liens on a debtor's property. (See "Liens.")

LIENS

A lien is a claim against a debtor's property for the amount of a debt. It gives the creditor the right to be paid from the proceeds if the property is sold or refinanced. A debtor may voluntarily take on a lien, by pledging collateral as security for a loan or purchase. More often, liens are placed on property by creditors.

Some liens do not require a court judgment in the creditor's favor, such as:

- **Tax liens.** The IRS can record a lien against a debtor's property for delinquent taxes.
- **Child support liens.** For unpaid child support debts.
- **Mechanic's or materialmen's liens.** Someone who performs work or supplies materials for a house, vehicle or other property can place a lien on that property if the bill is not paid.

Some liens can be used only by a creditor who has won a court judgment against the debtor. Among these judicial liens are:

- **Real estate liens.** A creditor who has a court judgment that is enforceable in California or a workers' compensation judgment may place a lien on the debtor's real estate. This lien must be recorded (put on file) at the county recorder's office; any real estate the debtor purchases in that county after the lien is placed will also be subject to the real estate lien. (Code of Civ. Proc. §§ 697.060, 697.330.)
- **Business property liens.** A creditor can create a lien that lasts for five years against a business' personal property (anything but real estate) by filing papers with the California Secretary of State. This lien applies to tools, equipment, harvested crops, accounts receivable and inventory items with a unit value of over $500, but not to cars, boats or other vehicles. The lien also applies to assets that the debtor acquires after the lien is placed. (Code of Civ. Proc. §§ 697.350, 697.510.) However, if business assets are transferred in the ordinary course of business and the purchaser is unaware of the lien, the creditor cannot collect from those assets.
- **Liens on pending legal action.** If a debtor is involved in a lawsuit, divorce or other legal action, a creditor may file a lien in the pending case. If the debtor wins the suit, he or she must pay the creditor before collecting his or her own judgment. (Code of Civ. Proc. § 708.440.)

LOANS

Under state and federal law, lenders must provide borrowers with certain information and options, and are restricted in the methods they can use to collect loans.

Disclosures

The Federal Truth In Lending Act requires lenders to disclose certain information in writing when someone applies for a loan, such as the total amount of the loan, the interest rate and amount, and any penalties for late payment or prepayment. (15 U.S.C. § 1638.)

Balloon Payments

If a loan includes a balloon payment—a large payment at the end of a loan period—you have the right to refinance that payment at the lender's prevailing rate when it comes due. (Civ. Code § 1807.3.)

Restricted Collection Practices

Lenders must follow certain procedures when trying to get borrowers to repay their loans. Several short-cuts have been restricted or banned.

- **Setoffs** happen when your lending institution removes money from your deposit account to cover a payment missed on your loan. This is legal only if the bank disclosed in writing, when you took out the loan, its right to use a setoff. Otherwise, you can sue for the amount taken out of your account plus any other fees or penalties. A bank cannot use a setoff in any circumstances if the aggregate balance of all your accounts with that bank is under $1,000. (Fin. Code §§ 864, 6660.)

- **Confession of judgment** is a loan provision that lets a lender automatically take a judgment against you if you default, without having to sue you. Federal law prohibits such provisions in any non-real estate consumer contract. (Fed. Trade Commission's Credit Practices Rule, 16 C.F.R. § 444.)

- **Security interest.** When you take out a secured loan, you give the creditor the right to take certain property, or a portion of it, if you don't pay. This is called a security interest. Federal law prohibits lenders from taking a security interest in the following, unless you are actually buying the item: clothing, furniture, appliances, linens, china, crockery, kitchenware, one radio and one television, wedding ring and personal effects. (Fed. Trade Commission's Credit Practices Rule, 16 C.F.R. § 444.)

- **Voluntary wage assignments.** Some lenders try to ensure your repayment by suggesting that you voluntarily agree to a wage assignment. This means that each time you are paid, a sum of money is deducted from your paycheck by your employer to pay the lender.

  With the exception of real estate loans, a voluntary wage assignment is allowed only if you have the power to revoke it. (Fed. Trade Commission's Credit Practices Rule, 16 C.F.R. § 444.) If you're married, your spouse must consent before the lender can take a voluntary wage assignment. (Lab. Code § 300.)

- **Waivers of exemptions.** If a creditor sues you and wins a court judgment, or you file for bankruptcy, some of your property is protected from your creditors—that is, it can't be taken to pay what you owe. This property is called your exempt property. (See "Debt Collection" for more information.)

  Some creditors try to get around these laws by including a provision in a loan agreement that says you waive your right to keep your exempt property. These provisions are prohibited in any non-real estate consumer contract. (Fed. Trade Commission's Credit Practices Rule, 16 C.F.R. § 444.)

REPOSSESSING PROPERTY

If you buy something on credit and pledge the item as security for the loan—for example, a new car—and then don't keep up your loan payments, the item can be repossessed. In California, a creditor must first sue you in court and obtain a court judgment before repossessing any property except a motor vehicle. Of course, if a creditor (or a "repo man") shows up without a court judgment and you give him permission to repossess your property—in other words, you give it back—it's perfectly legal. (Civ. Code § 1812.2.) You are under no obligation to give this permission, but if you don't and the creditor sues, attorney fees and court costs will probably be added to the amount you already owe.

Motor Vehicles

As mentioned, a lender doesn't need to sue and win a court judgment to repossess a motor vehicle; the lender is free to send a repossessor as soon as you default on your car loan payments. (Civ. Code § 2983.2.) A repossessor can't use force to get to your vehicle—repossessions must occur without any "breach of the peace." (Comm. Code § 9503.) But a repossessor can grab your vehicle almost anytime you're not in it or standing guard. It's legal to hotwire a car, use a duplicate key or remove a car from an open garage or carport. It's illegal to take a car from a garage where the door is closed but unlocked or to break into a locked garage, even by using a duplicate key.

When your car is repossessed, you often have a short time during which you can get it back by paying all past due installments and late fees, as well as the costs the lender incurred in taking and storing it. You can't reinstate the contract, however, if you have done any of the following:

- had the contract reinstated in the past
- lied on your credit application
- hid the car to avoid repossession
- didn't take care of the car, and its value has substantially diminished, or
- have committed violence against the lender or repossessor.

The lender must give you written notice that you have the right to reinstate the contract within 15 days after the notice is mailed. If it doesn't, you may have the right to get the vehicle back for nothing—but you will have to resume making payments on your loan. If you don't reinstate the contract within the time permitted, the lender will declare the entire balance due and send you a formal notice of its intent to sell the car. You then have an additional 10 days to pay the entire balance of what you owe in exchange for getting it back.

If you don't pay what you owe within the time provided in the lender's notice, the property will be sold at an auction. The lender must give you 15 days' notice of the time and place of the sale. Usually, the lender invites used car dealers and others who regularly buy repossessed cars. They bid very low, so the sale of your car will likely bring in far less than what you owe the lender.

The sale price is subtracted from what you owed the lender before the car was repossessed. Then, the cost of repossessing, storing and selling the property is added to the difference, and the total is called a deficiency judgment. You owe that amount to the lender. If you don't pay, the lender can sue you.

If the repossessor takes your car, you're entitled to get back all your belongings in the car when it was repossessed. You'll have to make a request, within the time allowed in your loan agreement.

STUDENT LOANS

Student loans fall into four categories. Repayment of all of these loans is guaranteed by the federal government. (20 U.S.C. § 1071.)

- Guaranteed Student Loans (GSLs; also called Stafford Loans). A GSL is made by a bank to finance college or graduate school education.
- National Direct Student Loans (NDSLs; also called Perkins Loans). An NDSL is a need-based loan made by your school to finance college or graduate school education.
- Non-need-based college loans—made directly by your school to finance college or graduate school education.
  — Parental Loans for Students (PLUS)—made to parents to help pay for their dependent children's education, and
  — Supplemental Loans for Students (SLS)—made directly to financially independent students.
- Miscellaneous loans created and funded by the federal government.
  — Health Professions Student Loans (HPSL)
  — Health Education Assistance Loans (HEAL).

Contact your school's financial aid office for details regarding deferment and cancellation of an HPSL or HEAL.

Canceling a Student Loan

Your obligation to repay a GSL, NDSL, PLUS or SLS depends on the kind of loan and when you borrowed the money.

- You become totally and permanently disabled or die. You can cancel a GSL, NDSL, PLUS or SLS Loan. PLUS Loans may be canceled if the child for whom you borrowed the money dies.
- You serve in the U.S. military. The Defense Department will repay a portion of a GSL, NDSL, PLUS or SLS Loan.
- You're a full-time teacher in a designated area serving low-income students. You can cancel up to 100% of an NDSL. You can cancel up to 100% of a GSL made before October 1, 1992.
- You're a full-time teacher of handicapped children. You can cancel up to 100% of an NDSL.
- You're a full-time professional provider of early intervention services for the disabled. You can cancel up to 100% of an NDSL made after July 23, 1992.
- You're a full-time teacher of math, science, foreign languages, bilingual education or other fields designated as teacher shortage areas. You can cancel up to 100% of an NDSL made after July 23, 1992. You can cancel up to 100% of a GSL made before October 1, 1992.
- You're a full-time employee of a public or nonprofit agency providing services to low-income, high-risk children and their families. You can cancel up to 100% of an NDSL made after July 23, 1992.
- You're a full-time nurse. You can cancel up to 100% of an NDSL made after July 23, 1992. You can cancel up to 100% of a GSL made before October 1, 1992.
- You're a full-time medical technician. You can cancel up to 100% of an NDSL made after July 23, 1992.
- You're a full-time law enforcement or corrections officer. You can cancel up to 100% of an NDSL made after November 29, 1990.
- You're a full-time staff member in a Head Start program. You can cancel up to 100% of an NDSL.
- You're a Peace Corps of VISTA volunteer. You can cancel up to 70% of an NDSL. You can cancel up to 100% of a GSL made before October 1, 1992.
- You return to school for a teaching certificate. You can cancel up to 100% of a Stafford Loan made before October 1, 1992.

Deferring Repayments

You can defer (postpone) the repaying certain student loans if you are not in default—that is, you must have made your payments on time or you are still in the grace period after graduation. (20 U.S.C. § 1077.) The rules depend on the kind of loan you have and when you obtained it.

Loans Disbursed After July 1, 1993

- You are enrolled in school at least half-time. You can defer only principal on PLUS and SLS Loans. You can defer interest and principal on an NDSL or GSL.
- You are enrolled in an approved graduate fellowship program or a rehabilitation program for the disabled. You can defer only principal on PLUS and SLS Loans. You can defer interest and principal on an NDSL or GSL.
- You are unable to find full-time employment. You can defer only principal on PLUS and SLS Loans. You can defer interest and principal on an NDSL or GSL. The deferment is for a maximum of three years.
- Your are suffering from economic hardship—that is, your student loan debt is at least 20% of your gross income. You can defer only principal on PLUS and SLS Loans. You can defer interest and principal on an NDSL or GSL. The deferment is for a maximum of three years.

GSLs Disbursed Before July 1, 1993

- You are in school full-time. Some banks will let you defer your repayment if you are in school half-time. The deferment lasts until six months after your schooling ends.
- You are disabled and enrolled in full-time rehabilitation training. The deferment lasts until six months after your training ends.
- You are temporarily totally disabled. The deferment is for a maximum of three years.
- You are in the military. The deferment is for a maximum of three years.
- You are a full-time volunteer in a tax-exempt organization, the Peace Corps or an ACTION program. The deferment is for a maximum of three years.
- You are on active duty with the National Oceanic and Atmospheric Administration Corps. The deferment is for a maximum of three years.
- You are a full-time teacher in a government-identified teacher shortage area. The deferment is for a maximum of three years.
- You are completing a professional internship. The deferment is for a maximum of two years.
- You are unemployed, but are looking for work. The deferment is for a maximum of two years.
- You are the mother of preschool children, are entering or reentering the work force and are earning no more than $1 above the federal minimum wage. The deferment is for a maximum of one year.
- You are on parental leave. The deferment is for a maximum of six months.

NDSL, PLUS and SLS Loans Disbursed Before July 1, 1993

- You are in school full-time. You can defer only principal on PLUS and SLS Loans; you cannot defer an NDSL.
- You are disabled and enrolled in full-time rehabilitation training. You may defer only principal on PLUS and SLS Loans; you cannot defer an NDSL.
- You are temporarily totally disabled. You may defer only principal on PLUS and SLS. You may defer principal and interest on an NDSL. The deferment is for a maximum of three years. If your NDSL is from before the fall of 1987, you cannot defer any of it.

- You are in the military. You may defer only principal on an SLS. You may defer principal and interest on an NDSL. You may defer principal and interest on a PLUS Loan made before August 15, 1983. The deferment is for a maximum of three years.
- You are a full-time volunteer in a tax-exempt organization, the Peace Corps or an ACTION program. You may defer only principal on an SLS. You may defer principal and interest on an NDSL. You may defer principal and interest on a PLUS Loan made before August 15, 1983. The deferment is for a maximum of three years.
- You are on active duty with the National Oceanic and Atmospheric Administration Corps. You may defer only principal on an SLS. You may defer principal and interest on an NDSL. The deferment is for a maximum of three years. If your NDSL is from before the fall of 1987, you cannot defer any of it.
- You are a full-time teacher in a government-identified teacher shortage area. You may defer only principal on an SLS. The deferment is for a maximum of three years. You cannot defer an NDSL or PLUS Loan.
- You are completing a professional internship. You may defer only principal on an SLS. You may defer principal and interest on an NDSL. The deferment is for a maximum of two years. You cannot defer a PLUS Loan.
- You are unemployed, but are looking for work. You may defer only principal on an SLS, PLUS or an NDSL. The deferment is for a maximum of two years.
- You are the mother of preschool children, are entering or reentering the work force and are earning no more than $1 above the federal minimum wage. You may defer only principal on an SLS. You may defer principal and interest on an NDSL. The deferment is for a maximum of one year. If your NDSL is from before the fall of 1987, you cannot defer any of it.
- You are on parental leave. You may defer only principal on an SLS. You may defer principal and interest on an NDSL. The deferment is for a maximum of six months. If your NDSL is from before the fall of 1987, you cannot defer any of it. Nor can you defer a PLUS Loan.

Consolidating Your Loans

You can consolidate any GSL, NDSL, HPSL, SLS, ALAS and PLUS loan payments you make if you owe at least $7,500, you are in the repayment period or grace period preceding repayment, and are no more than 90 days past due on any loan you want to consolidate. All consolidated loans are repaid at 9%. You can also extend your repayment period. A HEAL loan cannot be consolidated to reduce interest, but can be combined with the other loans so that you make only one payment a month.

Delinquent Student Loans

The Internal Revenue Service is authorized to deduct the amount of delinquent student loans from any income tax refund due you. (31 U.S.C. § 3720A; 26 C.F.R. § 301.6402-6T(b)(1).) You will be notified before the money is withheld and given at least 60 days to present written evidence to the agency collecting the loan showing that the loan is either not past due or not legally enforceable. Also, the Department of Education can garnish up to 10% of your wages—without first suing you and getting a judgment—if you've defaulted on your loan. At least 30 days before the garnishment is to begin, you will be notified and given the opportunity to object—on the ground that you returned to work within the previous 12 months after having been fired or laid off. Finally, you may be sued on a delinquent loan, no matter how old it is or how long ago you defaulted.

DOGS

State laws are covering more and more topics when it comes to animals, but local governments are still in charge of most basic animal regulations. Most cities:

- Require owners to buy a license for each dog.
- Limit the number of pets per household.
- Require dogs to be on a leash and under control whenever they're off their owners' property, except in areas designated for unleashed dogs. (Most trails and campgrounds of the California State Park system are closed to dogs.)
- Require dogs to have a rabies vaccination and sometimes other shots, such as distemper, as well.
- Require owners to immediately dispose of, in a sanitary manner, dog droppings deposited anywhere except on their own property.

Many of these local laws, however, don't apply to assistance dogs trained to help disabled owners.

TOPICS

> **DESTRUCTION OF LIVESTOCK BY DOGS**
> **DOG BITES AND OTHER INJURIES CAUSED BY DOGS**
> **DOG POUNDS AND SHELTERS**
> **DOGS IN VEHICLES**
> **GUIDE, SIGNAL AND SERVICE DOGS**
> **PET STORES**

RELATED TOPICS

> **COURTS AND LAWSUITS**
> Personal Injury Lawsuits
> **LANDLORDS AND TENANTS**
> Pets
> **REAL ESTATE**
> Noise

ADDITIONAL RESOURCES

Dog Law, by Mary Randolph (Nolo Press), is a guide to the laws that affect dog owners and their neighbors.

Canine Companions for Independence, P.O. Box 446, Santa Rosa, CA 95403, (707) 767-BARK, provides information about assistance dogs.

DESTRUCTION OF LIVESTOCK BY DOGS

Someone who owns, possesses or keeps a dog that injures or harasses livestock is liable to the owner of the livestock for his or her losses. The farmer who loses livestock doesn't have to prove that the dog's owner knew that the dog posed a danger to livestock.

A farmer who catches a dog in the act of harassing or wounding livestock may kill the dog without being liable to the dog's owner for the value of the dog. (Civ. Code § 3341.)

DOG BITES AND OTHER INJURIES CAUSED BY DOGS

In California, the owner of a dog that injures someone is almost always liable for the injury. Three different legal rules impose liability; someone injured by a dog has a choice of suing under any one of them.

- **The dog bite statute.** If a dog bites someone, the owner is liable for the injury. (Civ. Code § 3342.) The injured person does not have to prove that the dog owner did anything wrong. It doesn't matter, for example, that the owner didn't know the dog would hurt anyone or conscientiously tried to keep it from injuring anyone.

  The police and military cannot be sued if their trained dogs bite someone while they're working. This immunity applies only if the government agency in charge of the dog has a written policy on proper use of its dogs. (Civ. Code § 3342(b).)

- **The common law rule.** The statute above applies only to dog bites; to sue for other injuries, an injured person must prove that the dog's owner or keeper knew, or had reason to know:

  —the dog was vicious or dangerous to people; and

  —the specific tendency (for example, a tendency to knock people down) of the dog that caused the injury.

- **Negligence.** A dog owner may also be sued for negligence (unreasonable carelessness) if the owner's actions resulted in an injury. For example, a California man let his dog roam, in violation of a local leash law. The dog ran into the road, and a pickup truck crashed trying to avoid it. Two men riding in the back of the truck suffered serious permanent injuries. A judge ruled in 1987 that the dog owner's violation of the leash law was negligence, and awarded the injured men $2.6 million.

  A dog owner may be able to escape liability by proving that the injured person provoked the injury, or voluntarily and knowingly risked the injury.

What the Owner Is Liable For

A dog owner who is legally responsible for an injury to a person or property may be responsible for reimbursing the injured person for:

- medical bills (emergency room, office visits, hospital stays, surgery, medication, physical therapy)
- time off work
- pain and suffering
- property damage.

Who Is Responsible

Usually, a dog's owner is legally responsible for damage or injury the dog causes. But an injured person may also sue:

- The dog owner's parent, if the owner is less than 18 years old
- The dog owner's landlord, if he or she knew the dog was dangerous but didn't do anything about it, or
- Someone who was taking care of the dog for the owner.

Vicious Dogs

If a dog bites someone on at least two separate occasions, or if a dog trained to fight bites someone once and causes substantial injury, any person (or the district or city attorney) can sue the dog's owner in Municipal Court. The court will determine whether or not the dog is still a danger to people. The court may order the owner to take any action it decides is necessary to prevent future injury, including removing the dog from the area or destroying it. (Civ. Code § 3342.5.)

California law requires the owner of a dog that a judge finds to be "potentially dangerous" to keep the dog fenced or leashed at all times. The court may also prohibit the owner of a vicious dog from owning a dog for up to three years. (Food and Agric. Code § 31601 and following.)

DOG POUNDS AND SHELTERS

A dog running loose in violation of local law can be picked up and taken to the pound by municipal or county animal control officers. The owner will be fined and charged for the cost of impounding the dog. If the dog is unlicensed, there will be an additional fine.

Unless a dog is running at large, or an emergency requires immediate action, most courts would agree that an owner who has possession of a dog is entitled to:

- be notified before the dog is seized
- be notified before the dog is destroyed, and
- given a chance to argue, in court, that the dog shouldn't be destroyed.

If a dog isn't claimed or adopted within a certain time, a shelter may destroy it humanely, or sell it to a research lab unless local law prohibits it. Any animal shelter, public or private, that turns dogs over to a research facility must prominently post a large sign, stating that "Animals Turned Into This Shelter May Be Used For Research Purposes." (Civ. Code § 1834.7.)

DOGS IN VEHICLES

Dogs in the open back of a pickup must be either in a cage or cross-tied to the truck unless the sides of the truck are at least 46 inches high. The law doesn't apply to cattle or sheep dogs used by farmers and ranchers. Violators can be fined $50 to $100 for a first offense and up to $250 for a third offense. (Veh. Code §§ 23117, 42001.4.)

GUIDE, SIGNAL AND SERVICE DOGS

KINDS OF ASSISTANCE DOGS

- **Guide dogs** help visually-impaired owners navigate through public places.
- **Signal dogs** alert hearing-impaired people to important sounds: intruders, phones, crying babies, doorbells and smoke alarms. In cars, they alert owners to ambulance sirens and honking drivers.
- **Service dogs** are the arms and legs of many physically disabled people. They pull wheelchairs, carry baskets and briefcases, open doors and turn on lights.

Access to Public Places

Any person who is partially or totally blind, deaf or hearing-impaired or physically handicapped has the right to take a trained guide dog, signal dog or service dog into any public place. That includes hotels, trains, buses, planes and other places the public is invited. It is illegal to impose any extra charge for admitting an assistance dog to any place the dog is allowed by law. (Civ. Code § 54.2.) Zoos are allowed to keep these dogs out of areas where zoo animals aren't separated from the public by a physical barrier, but the zoo must maintain free kennel facilities for the dogs. (Civ. Code § 54.7.)

Guide dogs are also allowed in any building or property owned or controlled by the federal government. (40 U.S.C. § 291.)

AVOIDING PROBLEMS IF YOU HAVE AN ASSISTANCE DOG

It's a good idea for people who have assistance dogs to carry copies of the state laws that allow them access to public places. If they are refused admittance to a public place, they can show the management that the law forbids such discrimination.

Rental Housing

Generally, California landlords may refuse to rent to tenants with dogs. There are, however, a few exceptions.

Residents of public housing developments (those owned and operated by a state, county, city or district agency) who are over the age of 60 or disabled may keep up to two small pets per apartment. (Health & Safety Code § 19901.)

Tenants in "federally assisted" housing for the elderly or handicapped are allowed by law to own pets. (Housing and Urban-Rural Recovery Act of 1983, 12 U.S.C. § 1701r-1.) This rule applies even if the federal government does not own the rental housing—it's enough that a federal agency (the U.S. Department of Housing and Urban Development, for example) subsidizes it.

It is illegal to refuse to rent housing to someone because that person uses a guide, signal or service dog. (Civ. Code § 54.1(5).) These dogs are normally so well-trained and well-behaved that a landlord has little reason to object to them anyway. The law allows landlords to include reasonable regulations in the lease or rental agreement. The owners, like all dog owners, are liable for any damage the dogs cause.

Government Assistance for Low Income Owners

The Internal Revenue Service recognizes guide dogs as a legitimate medical expense, which can be deducted for federal income tax purposes. (Treas. Reg. § 1.213-1(e)(1)(iii).)

To help with the expenses of keeping a guide dog, California gives a monthly payment for dog food to low-income disabled owners. (Welf. & Inst. Code § 12553.)

The federal government may also pay for a guide dog for a veteran who is entitled to federal disability compensation. (38 U.S.C. § 614.) The costs paid for may include travel expenses incurred when the veteran goes to pick up the dog from a training center.

PET STORES

To prevent California consumers from buying an unhealthy puppy imported into the state from a midwestern "puppy mill," California retail pet dealers must post, on the dog's cage, a sign giving the state where the dog was bred. They must also post, close to the cages, a notice stating that information about the source and health of the dogs is available to prospective buyers.

Every retail seller of a dog must also fill out and give the buyer a written form, which is provided by the state Department of Consumer Affairs. The form lists:

- where the dog came from, if it came from a licensed dealer
- its birth date
- its immunization record
- a record of any known sickness the dog has, and
- a record of any veterinary treatment or medication received by the dog while with a retail pet dealer.

The dealer must also give the buyer one of the following:

- a statement that the dog has no known disease or condition that requires hospitalization or surgical procedures at the time of sale, or
- a record of any known disease or condition that the dog is afflicted with at the time of sale, along with a statement signed by a licensed veterinarian that authorizes the sale, recommends necessary treatment, if any, and verifies that the disease or condition does not require hospitalization or surgical procedures.

They are also required to give prospective buyers additional information on the breeder and broker, purebred registration, past disease and the dog's parents' registration number, if any, from the Orthopedic Foundation for Animals.

Dealers who knowingly sell sick animals are subject to a penalty of up to $1,000 and may be prohibited from selling dogs for up to 30 days for a first offense. (Health & Safety Code §§ 25995.3, 25995.8, 25996.90, 25996.91.)

EMPLOYEES' RIGHTS

Both California and federal law protect the rights of workers. Employees have the right to work free of discrimination, harassment, environmental hazards and violations of their privacy. However, many benefits that employers have traditionally offered employees, such as insurance plans or pensions, are not legally required.

TOPICS
- AIDS
- CHILD CARE WORKERS
- CHILD LABOR
- DISCRIMINATION
- DRUG TESTING
- ENGLISH-ONLY RULES
- EQUAL PAY
- FIRING
- HEALTH AND SAFETY REGULATIONS
- HEALTH INSURANCE
- IMMIGRANT WORKERS
- INDEPENDENT CONTRACTORS
- LIE DETECTOR TESTS
- PARENTAL LEAVE
- PENSIONS
- PREGNANCY
- PRIVACY
- PSYCHOLOGICAL TESTING
- SEXUAL HARASSMENT
- SICK LEAVE
- SMOKING POLICIES
- UNEMPLOYMENT INSURANCE
- UNIONS
- VACATIONS
- WAGE AND HOUR LAWS
- WORKERS' COMPENSATION

RELATED TOPICS
- CONSUMERS' RIGHTS
    - Health Insurance
- COURTS AND LAWSUITS
    - Jury Duty

GOVERNMENT BENEFITS
Disability Insurance
SMALL BUSINESSES
Responsibility to Employees

ADDITIONAL RESOURCES

Sexual Harassment on the Job, by William Petrocelli and Barbara Kate Repa (Nolo Press), explains what sexual harassment is and how to stop it.

Your Rights in the Workplace, by Barbara Kate Repa (Nolo Press), is a comprehensive guide to workplace rights, and explains the latest sweeping changes in laws passed to protect workers.

COBRA Continuation Coverage, available from the International Foundation of Employee Benefit Plans for $10, explains COBRA health insurance and exclusions.

The California Department of Fair Employment and Housing, 2000 O St., Suite 120, Sacramento, CA 95814, (916) 445-9918, takes complaints about discrimination and harassment, and can give specific legal information on state employment law.

The Western Service Center of the Immigration & Naturalization Service, 24000 Avila Road, 2nd Floor, Laguna Niguel, CA 92656, (714) 643-4236, takes complaints about violations of the Immigration Reform and Control Act (IRCA).

Equal Rights Advocates, 1663 Mission Street, Suite 550, San Francisco, CA 94103, provides general information, (415) 621-0672 and advice and counseling, (415) 621-0505.

9to5, National Association of Working Women, 614 Superior Ave., NW, Cleveland, OH 44113, (800) 522-0925, has a toll-free hotline and provides referrals to local groups.

ACQUIRED IMMUNE DEFICIENCY SYNDROME (AIDS)

Government polls indicate that roughly one in every 100 American workers already has been infected by HIV, the virus that can cause Acquired Immune Deficiency Syndrome (AIDS). In some communities with high-risk populations, such as San Francisco, the infection rate is reported to be as high as one in every 25 workers. Additional recent polls reveal that even these high estimates are unrealistically low. Although the virus is not spread through the kind of casual contact that typically takes place at work, some employers and employees have reacted to the spread of AIDS with panic—and a strong prejudice against working with people who are infected with the HIV virus.

California courts have ruled that AIDS and HIV infection are disabilities, so infected workers are protected by federal, state and local laws prohibiting discrimination against the disabled. The federal Americans with Disabilities Act (ADA) also covers HIV infection and AIDS. Under the ADA, it is illegal for any company employing 15 or more people to discriminate against workers because they are HIV infected or suffering from AIDS.

Employers covered by the ADA must also make reasonable accommodations to allow employees with AIDS to continue working. Such accommodations may include extended leave policies, re-assignment to vacant positions within the company that are less strenuous physically and flexible work schedules.

California law prohibits using HIV test results to determine suitability for employment. (Health & Safety Code §§ 199.21(f), 199.38.) Most California courts have ruled that HIV or AIDS-infected workers must be allowed to continue on the job if they can continue working when the employer makes some reasonable accommodation.

In addition, a number of California cities, including Los Angeles and San Francisco, have enacted laws prohibiting discrimination in employment based on AIDS. San Francisco specifically prohibits AIDS testing unless the employer can show that the absence of AIDS is a necessary occupational qualification.

AIDS Testing

An employer cannot test job applicants or employees for AIDS unless having AIDS could be considered "job-related and consistent with business necessity." So far, under the ADA, the only jobs that have met this strict criteria are a few positions involving food handling.

The laws on job discrimination based on AIDS are evolving rapidly. For more information, contact the AIDS Legal Referral Panel (415) 291-5454 or the Human Rights Commission of San Francisco (415) 558-4901.

CHILD CARE WORKERS

A babysitter, au pair or nanny who works regularly or frequently for a family, in the family's home, is usually considered an employee by the IRS and other government agencies.

A child care worker is covered by the federal Fair Labor Standards Act (FLSA) if he or she is paid at least $50 in wages per calendar quarter and works at least eight hours a week for one or more employers. This means the employee is entitled to the minimum wage and other benefits guaranteed by the FLSA. There are, however, a few exceptions.

- employers can count the reasonable cost or fair value of food, lodging or other facilities customarily furnished the employee when determining wages.
- an employer does not have to pay overtime to an au pair or in-home child care worker, but must pay minimum wage for each hour worked.

For more information on the FLSA, contact the local Wage-Hour Office, listed in most phone books under U.S. Government, Department of Labor, Wage and Hour Division.

Employers of in-home child care workers must comply with:

- federal tax requirements, which include withholding Social Security and Medicare taxes (FICA) and paying federal unemployment taxes. These requirements are outlined in IRS Publication 926: Employment Taxes for Household Employers, available from the IRS at (800) 829-FORM.
- state laws regarding taxes (income, unemployment insurance and state disability insurance fund) and workers' compensation coverage. For more information, contact the nearest office of the State Department of Industrial Relations.
- immigration law, including filing INS Form I-9 and verifying an employee's eligibility to work in the U.S. For more information, contact your local immigration and Naturalization Service office listed in the telephone book under U.S. Department of Justice or call (800) 755-0777.

An employer who fails to meet these legal obligations may be assessed substantial financial penalties and will not be able to take a federal child care income tax credit.

CHILD LABOR

Federal law generally prohibits employing children under the age of 14. A person who is at least 16 years old may be employed in most non-hazardous jobs (most jobs except for mining, manufacturing, meatpacking, roofing and excavation), as long as the job doesn't have a bad effect on the young employee's schooling or health. To work in occupations that the Department of Labor deems hazardous, the employee must be at least 18 years old. To determine which types of jobs are currently considered hazardous for the purposes of the Federal Fair Labor Standards Act, call your local office of the Labor Department's Wage and Hour Division.

The law restricts when and for how many hours that workers ages 14 and 15 may be employed. Here are the rules.

- They may work no more than three hours on a school day and no more than 18 hours in a school week.
- They may work no more than eight hours on a non-school day and no more than 40 hours in a non-school week.
- During the period that starts with the day after Labor Day and ends at midnight May 31, their workday may not begin earlier than 7 a.m. or end later than 7 p.m.
- From June 1 through Labor Day, their workday may not begin earlier than 7 a.m., but it can end as late as 9 p.m.

Jobs Without Restrictions

Some industries have obtained special exemptions from the legal restrictions on child labor. Children of any age may deliver newspapers, for example, or perform in television, movie or theatrical productions.

Farm Labor

The following less-stringent child labor restrictions apply only to farm work.

- Workers who are 16 and older may perform any farm job, hazardous or not, for unlimited hours.
- Workers who are 14 or 15 years old may perform any non-hazardous farm job outside school hours.
- Workers who are 12 or 13 years old may perform any non-hazardous farm job outside of school hours if they have their parents' written consent or are employed on the same farm as their parents.
- Children under 12 years old may perform jobs on farms owned or operated by their parents or, with their parents' written consent, outside of school hours and in non-hazardous positions on farms that use less than 500 days of paid labor in a calendar quarter.

DISCRIMINATION

Many kinds of discrimination in the workplace are prohibited by local, state and federal law.

Title VII

Title VII of the Civil Rights Act of 1964 is the primary federal law outlawing discrimination on the basis of race, skin color, sex, religious beliefs or national origin. The Equal Employment Opportunity Commission (EEOC) is the federal agency that administers and enforces Title VII.

Title VII applies to all companies and labor unions with 15 or more employees. It also governs employment agencies, state and local governments and apprenticeship programs. Title VII covers discrimination in every aspect of the employment relationship, from pre-hiring ads to working conditions, performance reviews and post-employment references.

A number of other federal laws are used in conjunction with Title VII to fight unfair workplace discrimination.

- The Equal Pay Act, enacted about one year before Title VII, specifically outlaws discrimination in wages on the basis of sex.
- The Age Discrimination in Employment Act (ADEA) prohibits workplace discrimination on the basis of age. It applies only to employees who are at least 40 years old. The Older Workers Benefit Protection Act is an amendment to the ADEA that specifically outlaws discrimination in employment benefit programs on the basis of employees' age, and it too applies only to employees age 40 and older. It also deters employers' use of waivers in which employees sign away their rights to take legal action against age-based discrimination.
- The Pregnancy Discrimination Act (PDA) makes it illegal for an employer to refuse to hire a pregnant woman, terminate her employment or compel her to take maternity leave.
- The Americans With Disabilities Act (ADA) makes it illegal to discriminate against people because of their physical condition.

California Department of Fair Employment and Housing

California workers also are covered by state law, which prohibits discrimination based on race, religion, color, national origin, ancestry, physical handicap, medical condition, marital status, sex, pregnancy, childbirth or related medical conditions, political activity, or arrests or detentions that did not result in a criminal conviction. California law covers all workplaces with five or more employees, and covers the entire employment relationship, like Title VII. (Gov't. Code §§ 12900-12996.)

A law signed in September 1992 (Assembly Bill 2601) made it illegal to discriminate against gays and lesbians in the workplace—a practice already declared illegal by court rulings.

DRUG TESTING

Employers have the right to test new job applicants for traces of drugs in their systems as long as the applicants know that the testing will be part of the screening process and agree to it in writing. Any company that intends to conduct drug testing on job candidates usually includes in its job application an agreement to submit to such testing. The applicant agrees by signing the application. If, in the process of applying for a job, you are asked to agree to drug testing, you have little choice but to agree to the tests or drop out as an applicant.

The rules are somewhat different when it comes to people who have already been hired. Many employers connected with the federal government are specifically authorized to test employees, not just applicants, periodically for drug use. For example, the Department of Defense authorizes employers with which it does business to test for drugs in certain circumstances, and the Department of Transportation requires drug testing for some critical positions, such as airline pilots.

Other private employers can test for drug and alcohol use only if it relates to performance and behavior on the job. Unless a problem surfaces that indicates an employee may be working below par or endangering the safety of others because of substance abuse, there is generally no legal right to perform a drug test.

Companies that conduct blanket drug tests of all employees or randomly test employees without justification can be sued for invasion of privacy and infliction of emotional harm. And California courts have repeatedly held that drug tests given without notice violate public policy.

ENGLISH-ONLY RULES

Some employers require employees to speak only English on the job, even if their jobs do not involve working with the public.

The Equal Employment Opportunity Commission and the courts regard English-only rules in the workplace to be illegal discrimination on the basis of national origin under the Civil Rights Act of 1964. Exceptions are allowed only in cases where there is a clear business necessity, such as for air traffic controllers. Employers who have a workplace rule requiring employees to speak English must first notify all employees of the rule, inform them about when English must be spoken and explain the consequences of breaking the rule.

EQUAL PAY

The Equal Pay Act is a federal anti-discrimination law, enforced by the Equal Employment Opportunity Commission, that requires employers to pay all employees equally for equal work, regardless of their sex. It also provides that fringe benefits, including pension retirement plans, must not discriminate between men and women performing equal work. Although the Act protects both men and women, it has almost always been applied to situations where women are paid less than men for doing similar jobs.

Pay systems that result in employees of one sex being paid less than the other for equal work are allowed under the Equal Pay Act only if the pay system is actually based on a factor other than sex, such as seniority, merit or quantity or quality of production.

Jobs don't have to be identical for the courts to consider them equal. In general, courts have ruled that two jobs are equal when both require equal levels of skill, effort and responsibility and are performed under similar conditions.

FIRING

The century-old legal doctrine of "employment-at-will" states that employers do not need a reason to fire employees—they may fire any or all of their workers at will. Although an employer may fire someone for no reason, it is illegal for an employer to fire an employee for a reason that violates public policy. This is the basis of most wrongful discharge claims.

At-will employees who are fired have no right to notice, no right to contest their dismissals, no right to severance pay. The only thing you're entitled to is your final paycheck, including all vacation pay already earned. State law says that you have the right to get your final paycheck immediately, with some special exceptions for employees of the movie, petroleum and farming industries.

Wrongful Discharge

Because courts are gradually establishing more rights for fired employees, many company owners and managers now are careful to provide at least the appearance of fair and even-handed treatment of employees who are fired. Most do this by carefully documenting what is considered to be the employee's unacceptable work performance.

But if you have been fired, several legal theories may help you fight your dismissal.

- **Violation of public policy.** The most common challenge is to show that your ex-employer violated public policy—that is, fired you for a reason that the law specifically says employers may not use for firing, or for a reason that most people would find morally disgusting.

- **Breach of an implied contract.** Employees who challenge a dismissal often argue that an employer offered them a job for a certain period of time at a stated salary, and that the firing violates this contract. Often, an employee claims that a contract was formed when an employer referred to permanent employment in the hiring process or the employee manual implied there would be no lay-offs. However, most employers clearly state that there is no employment contract, or did not put any promise of permanent employment in writing, so this argument is difficult for an employee to win.

- **Defamation.** When someone makes or distributes false statements about someone that lower his or her public image, that is defamation. There are a lot of opportunities in the typical firing process for an employer to do just that. But defamation is usually difficult to prove. Typically, the employee must show that, in the process of dismissing him or her from the job, or subsequently providing references to potential new employers, the ex-employer significantly damaged the employee's good name and reduced the chances for gaining new employment.

HEALTH AND SAFETY REGULATIONS

California has its own occupational safety and health program—Cal/OSHA—that protects workers' rights to safe and healthful work conditions. The law covers all workers in the state, including those employed by state and local government, but does not cover federal employees. (Cal. Code of Regs., Title 8, Industrial Relations.)

Cal/OSHA requirements. Employers must have an Injury and Illness Prevention Program, which must be in writing and tailored to the needs of the individual workplace. At a minimum, each program must:

- identify who at the company is responsible for enforcing health and safety measures
- set out regulations for safe work practices, which may include training and discipline
- spell out how employees can complain about unsafe conditions and hazards in the workplace, and
- schedule periodic inspections to identify unsafe conditions and work practices.

Depending on the types of hazards and workplaces involved, the employer's responsibility for creating and maintaining a safe workplace can include such diverse things as labeling potentially hazardous substances, upgrading or removing machinery that poses a danger, providing employees with special breathing apparatus to keep dust created by a manufacturing process from entering workers' lungs, improving lighting above work areas, vaccinating against diseases that can be contracted at work, or even tracking the effects of workplace conditions on employees' health through periodic medical examinations.

The need to post. The most important protection of the law is that employers must give employees access to the laws on workplace health and safety. To that end, employers must display six posters in a place where they can easily be read by all employees: Regulations for Wages, Hours and Working Conditions; Pay Day Notice; Safety and Health Protection on the Job; Discrimination in Employment Is Prohibited; Notice of Workers' Compensation Carrier; and Notice of Unemployment and Disability Insurance.

Although the prime responsibility for keeping the workplace safe and healthy falls on employers, the law also requires employees to obey all workplace safety rules and not interfere with other workers' use of safety equipment.

Retaliation is prohibited. It is illegal for an employer to fire or punish an employee for filing a safety complaint or participating in an investigation of a safety violation. Cal/OSHA can order an employer who violates this rule to return the employee to the job and to reimburse him or her for damages such as lost wages, the value of lost benefit coverages and the cost of searching for a new job.

Enforcing your OSHA rights. If you've tried to take action inside your company to correct a workplace safety hazard but the danger continues, you can file a complaint by contacting the nearest OSHA office. Look in the phone book under California, State of—Department of Industrial Relations, Division of Occupational Safety and Health or Division of Labor Standards Enforcement.

Walking off the job. OSHA gives you the right to refuse to continue doing your job in extreme circumstances that represent an immediate and substantial danger to your personal safety. If you walk off a job because of a safety hazard, be sure to contact the nearest OSHA office as soon as you're out of danger.

HEALTH INSURANCE

Contrary to what many people believe, employers are not required to offer health insurance coverage to employees. However, if health insurance is provided for one employee, it must also be available to the others.

Workers who have been covered by health insurance on the job and who have not been fired for gross misconduct may have the right to continue health insurance coverage when employment ends. Under the federal Consolidated Omnibus Budget Reconciliation Act (COBRA), employers must offer a former employee the option of continuing to be covered by the company's group health insurance plan at the worker's own expense for at least 18 months after employment ends. Coverage for family members is also included. In some other circumstances, such as the death of the employee, that employee's dependents can continue coverage for up to 36 months.

COBRA also requires that, for the former employee, the cost of continuing group health coverage must be similar to the cost of covering people who are still working for the employer.

In California, there is no state law that gives you the right to continue group health insurance after you leave a job where insurance was available.

IMMIGRANT WORKERS

The Immigration Reform and Control Act (IRCA) is a federal law that restricts the flow of foreign workers into American workplaces. IRCA covers all employees hired since November 6, 1986, except those who work occasionally in private homes as domestic workers. Independent contractors aren't covered.

Under IRCA, it is illegal for an employer to:

- hire a worker who the employer knows has not been granted permission by the Immigration and Naturalization Service (INS) to be employed in the United States (through a green card or visa)
- hire any worker who has not completed INS Form I-9, the Employment Eligibility Verification Form
- continue to employ an unauthorized worker—often called an illegal alien or undocumented alien—hired after November 6, 1986.

Filing INS Form I-9

Employees must fill out the employee's section of Form I-9 by the end of the first day on a new job. They then have three business days to present the new employer with documents that prove their identity and eligibility to work in the United States. A current U.S. passport is usually sufficient to prove both.

If you don't have a passport, a current California driver's license or photo identification card will typically prove your legal identity. You may have to provide a form of verification such as a military ID card, a draft record, a voter registration card or Native American tribal documents. For young workers, a school report card or a hospital record such as a birth certificate is acceptable as proof of identity.

Native-born adults can typically prove employment eligibility by producing a Social Security card or a birth certificate issued by the state of birth. If you look or sound as though you might be an immigrant, you may have to produce both a Social Security card and a birth certificate.

Illegal Discrimination Under IRCA
IRCA makes it illegal for an employer with three or more employees to:
- discriminate in hiring or firing anyone on the basis of what country they were born in or the fact that they became or are in the process of becoming naturalized U.S. citizens, or
- retaliate against an employee for exercising any rights under IRCA.

INDEPENDENT CONTRACTORS
Most workplace rights guaranteed by law to employees are not guaranteed to people who work as independent contractors. The relationship between independent contractors and the company or person paying for their work is covered not by the law of the workplace, but by contract law and the laws of California.

To be considered an independent contractor, a person must control both the outcome of the project and how it is accomplished. Also, an independent contractor must offer services to the public at large, not just to one company.

Employee or Independent Contractor?
Common examples of those who work as independent contractors are lawyers, accountants, decorators or computer consultants. But to avoid paying benefits, some employers try to classify people who should be considered full- or part-time employees as independent contractors. If it is unclear whether a person should be classified as an employee or independent contractor, consider the factors that the IRS looks at:
- **Training.** An employee is trained by the employer to perform services in a particular manner. Independent contractors use their own methods and receive no training from those who pay for their services.
- **Hiring assistants.** An employee works for an employer who hires, supervises and pays assistants. An independent contractor hires, supervises and pays assistants under a contract that requires him or her to provide materials and labor, and is responsible only for the result.
- **Continuing relationship.** An employee has a continuing relationship with an employer, even if the work hours vary.
- **Set hours of work.** An employee has set hours of work established by an employer. An independent contractor establishes his or her own work schedule.
- **Work done on premises.** An employee works on the premises of an employer, or works on a route or at a location designated by an employer.
- **Pay.** An employee is paid by the hour, week or month. An independent contractor is paid by the job or on a straight commission.
- **Expenses.** An employee's business and travel expenses are paid by the employer, showing that the employee is subject to the employer's regulation and control.
- **Tools and materials.** An employee is furnished with tools, materials and other equipment by an employer.
- **Right to fire.** An employee can be fired by an employer. An independent contractor cannot be fired as long as he or she produces a result that meets the specifications of the contract.

- **Right to quit.** An employee can quit his or her job at any time without incurring liability. An independent contractor usually is legally obliged to make good for failure to complete an agreed-upon project.

LIE DETECTOR TESTS

The federal Employee Polygraph Detection Act (29 U.S.C. § 2001) virtually outlaws using lie detectors (polygraphs) in connection with employment. That law covers all private employers in interstate commerce, which includes just about every private company that uses the U.S. mail or the telephone system.

Under the Act, it is illegal for all private companies to:

- require, request, suggest or cause any employee or job applicant to submit to a lie detector test

- use, accept, refer to or inquire about the results of any lie detector test conducted on an employee or job applicant, or

- dismiss, discipline, discriminate against or even threaten to take action against any employee or job applicant who refuses to take a lie detector test.

The polygraph law also prohibits employers from discriminating against or firing those who use its protections.

When Polygraph Tests Can Be Used

The Employee Polygraph Protection Act allows polygraph tests to be used in connection with jobs in security and handling drugs, or in investigating a specific theft or other suspected crime. However, before an employee can be required to take a test as part of an investigation of an employment-related crime, he or she must be given written notice that he or she is a suspect.

The Act does not apply to—and lie detector tests are allowed for—employees of federal, state or local government, nor to certain jobs that handle sensitive work relating to national defense.

Illegal Lie Detector Tests

The Employee Polygraph Protection Act is enforced by the U.S. Department of Labor. If you have questions about whether the Act applies to your job or if you suspect that you have been illegally subjected to polygraph testing, call the Labor Department's Wage-and-Hour Division.

If the Labor Department finds that your rights under the Act were violated, it can fine the employer up to $10,000 and issue an injunction ordering the employer to reinstate you to your job, promote you, compensate you for back wages, hire you or take other logical action to correct the violation.

PARENTAL LEAVE

California law gives employees in private industry the right to take time off from work to deal with specific parental responsibilities. State law provides that:

- An employer may not discriminate against an employee who takes time off to attend a child's school conference, provided that the employee gives the employer reasonable notice of the need to attend the conference. (Labor Code § 230.7.)

- Companies with 25 or more employees may not fire or discriminate against an employee who is a parent or guardian of any child in kindergarten through 12, for taking one four-hour leave from work each school year, per child, to visit the child's school. The employee must give the employer reasonable notice of the need for the leave. (Labor Code § 230.8.)

In addition, the federal Family and Medical Leave Act (FMLA) requires that employees must get up to 12 weeks of unpaid leave if they have or adopt or give up a child for placement—or if they have a serious health problem or must take off work to care for a spouse, child or parent. Because the FMLA applies only to workplaces with 50 or more employees and is in other respects less liberal than the state law on family leave, most California employees invoke the protection of the state law.

Federal and state law require that an employer grant men the same options for taking leave from their jobs to care for a child as it grants to women. To do otherwise is illegal discrimination based on sex. However, a study released by the U.S. Small Business Association in 1991 showed that this law is routinely violated. Most companies offer some type of leave for childbirth to female workers, the study found, but less than 8% offer the same option to their male employees.

California law also prohibits workplace discrimination based on marital status. If an employer offers parental leave only to married employees, that violates this law. (Gov't. Code §§ 12900-12996.)

PENSIONS

Pensions include any program that provides income to people after they've left the workforce because of advancing age. No law requires an employer to offer a pension plan.

Eligibility for pension coverage. If a company chooses to offer a pension plan, the Employee Retirement Income Security Act (ERISA), a federal law, requires that the plan spell out who is eligible for coverage. Plans don't have to include all workers, but they must be structured so that they benefit a fair cross-section of employees and don't discriminate in favor of officers, shareholders or highly-paid employees. If you're eligible to participate in your employer's pension program, the plan administrator at your company must provide you with the documents you need to understand the plan: a summary plan description, summary annual report, and survivor coverage data—a statement of how much your plan would pay to any surviving spouse should you die first.

Once a year, your plan administrator must also provide you with a detailed, individual statement of the pension benefits you've earned, but only if you request it in writing or are going to stop participating in the plan because, for example, you change employers.

Early retirement. Each pension plan has its own rules on the age you must reach before filing for benefits. Most private pension plans consider 65 the normal retirement age, but an increasing number offer the option of retiring early, usually at age 55. If you elect early retirement, expect your benefit checks to be much smaller than they would be if you waited until the later retirement age, since most pension payments are calculated based on the number of years you have been enrolled in the plan.

Many corporations now use the early retirement option to cut staff. By making a temporary offer to increase the benefits available to those who retire early, these corporations create an incentive for employees to volunteer to leave the company's payroll before turning age 65.

Filing for benefits. The summary plan of your pension program will spell out when you become eligible for benefits and how to file a claim for them. It will also describe how you can appeal the decision if you are denied benefits under your pension plan.

Under ERISA, the administrator of your pension plan must approve or deny your claim for benefits within 90 days after you file it. ERISA makes it a crime for an employer to fire, suspend or otherwise discriminate against or punish employees or their beneficiaries for pursuing their rights to pension benefits.

Appealing a denial of benefits. Each pension plan has its own system for appeals. If your pension plan denies you benefits to which you're entitled, its administrator is required to advise you about how to appeal that decision. You'll have 60 days to request such an appeal, and the group that reviews your appeal will usually have 120 days after you file it to issue its decision. ERISA requires that you be given a plain English explanation of the decision on your appeal.

PREGNANCY

The federal Pregnancy Discrimination Act (which amended Title VII of the Civil Rights Act of 1964) outlaws discrimination against women on the basis of pregnancy, childbirth or any related medical condition.

The Act provides that if an employee is temporarily unable to perform her job because of a pregnancy-related condition, an employer must treat her as it does any other "temporarily disabled employee." It may arrange for a pregnant woman to do modified tasks, give alternate work assignments, give her disability leave or provide for leave without pay—and it must make such arrangements if it does so for other disabled employees.

The law also specifies that:

- An employer cannot refuse to hire or promote a woman solely because she is pregnant, as long as she is able to perform the key functions of the job.
- Pregnant employees who need time off from work must receive the same treatment as employees who take time off because of other medical conditions. This protection includes women who must take time off from work to recover from an abortion.
- An employer cannot refuse to provide health insurance benefits that cover pregnancy if it provides such benefits to cover other medical conditions.
- A woman cannot be required to take a leave from work during her pregnancy if she remains able to do her job.
- A woman cannot be forced to take a minimum amount of time off from work after giving birth.

California law specifically requires that a female employee must be allowed to take up to four months of unpaid leave for pregnancy or childbirth. (Gov't. Code § 12945.) Her job must be held open for her on return just as jobs are held open for employees on sick leave or other disability leave.

PRIVACY

Employers are entitled to intrude on your personal life no more than is necessary for legitimate business interests. If a company has abused its power to check up on you, you can file a lawsuit claiming invasion of privacy. The most likely way to win such a case is to show that in the process of collecting information on you, the employer was guilty of one or more of the following wrongs.

- **Deception.** Your employer asked you to submit to a routine medical examination, for example, but mentioned nothing about a drug test. However, the urine sample that you gave to the examining physician was analyzed for drug traces, and because drugs were found in your urine, you were fired.
- **Violation of confidentiality.** For instance, your employer asked you to fill in a health questionnaire and assured you that the information would be held in confidence for the company's use only. But you later found out that the information was divulged to a mortgage company that inquired about you.
- **Secret, intrusive monitoring.** Installing visible video cameras above a supermarket's cash registers would usually be considered a legitimate method of ensuring that employees aren't stealing from the company. But installing hidden video cameras above the stalls in an employee restroom would probably qualify as an invasion of privacy in all but the most high-security jobs.
- **Intrusion on your private life.** Your employer hired a private detective, for example, to monitor where you go in the evening when you're not at work. When the company discovered that you are active in a gay rights organization, you were told to resign from that group or risk losing your job.
- **Workplace searches.** In general, it is legal for employers to monitor business-related telephone calls to and from their own premises. Employers may also search through items owned by an employee but kept at work—unless the

employee logically expects that the spot in which those items are stored is completely private.

- **Use of criminal records.** California law has restrictions against using criminal records in making employment-related decisions. But since criminal court proceedings are matters of public record, there is little a job applicant or employee can do to stop an employer from discovering criminal records. In fact, some credit reporting companies also do routine checks of criminal court records throughout the country and then use those records to create reports on individuals—reports which they then sell to employers who inquire about those individuals.

HOW TO CHECK YOUR PERSONNEL FILES

The best way to find out what a company knows about you, or what it is saying about you to businesses and people outside the company who inquire, is to obtain a copy of your employment file. California law gives employees broad access to their employment records. Employees have the right to see their personnel files and to demand a copy of any document relating to employment that they have signed. Employers must keep a copy of the employee's personnel file where the employee reports to work, or must make the file available at that location within a reasonable time after the employee asks to see it. (Labor Code §§ 432, 1198.5.)

PSYCHOLOGICAL TESTING

Some employers use written questions to predict whether or not a person would lie, steal or be unreliable if hired for a particular job. Because lie detector tests are now generally illegal in the workplace, these questionnaires—which are usually called integrity tests—are often used as a substitute in screening applicants for job openings.

Because psychological testing is relatively new, there have been very few legal challenges to the practice. However, courts have imposed these restrictions:

- Psychological tests cannot be used only to screen out job applicants in a protected group, such as women or African-Americans.
- Employers cannot use psychological tests to ask prospective employees about their sexual orientation.

Tougher standards are in sight. Several California courts have asked that boundaries be set in the types and timing of screening questions.

SEXUAL HARASSMENT

Sexual harassment on the job is any unwelcome sexual advance or conduct that creates an intimidating, hostile or offensive work environment. Both federal and state laws prohibit such behavior. In workplaces, sexual harassment ranges from sexist jokes and innuendos to outright sexual assault. Although the laws protect men as well as women from being harassed at work, most cases and complaints involve a man harassing a woman.

The U.S. Supreme Court recently held that courts must look at all the circumstances to determine whether or not sexual harassment has occurred, including:

- how often the conduct occurred
- how severe the conduct was

- whether the conduct was physically threatening or humiliating, or merely offensive words, and
- whether the conduct interfered with an employee's work performance. (*Harris v. Forklift Sys., Inc.*, No. 92-1168, 11/9/93)

What Employees Can Do About It

If you feel you are being harassed at work, you have several options. In addition to the steps you can take within your workplace, such as confronting the harasser and demanding a stop to the harassment, or using a company grievance procedure to complain, you have legal options as well. You can:

- **File a complaint with a government agency.** Filing a complaint under federal or state law sets in motion an investigation that may resolve the complaint, and is also a necessary first step if you want to later file an independent lawsuit stemming from the harassment.

  Since sexual harassment is prohibited under both state law (the Fair Employment and Housing Act or FEHA, Gov't. Code §§ 12900 to 12996) and federal law (the Civil Rights Act of 1964), you may file your complaint with either a state or federal agency. If your employer has fewer than 15 employees (the minimum for federal discrimination claims), you should file with the state, since California's minimum is five employees. Because a claim filed in the FEHA office is considered to be automatically filed with the EEOC as well, you need not agonize over which to choose. But you should file your complaint within one year of the last act of harassment.

  The advantage of filing and pursuing a state claim is that you are allowed to collect as high an amount in damages as you are able to prove. In federal claims, the amount you can collect will be limited—from $50,000 to $300,000—depending on how many employees there are in your workplace.

FILING A HARASSMENT CLAIM

To file a harassment claim with the state agency, contact:
California Department of Fair Employment and Housing
(916) 445-9918
File a federal claim at any one of the six EEOC offices in California.

- **File a lawsuit.** You can also file a private lawsuit for sexual harassment or under some other legal theory, such as intentional infliction of emotional distress or assault. You will usually need to hire a lawyer to help.

SICK LEAVE

No state or federal law requires an employer to offer sick leave, although many employers offer a number of paid days off each year to attend medical appointments or recover from an illness. If this benefit is offered to one employee or group of employees in a workplace, it must also be offered to all other employees there.

SMOKING POLICIES

The legal issues surrounding tobacco smoke in the workplace are unsettled. Airline flight attendants have secured some indirect protection from second-hand smoke in their workplace from Federal Aviation Administration restrictions on in-flight smoking by passengers. And while here is no federal law that directly controls smoking at work, many cities—including San Francisco, Palo Alto and Los Angeles—

have laws restricting smoking in privately owned workplaces.

Because of the potentially higher costs of health insurance, absenteeism, unemployment insurance and workers' compensation insurance associated with employees who smoke, many companies now refuse to hire anyone who admits to being a smoker on a job application or in pre-hiring interviews. There is no law against this practice.

UNEMPLOYMENT INSURANCE

Unemployment insurance, also called UI or unemployment compensation, provides you with a regular paycheck after you're let go from a job, until you're either called back to that job or find a new one. The UI program is run jointly by the federal government and the states, and is paid for primarily by a tax on employers. UI benefits are usually limited to 26 weeks, but in recent bad economic times, that period has been extended.

Unemployment insurance covers most employees of all levels, including part-time and temporary workers. To be covered, you must have been employed for at least six months during the year before your job loss and have earned $1,200 in a three-month base period, or $920 in each of eight calendar weeks.

Those not covered include people employed by small farms, casual domestic workers and babysitters, newspaper carriers under age 18, children employed by their parents, their spouses or their children, employees of religious organizations and elected officials.

Eligibility for benefits. To qualify for benefits, you must have left your job for "good cause," which includes leaving because you were laid off, the job was eliminated, your employer went bankrupt. Good cause includes leaving because of excessive cost or time to travel to work, a doctor advised you to change jobs for health reasons, or to accompany your spouse to a new locality. In addition, you must:
- be available to be recalled to your old job or to work in a similar one
- be physically able to perform your old job or a similar one, and
- be actively seeking work in a reasonable and customary way.

Even if you're covered by unemployment insurance and otherwise eligible to receive it, you may be disqualified from receiving benefits if you:
- refused to accept a similar job without good reason
- quit your job without a good reason
- lied or failed to disclose a material fact in applying for benefits, or
- were fired from your job for misconduct—such as stealing, drinking or sleeping on the job.

However, the UI Board has held that mere inefficiency, poor job performance because of inability or incapacity, or inadvertent mistakes will not be considered job misconduct that will disqualify you from receiving benefits.

Calculating your benefits. You become eligible for unemployment insurance benefits after you've been unemployed for one week. To calculate your benefits, the unemployment insurance office uses a rather complicated formula premised on the base period of your wages. Your benefits should total roughly half your total base earnings.

To file a claim, go to the nearest unemployment insurance office. After you file, you will have to follow up periodically to state that you are still unemployed, and to show that you are actively seeking work.

If your claim is denied, you'll be notified in writing of that decision, the reason for it and the number of days you have to indicate that you want to appeal.

UNIONS

The National Labor Relations Act (NLRA) requires most employers and unions to negotiate fairly with each other until they agree to a contract that spells out the terms and conditions of employment for the workers who are members of the union—including pay rates, hours and work conditions. The National Labor Relations Board (NLRB) enforces this requirement by using mediators, administrative law judges, investigators and others.

Generally, the courts have ruled that employees have rights to:

- discuss union membership and read and distribute literature concerning it during non-work time in non-work areas such as an employee lounge
- sign a card asking an employer to recognize a union and bargain with it, sign petitions and grievances concerning employment terms and conditions and ask co-workers to sign petitions and grievances
- display pro-union sentiments by wearing message-bearing items as hats, pins and T-shirts on the job.

An employer may not:

- grant or promise employees a promotion, pay raise, a desirable work assignment or other special favors if they oppose unionizing efforts
- dismiss, harass, reassign or otherwise punish or discipline employees—or threaten to—if they support unionization
- close down a worksite or transfer work or reduce benefits to pressure employers not to support unionization.

The NLRA also prohibits unions from interfering with employees' rights to reject or change union membership.

Unions may not:

- restrain or coerce employees from exercising their rights under the NLRA; this includes violence and threats of violence against people who reject union membership
- cause or encourage an employer to discriminate against an employee or group of employees because of their de-unionization activities
- interfere in any way with an employee's right to freely express opinions on union membership
- fail or refuse to bargain in good faith with an employer
- prevent employees from going to work by using such tactics as mass picketing.

In general, the courts have recognized an employee's right to refuse to join a union on religious grounds. However, the employee can still be required to pay union dues and fees.

Additional Information

Contact the local office of the NLRB, listed in the federal government section of the telephone directory. If you are having specific problems with a union at work, contact the California AFL-CIO headquarters at the California Labor Federation, 417 Montgomery Street, Suite 300, San Francisco, CA 94104, (415) 986-3585.

VACATIONS

No state or federal law requires an employer to offer vacation, although offering a number of paid days off each year has become a standard amenity in most workplaces. However, if an employer chooses to offer paid vacation time to one employee or a group of them in a workplace, it must also be offered to all other employees there.

WAGE AND HOUR RESTRICTIONS

The federal Fair Labor Standards Act (FLSA) establishes minimum pay and hour rules. The FLSA applies to employers with annual sales of $500,000 or more or that are engaged in interstate commerce, which covers nearly all workplaces.

Some employees are exempt from the FLSA, including:

- executive, administrative and professional workers

- employees in training
- transportation industry workers
- employees who work out of the country
- people with severe physical handicaps employed in special workshops
- volunteers in nonprofit organizations
- mental patients or patient-workers at rehabilitation facilities, and
- prison laborers.

Complaints about possible violations of the FLSA should go to a local office of Wage and Hour Division of the U.S. Department of Labor, listed in the U.S. government section of the telephone directory.

Minimum Wage

The FLSA requires that you be paid at least the minimum wage—currently $4.25 per hour. Employers may pay on the basis of time at work, piece rates or some other measurement, but in all cases, an employee's pay divided by the hours worked during the pay period must equal or exceed the minimum wage. Some additional rules on pay rates:

- **No pay required for time off.** Employers are not required to pay employees for time off, such as vacation, holidays or sick days.
- **Tips.** When employees routinely receive at least $30 per month in tips as part of their job, their employers may credit up to 50% of those tips against the minimum wage requirements.
- **Commissions.** Commissions paid for sales may take the place of wages for purposes of the FLSA. However, if the commissions do not equal the minimum wage, the employer must make up the difference.

Overtime

The FLSA requires that anyone who works more than 40 hours in one week must be paid at least one-and-one-half times their regular rate of pay for all hours worked in excess of 40. Your employer can calculate and pay overtime by the week—which can be any 168-hour period made up of seven consecutive 24-hour periods.

Employers may offer employees compensatory time off from work in place of cash, as long as the comp time is awarded at the rate of one-and-one-half times the overtime hours worked, and the comp time is taken during the same pay period that the overtime hours were worked.

Calculating your rate of pay. Your regular rate of pay includes your base pay plus any shift premiums, hazardous duty premiums, cost-of-living allowances, bonuses used to make otherwise undesirable worksites attractive, and the fair value of such things as food and lodging that your employer routinely provides as part of your pay. If you work on an hourly or salary basis, calculate how much your employer owes you for overtime hours under the FLSA by multiplying your regular hourly rate by 150% to determine the pay you're entitled to receive for each hour over 40 you worked during a week.

Calculating your on-the-job time. When a work period begins and ends is determined by a federal law called the Portal-To-Portal Pay Act (29 U.S.C. § 251). It requires that an employee be paid for any time spent that is controlled by the employer. In general, on-the-job time does not include the time employees spend washing themselves or changing clothes before or after work, meal periods during which employees are free from all work duties or time spent commuting between home and work.

Pay intervals. State laws, not the FLSA, govern how often you must be paid. These laws are complex, usually covering only certain types of companies and employees. If you have a question about how often you must be paid, contact the local office of the California Labor Department.

Final paychecks. State law also controls how soon your final paycheck must be given to you if you are fired or quit work. In California, if you're fired, you have the right to get your final paycheck immediately—with some special exceptions for employees of the movie, petroleum and farming industries. If you quit, you are entitled to your paycheck within 72 hours, or immediately if you've given 72 hours' notice. (Lab. Code § 202.)

Local laws. Some counties, cities and towns have passed their own wage laws. Check with the law department of the county or municipality in which you work.

WORKERS' COMPENSATION

The workers' compensation system replaces income of employees who are injured or become ill because of their jobs. Benefits may also extend to workers' dependents and to the survivors of workers who are killed on the job. In some circumstances, workers' compensation also protects employers from being sued for those injuries or deaths. The insured worker pays no deductible amount; the system is funded primarily by insurance premiums paid by employers.

Injuries covered. To be covered by workers' compensation, the injury needn't be caused by a sudden accident such as a fall. With a few exceptions, any injury that occurs in connection with work is covered.

Illnesses covered. A common illness becomes an occupational illness for purposes of workers' compensation when the nature of a job increases the worker's chances of suffering from that disease. Illnesses that are the gradual result of work conditions—for example, emotional illness, repetitive motion injuries and stress-related digestive problems—increasingly are being recognized by the courts as being covered by workers' compensation insurance.

Benefits available. The California workers' compensation system entitles workers to be paid for all medical treatment necessary to cure or relieve the effects of an accident or injury caused at work.

This includes doctors' bills, hospitalization, physical restoration, surgical and chiropractic care, nursing services, dental care, prescriptions, X-rays, laboratory studies and all other necessary and reasonable care ordered by a physician. The employee is also entitled to a portion of his or her wages while off work: about 2/3 of gross weekly wages for a temporary disability, up to $148 weekly for a permanent disability.

If workers' compensation sounds almost too good to be true to the ears of an injured worker, that's because it may be. In reality, many of those who try to get compensated by the system, which is dominated by doctors and lawyers, come away with lots of frustration and very little money. Most glitches arise over whether or not a particular medical treatment is actually "reasonable and necessary" in the eyes of those who administer the funds.

Filing a workers' compensation claim. The first step in every workers' compensation claim is to inform your employer of your injury as soon as possible after getting any medical care required.

Typically, your employer will have claim forms for you to fill out and submit, or can obtain a form quickly. It then becomes your employer's responsibility to submit the paperwork to the proper insurance carrier and to your state's workers' compensation agency.

If your employer refuses to cooperate with you in filing a workers' compensation claim, a call to your local workers' compensation office will usually remedy the situation. Look in the state government section of your local telephone directory.

GOVERNMENT BENEFITS

Many government programs provide food, housing, income and medical benefits to needy Californians. Here we cover those programs that are run by the state or are jointly administered by federal and state agencies. There are some strictly federal programs, such as veterans' benefit programs, that we mention only briefly.

California or United States residency or citizenship is required for nearly all government benefit programs.

TOPICS

AID TO FAMILIES WITH DEPENDENT CHILDREN
DISABILITY INSURANCE
FOOD STAMPS
GENERAL ASSISTANCE
HOUSING
MEDI-CAL
MEDICARE
SOCIAL SECURITY
SUPPLEMENTAL SECURITY INCOME
VETERANS' BENEFITS

RELATED TOPICS

CITIZENS' RIGHTS
California Citizenship and Residency
United States Citizenship
LANDLORDS AND TENANTS
Evictions

ADDITIONAL RESOURCES

Social Security, Medicare and Pensions, by Joseph Matthews and Dorothy Matthews Berman (Nolo Press), explains the rules of these programs and discusses how to deal with the government bureaucracies.

The Food Stamp Sourcebook (Food Research Action Coalition) explains federal food stamp rules.

The Clearinghouse Review, a periodical published primarily for Legal Aid and Legal Services lawyers, contains articles on all federal government benefits programs.

How To Get a Green Card, by Loida Nicolas Lewis with Len T. Madlansacay (Nolo Press), explains many ways to get permanent resident status.

Insider's Guide: U.S. Immigration Made Easy, by Laurence A. Canter and Martha S. Siegle (Sheridan Chandler), is an extensive discussion of immigration law.

The Veteran's Guide to Benefits, by Ralph Roberts (Signet), is an inexpensive paperback that's full of great information for veterans.

AID TO FAMILIES WITH DEPENDENT CHILDREN

The Aid to Families with Dependent Children program (AFDC) is a joint federal-state program that provides assistance to almost five million families nationwide every month. It is the main source of income for families with children and no parent who is employed full-time.

Who Is Eligible for AFDC Benefits

A family must meet all these requirements to be eligible for the AFDC program:

- Family income and resources must be within limits set by the state. The family must own less that $1,000 worth of resources. Many types of property are exempt from this limit, including most furniture and clothing, a burial plot, the full value of a home and the value of a car up to $1,500.

  The family's gross income must be no higher than 185% of the state subsistence level.

- The children in the family must be deprived of parental support or care. This means at least one of the child's parents must be absent from the home or incapacitated, or the family's main breadwinner must be employed less than 100 hours per month. Most often, the "deprivation" requirement is met because only one parent lives in the home.

- The children must be living either with a parent or with another relative who qualifies as a caretaker relative (most relatives qualify).

- The family must be residing in California.

- The family must either be U.S. citizens or have legal alien status.

- The caretaker must not be involved in a strike on the last day of the month for which benefits are sought.

Benefit Amounts

Families don't necessarily get what they need under this program, only what the state is willing to pay.

Current 1993 payment standards in California are as follows:

— $351 for a family with one child
— $576 for a family with two children
— $715 for a family with three children, and so on.

These amounts are subject to change by the state legislature, and when budget constraints exist, families may be paid even less.

With some exceptions, if the family has income, it is deducted from the need standard (which is always a little higher than the payment standard), and AFDC pays the difference. Generally, all cash receipts count as income, except:

- the first $50 per month in child support received by the family
- a small portion of earned income
- certain expenses (such as child care) associated with the job
- all of the earned income of a student under 16, and
- educational loans and grants.

How To Stay Eligible

Once a family qualifies for AFDC, it must meet certain requirements to stay eligible. It must:

- report its income and resources accurately to the welfare department
- provide a Social Security number for each member of the family
- cooperate with work or education requirements, which means looking for a job or undergoing training, and
- cooperate with the District Attorney's office in collecting child support from an absent parent.

Termination of Benefits

A family that is denied AFDC or has its benefits cut or terminated is entitled to a hearing before a judge. The judge is employed by the welfare department but is required to be impartial. The judge will examine the facts in light of the welfare rules and decide whether or not the welfare department's actions were appropriate. For families already on AFDC, the hearing is held before the actions take effect.

DISABILITY INSURANCE

State and federal disability insurance programs are both designed to help disabled workers who can't work, but they differ regarding eligibility, benefit amounts and duration of coverage. You may also be eligible for private disability benefits from your employer.

Federal Benefits

If you have a permanent or long-term disability, you should apply for federal disability benefits distributed through the Social Security program. To qualify, you must not only be disabled, but also be eligible for Social Security based on your work history. Your dependents can also receive benefits under this program.

To be eligible, you must:

- Be disabled. This means that you have a physical or mental impairment that prevents you from doing any substantial gainful work—that is, work for which you can expect to receive more than $500 per month. The impairment must be expected to last at least 12 months or to result in your death. Your disability must be verified by a doctor. The Social Security Administration has published a list of what it considers to be disabling conditions, including mental illness, brain damage, progressive uncontrolled cancer, kidney failure, and heart disease that doesn't respond to medical treatment.

- Have the required number of work credits. These credits are calculated in the same way as for Social Security retirement benefits. Most people who have worked at least a few years, paying into the Social Security fund, are covered.

You can apply for Social Security benefits at any Social Security Administration office. Once you complete the application, you must wait five months before you receive your first payment. You may be eligible for back payments if you wait to apply, but back payments are limited to the 12 months before you filed your application.

The amount of your payments is based on your salary or wage history. The amount won't be as much as you made before your injury.

State Disability Insurance (SDI)

SDI is a California program for workers who are temporarily or permanently disabled. It is much more inclusive than the federal program. (Unemp. Ins. Code § 2601 and following.)

You are eligible to receive SDI if you have any physical or mental illness or injury that prevents you from doing your regular or customary work. Pregnancy, childbirth and related conditions, and elective surgery are all included as disabilities. The usual disability period for a normal pregnancy is up to four weeks before the expected delivery date and up to six weeks after the actual delivery date.

You cannot receive SDI if:

- you left your job before becoming disabled
- you are already collecting workers' compensation in an amount greater than or equal to what your SDI benefit would be (you can collect the difference if your workers' compensation payments are less than your SDI benefits)
- you are receiving unemployment insurance benefits

- you are incarcerated, or
- you are receiving full wages from your employer.

To apply, you and your doctor must fill out a form. You can get the form from your local SDI office (a division of the Employment Development Department) or from the Employment Development Department in Sacramento. You must file for benefits within 49 days of the beginning of your disability.

For the first week after you file your application, you are not eligible for any benefits. After that week, if you meet the other requirements, you will begin receiving checks. It may take up to two weeks for your first check to arrive.

The amount of benefits is based on your earnings during a 12-month period ending about six months before your disability. Your weekly disability check will be about one-half of the amount you used to make in a week during your highest paid three months of the 12-month period. When you get an application form, you will also receive instructions for figuring out your precise benefit amount.

FOOD STAMPS

Food stamps are coupons, issued by the federal government, that can be used to buy food at participating stores. Most people who receive AFDC are eligible for food stamps, but you don't have to be receiving other government aid to be eligible. Food stamps can be used to buy most food products; they cannot be used for alcohol, cigarettes or other tobacco products, soap, paper products such as paper towels or toilet paper, or pet food. Stores cannot charge sales tax for products bought with food stamps.

You must apply for food stamps with all members of your household—everyone who regularly buys food and prepares meals together. It is the household, rather than individual members, who must meet the income requirements to qualify for food stamps. If you live with other people but make your meals separately, you can apply on your own unless you live with your spouse, sibling or child—they are almost always considered a part of your household for food stamp purposes.

How Food Stamps Are Issued

The food stamp program is administered by the U.S. Department of Agriculture. To apply, you must either call and request an application or go to the food stamp or county welfare office in person and fill one out. The application requests information regarding your household, income, expenses and immigration status. You may be required to present some proof of your responses. However, written proof may not be necessary; you can also give the names of people who can verify the information in your application, such as your employer. You must also have an interview.

If you qualify, you are eligible for food stamps beginning on the date you apply. In most cases, you must receive the food stamps (including those you were entitled to after you applied, during the time the office took to process your application) within 30 calendar days of the date you apply.

Emergency Food Stamps. If your household has an urgent need, you may be eligible for expedited service, which will get you food stamps within five calendar days of your application. To qualify, your household must meet one of these tests:

- The household has less than $100 in liquid assets and less than $150 gross monthly income.
- The household's gross income and resources together are less than the household's monthly expenses for rent or mortgage payments and utilities.
- Every member of the household is homeless, or
- Every member of the household is a migrant or seasonal farmworker, the household has less than $100 in liquid assets, the household has already

received all its income for the month from a job that has been discontinued, and the household doesn't anticipate earning more than $25 from any new job in the next ten days.

Eligibility

A household must meet three conditions to be eligible for food stamps:

1. Everyone in the household must be a U.S. citizen or a legal alien.

2. The household's net income cannot exceed the federally determined poverty line. In 1991-92, for example, a household with two persons had to have a monthly net income below $740 to qualify. In addition, the family's monthly gross income cannot exceed 130% of poverty income; for a two-person household in 1991-92, this amount was $962.

Monthly net income means money made in the month minus deductions allowed by the government. These deductions include a standard deduction per household of $122 in 1991-92, a deduction for work expenses and taxes, and a deduction for money spent on child or dependent care. Certain things don't count as income, including: non-monetary benefits such as public housing, money earned by a child under 18 who is in school at least half-time, student loans for tuition and school supplies (but not for living expenses), and irregular lump-sum payments such as tax refunds.

3. The family's resources cannot exceed $2,000 ($3,000 if the household has a member over the age of 62). Resources are liquid assets, such as money in bank accounts and property that could easily be converted to cash. Some things do not count as resources: the household's home, personal belongings, burial lots, life insurance policies, tools of trade, or cars used by household members to make a living or travel a long distance to work. A household in which every member is receiving AFDC does not have to comply with these resource limits.

Exceptions. Households may not receive food stamps, regardless of their income or resources, if any of the following is true:

- A member is on strike, unless the household was eligible before the strike, or the striker has been locked out or permanently replaced.
- A member is an illegal alien.
- The members live in certain institutions that serve meals, such as a boarding school or jail.
- All members are enrolled half-time in college or university, unless they work 20 hours per week, are receiving federal work-study money, are under 18 or over 60 years of age, are physically or mentally unfit, are receiving AFDC or taking care of a small child, or are enrolled in the Job Training Partnership Act (JTPA) program.
- All members are receiving Supplemental Security Income.

If you are eligible for food stamps, you will be certified to receive them for one to twelve months. At the end of your certification period, you must reapply, have another interview and prove your continuing eligibility.

How Many Food Stamps Will You Receive?

The amount of a food stamp award is based on household size and income. The food stamp office subtracts 30% of the household's net income from the maximum award allowed for that household size to determine the food stamp allotment. For example, here's how it would be calculated for a household of three people that earned $300 net monthly income:

Maximum award for family of three	$292
30% of $300 net income	-90
	$202 food stamp allotment

Changes in Eligibility and Amounts

You must notify the food stamp office within 10 days of any change in the circumstances that make you eligible for food stamps or determine the amount of your award. This includes a change in income or household size.

If the office decides to reduce or cut off your food stamps, you must receive notice and an opportunity to ask for a hearing on the subject. If you request a hearing within 10 days of receiving this notice, you will continue to receive food stamps while your hearing is pending. In any case, you must request a hearing within 90 days of receiving this notice, or you will not be allowed to protest the action. At the hearing, you will be able to present arguments and proof that your household should still receive food stamps.

GENERAL ASSISTANCE

General Assistance (GA) is a form of welfare available to needy people who don't qualify for other governmental relief programs, such as AFDC or Social Security. General Assistance is a state-mandated program, but the state doesn't pay for it. Instead, the state requires that all counties relieve and support their poor, incompetent, indigent and otherwise incapacitated residents. (Welf. & Inst. Code § 17000.) Each county has great discretion in deciding who qualifies for benefits, what they have to do to receive benefits, and how much money they receive.

Residency

Only California residents who are U.S. citizens or legal aliens are eligible for General Assistance. A recipient must apply in the county of which she is a resident—this means the county where she has lived for at least one year before applying. If she has not lived in any county for one year before applying, she can apply in the county where she has lived for at least one year in the last three years. Someone who has not lived in any county for one year must apply in the county where she has spent the most time in the three years before applying.

Eligibility and Amounts

To qualify for GA, an applicant must have very limited income and limited property. The exact requirements are up to each county. Many counties try to prevent fraud by disqualifying any person who has given away or sold property for less than its value for a certain period before applying. Almost every county requires applicants to register to work, if they are able, and many counties cut off the benefits of someone who refuses an offered job without a good reason.

GA payments are rarely sufficient to cover basic needs, despite the fact that state law requires counties to tie their payments to housing and food costs in the area. For example, Alameda County, which is considered one of the highest paying counties, currently provides about $340 a month for one person.

HOUSING

Housing benefits come in many forms. All are funded by the federal government, although state agencies help administer the programs. The primary federal housing programs are: public housing, Section 8 housing, housing vouchers and subsidized housing.

Many aspects of these programs are similar, including eligibility requirements, preferences for who receives housing first, and calculations of how much rent the government will pay on the tenant's behalf. However, the programs differ regarding how much freedom private landlords or housing owners have in deciding who to rent to, how much rent to charge and when to evict a tenant.

Eligibility

Several categories of persons are eligible for housing benefits:
- Families, including unmarried couples, single pregnant women and single parents with physical custody of their children.
- Persons over age 62.
- Handicapped or disabled persons. A handicapped person is anyone with a physical or mental impairment of indefinite duration that substantially impedes his ability to live independently, and whose abilities could be improved by more suitable housing. A disabled person is anyone defined as disabled under Social Security regulations.
- Remaining members of a tenant family: someone whose name is on the lease and who remains in the apartment after all other family members have gone.
- Displaced persons whose income is 80% or less of the median income for the area, and whose resources do not exceed the limits established by federal law. (24 C.F.R. 912, 42 U.S.C. 1437a (b)(2), (3).) A displaced person is someone who has lost her home due to government action or a federally recognized disaster.

Preferences

In most housing programs, there are significantly fewer housing units than there are people who qualify for them. To decide who gets the available housing, preferences are used. At least 70% of all units must be available to people who:
- are homeless, or live in shelters or substandard housing
- pay more than 50% of their income for rent and utility payments, or
- are involuntarily displaced by a disaster, government action, action taken by a housing owner that forces a tenant to leave (other than a rent increase), or domestic violence.

The remaining 30% of the units must be rented according to locally determined preferences. People who do not qualify for a federal or local preference are much less likely to receive housing, especially in public housing units.

Rent

Most tenants receiving housing benefits pay whichever of these amounts is higher:
- 30% of the household's adjusted monthly income (actual income less various deductions, including a standard deduction per child, a deduction for family members who are elderly, disabled or handicapped, and a deduction for child care expenses)
- 10% of the household's gross monthly income, or
- that part of a welfare benefit that is specifically intended to pay for housing.

This payment is intended to cover both rent and utilities. If the agency does not pay the tenant's utilities, the tenant is entitled to subtract utility payments and pay only the remainder for rent.

Public Housing

Public housing is housing owned by a local public housing authority, with assistance from the U.S. Housing and Urban Development Department (HUD). The local authority can use some discretion in deciding whom to rent to among eligible tenants. Tenants can be evicted from public housing only for a good reason, such as serious lease violations or criminal activity by a household member. To evict someone, the housing authority must follow specified federal procedures, in addition to state requirements.

Section 8 Housing

The Section 8 Program is also run jointly by a local housing authority and HUD. The housing authority enters into a contract directly with the landlord of a privately owned housing unit. The tenant pays a percentage of his or her income for rent (under the guidelines discussed above), and the housing authority pays the rest of the rent charged. The tenant and landlord also enter into a lease, which must be approved by the housing authority. In most cases, the apartment must be renting for a fair market price, as determined by housing authority guidelines. Tenants may be required to pay more than the guidelines indicate if they wish to live in an apartment that is renting for more than what the housing authority considers the fair market price.

A household that qualifies for assistance, as described above, must be allowed to participate in the Section 8 Program unless it currently owes rent or other money to the housing authority, it has committed fraud, any member has been involved in violent or drug-related criminal activity or the household has failed to comply with housing authority rules, such as allowing inspection of the apartment.

Housing Vouchers

The housing voucher program is available only to tenants who:
- make 50% or less of the median income for the area, or
- make 80% or less of the median income for the area and have been continuously eligible for some form of housing benefits or were physically displaced because their old premises are being rehabilitated.

Tenants must apply to the local housing authority for a housing voucher. A tenant who receives a voucher must find housing that is available and meets the housing authority's standards. The housing authority will pay the difference between what it determines to be the fair market rent for the unit, and what the tenant is required to pay under the guidelines mentioned above. However, since the landlord is free to charge more than the fair market rent, the tenant may have to pay more for the unit.

Subsidized Housing

A number of programs fall into this category. They all involve privately owned apartment complexes whose owners either receive rental subsidies or have low-interest mortgages insured by the Federal Housing Administration (FHA). All are required to charge lower than market rents. The amount of rent a tenant must pay is determined by the program's regulations. Landlords have a substantial amount of discretion in determining who to choose as tenants (among those who qualify under the guidelines above). Good cause is required to evict.

MEDI-CAL

Medi-Cal (called Medicaid outside of California) is a program established by the federal government and administered by the state which helps pay medical costs for qualified needy people. For low-income seniors, Medi-Cal covers some of the medical costs Medicare doesn't cover.

Eligibility

If you are receiving Supplemental Security Income (SSI) or AFDC, you are automatically eligible for Medi-Cal. Otherwise, to apply for Medi-Cal, you must fall into one of these categories:

- have children under 21 years old living in your home
- be under 21 yourself
- be 65 or over
- have a disability or be blind
- be pregnant
- be a refugee living in the U.S. less than a year, or
- currently be living in a skilled nursing facility.

Only those who have limited resources qualify for Medi-Cal. One person can have assets worth up to $2,000, two people can have assets worth up to $3,000, three people can have assets worth up to $3,150 and so on. There is no income limitation for eligibility, but people who make more than these amounts may be required to pay for some of the costs of care.

Generally, Medi-Cal won't consider the income or assets of your children or any other relatives in deciding your eligibility, unless you receive regular financial support from a relative. If you live with your spouse, his or her income and assets will be counted as your income. Different rules apply if your husband or wife is in a nursing facility.

To apply for Medi-Cal, you or your representative must file a written application in person at the local office of the State Department of Social Services.

Medi-Cal Benefits

Medi-Cal covers the following medical services:

- inpatient hospital or skilled nursing facility care
- outpatient hospital or clinic services
- independent laboratory and X-ray services
- physicians' services
- home health care services
- transportation (ambulance, if necessary) to and from the place you receive medical services
- state-licensed practitioner's care (chiropractor, optometrist, podiatrist, acupuncturist)
- eye glasses
- dental care
- prosthetic devices
- prescribed drugs
- physical, speech and occupational therapy
- private-duty nursing
- diagnostic, preventive, screening and rehabilitative services, and
- inpatient psychiatric care for those 65 and over.

In addition, Medi-Cal will pay some of the costs not covered by Medicare, including:

- the inpatient hospital insurance deductible that Medicare doesn't pay
- the Medicare medical insurance deductible
- the 20% of the "reasonable charges" that Medicare medical insurance doesn't pay of doctor bills and other outpatient care
- the monthly premium charged for Medicare medical insurance.

Coverage

The care or service must be prescribed by a doctor and provided by a doctor or facility that "participates" in Medi-Cal. Also, inpatient services must be approved as "medically necessary" by the facility. And Medi-Cal coverage for certain medical services must be approved by a Medi-Cal consultant before you receive them.

Hospitals, doctors and other providers of medical care that accept Medi-Cal patients must accept Medi-Cal's payment as payment in full. If you're eligible for both Medicare and Medi-Cal, and you're treated by a medical facility or doctor that accepts Medi-Cal patients, the treating physician must accept from Medicare and Medi-Cal the total fee that Medicare determines is reasonable. You cannot be billed for any extra amounts for the covered services.

MEDICARE

Medicare is a federal program designed to help seniors and some disabled Americans pay for medical costs. The program is divided into two parts: Part A is hospital insurance, and Part B is medical insurance.

Part A: Hospital Insurance

These people are automatically eligible to receive Part A coverage:

- those 65 or older and eligible for Social Security retirement benefits or for Railroad Retirement benefits
- those under 65 who have been entitled to Social Security disability benefits for 24 months, or
- anyone with a spouse or dependent who has permanent kidney failure.

If you're 65 or over but not automatically eligible for Part A insurance, you can still enroll in the Medicare hospital insurance program. You must pay a monthly premium of at least $156; the premium increases by 10% for each year after your 65th birthday during which you're not enrolled. You will also have to pay an initial "hospital insurance deductible" of about $650, which increases every year.

Part A hospital insurance pays a portion of hospital and inpatient treatment costs. However, only treatment that is medically reasonable and necessary is covered. The hospital or skilled nursing facility must be approved by Medicare and accept Medicare payment, and the specific care and treatment you receive must be prescribed by a doctor.

Among the specific things Part A Insurance pays for:

- a semi-private room (two to four beds per room) and all your meals, including any special, medically-required diets
- regular nursing services
- special care units, such as intensive care, coronary care or a private hospital room if medically necessary
- drugs, medical supplies and appliances furnished by the facility (casts, splints, wheelchair)
- hospital lab tests, X-rays and radiation treatment billed by the hospital
- operating and recovery room costs
- rehabilitation services while you're in the hospital or nursing facility, and
- part-time skilled nursing care and physical therapy and speech therapy provided in your home.

Part A Insurance *does not* pay for:

- television, radio or telephone in your hospital room
- private-duty nurses
- a private room, unless medically necessary, or
- the first three pints of blood you receive, unless you make arrangements for their replacement.

Part B: Medical Insurance

Part B Medical Insurance pays some of the costs of treatment by your doctor either in or out of the hospital, and some medical expenses incurred outside the hospital.

Anyone who is age 65 or older and a U.S. citizen or five-year resident is eligible. If you want Part B medical insurance, you must enroll in the program and pay a monthly premium ($31.80 in 1992). This premium is adjusted each year based on the cost of living.

Part B insurance pays only a fraction of most people's medical bills. Many major medical expenses are not covered. For treatment that is covered, Medicare pays only 80% of what it considers to be a reasonable charge for the doctor's services—which may be much less than the doctor charged you.

Part B insurance pays for:

- doctors' services, including surgery, provided at a hospital, at the doctor's office or at home
- mammograms and PAP smears for women patients
- medical services provided by nurses, surgical assistants, or laboratory or X-ray technicians
- services provided by pathologists or radiologists while you're an inpatient at a hospital
- outpatient hospital treatment, such as emergency room or clinic charges, X-rays and injections
- an ambulance, if required for a trip to or from a hospital or skilled nursing facility
- drugs or other medicine administered to you at the hospital or doctor's office;
- medical equipment and supplies, such as splints, casts, prosthetic devices, body braces, heart pacemakers, corrective lenses after a cataract operation, oxygen equipment, wheelchairs and hospital beds
- some kinds of oral surgery
- some of the cost of outpatient physical and speech therapy
- manual manipulation of out-of-place vertebrae by a chiropractor, and
- part-time skilled nursing care and physical therapy and speech therapy provided in your home.

Medicare Part B medical insurance *does not* pay for:

- routine physical examinations
- treatment that isn't "medically necessary," including some elective and most cosmetic surgery and virtually all alternative forms of medical care such as acupuncture, acupressure and homeopathy
- vaccinations and immunizations
- drugs—prescription or not—which you can administer or take yourself at home;
- routine eye or hearing examinations, eye glasses, contact lenses (except after a cataract operation) or hearing aids
- general dental work, and
- routine foot care.

SOCIAL SECURITY

Social Security is a combination of federal programs designed to pay benefits to workers and their dependents. Benefits are paid based on the worker's average wage in jobs covered by Social Security over his or her working life. The three basic categories of benefits under Social Security are:

- **Retirement Benefits.** You may choose to begin receiving your retirement benefits any time after you reach age 62, but the amount of benefits goes up for each year you wait to retire.
- **Dependents' and Survivors' Benefits.** If you're the spouse of a retired or disabled worker, or the surviving spouse of a deceased worker who would have qualified for retirement or disability benefits, you and your children may be

entitled to benefits based on the worker's earning record. You may also be eligible for these benefits if you're 62 or older and divorced—if your marriage to the worker lasted at least 10 years, you've been divorced at least two years and have not remarried.

- **Disability Benefits.** See Disability Insurance.

Qualifying for Benefits

The specific requirements within each program vary. However, to qualify for all benefits, the worker must have worked in "covered employment" for a sufficient number of years, which differs depending on when he or she reaches age 62, becomes disabled or dies. Any job or self-employment from which Social Security taxes are reported is covered employment.

You must have accumulated enough "work credits" from covered employment to reach insured status. Work credits are measured in quarter-years (January through March is the first quarter of each year, April through June is the second, and so on). You receive credit for every quarter in which you earned more than the required minimum amount of money in covered employment. The number of work credits you need depends on the benefit you're applying for and your age when you apply.

If you're eligible for benefits, the amount you will receive is determined by the history of all your reported earnings in covered employment since you began working. The amount of your benefits will depend on your average reported income.

SUPPLEMENTAL SECURITY INCOME

Supplemental Security Income (SSI) is a joint federal-state program intended to guarantee a minimum income to elderly, blind and disabled people. To be eligible for SSI, you must meet three requirements.

1. You must be 65 or over, blind or disabled. You're considered legally blind if your vision is no better than 20/200, or your field of vision is limited to 20 degrees or less, even with corrective lenses. You're considered disabled if you have a physical or mental impairment that prevents you from doing any substantial work and that is expected to last at least 12 months or to result in death.

2. Your monthly income must be less than $719 for an individual blind person, $645 for an individual elderly or disabled person or $514 for a disabled minor. (Income limits for married couples are higher.) Any income you earn in wages or self-employment, and any money you receive from investments, Social Security benefits, pensions, annuities, royalties, gifts, rents or interest on savings, regular food and housing provided by others is counted against the SSI limits.

Some things don't count as income, including:
- the first $20 per month you receive from any source (except other public assistance based on need)
- the first $65 per month of your earned income (wages or self-employment)
- one-half of all your earned income over $65 a month
- irregular or infrequent earned income (such as from a one-time only job) if such income isn't more than $10 a month
- irregular or infrequent unearned income (such as a gift or dividend on an investment) up to $20 per month
- food stamps or housing assistance from a federal housing program run by a state or local government agency
- some work-related expenses for blind or disabled people paid for through public assistance.

3. Your assets, not counting your home and car, must not be worth more than $2,000 ($3,000 for a married couple), although some items are excepted, including:
- your automobile, up to a current market value of $4,500. If you use your car for work, or to get to and from a job or regular medical treatment, or it is specially

equipped to transport a handicapped person, the value of your car isn't counted, no matter how much it's worth
- your personal property and household goods up to a total current or "equity" value of $2,000; wedding and engagement rings aren't counted, regardless of their value
- property essential to self-support, such as tools or machines used in your trade, and
- life insurance policies with a total face value of $1,500 or less per person, burial policies, or term life insurance policies with no cash surrender value, as well as a burial plot for each spouse.

Amount of Benefits

The maximum federal SSI payment is the same as the monthly income limits for eligibility. These maximum benefit amounts, though, are reduced by any income you make.
- your benefit check will be reduced by one dollar for every two dollars you earn in current wages or self-employment over $65 a month.
- your payment will be reduced dollar for dollar by the amount of unearned income you receive over $20 a month; such income includes your Social Security benefits, pensions, annuities, interest on savings, dividends, or any money from investments or property you own.
- your SSI payment will be reduced by one-third if you live in a friend or relative's home and receive food or clothing there.

How To Apply for SSI Benefits

Apply for SSI benefits at your local Social Security office. After you complete the necessary paperwork, it will take from four to eight weeks to receive your first regular monthly SSI check.

VETERANS' BENEFITS

Veterans may be entitled to numerous benefits, based on their service history. Although the eligibility requirements for each benefit are different, almost all benefits require that you have been honorably or generally discharged. In addition, most benefits require you to have been in active service; to qualify for a pension, you must have actually served during wartime.

These programs are managed by the federal Veterans' Administration (VA).

Types of Benefits Available

The complexity of the eligibility requirements and the multitude of benefits available make it impossible to detail them here. But generally speaking, the veteran's benefits that may be available include:
- medical care: both in VA hospitals and outpatient treatment, as well as nursing home facilities
- disability compensation: for service-connected injuries
- housing for older veterans
- death and burial benefits
- education and training—including low-cost student loans and grants and rehabilitation training
- employment preferences for civil service and other government jobs
- low-cost loans for veterans in business
- inexpensive housing loans
- life insurance, and
- pensions.

INHERITANCE AND WILLS

There are many ways to get your property to those you want to have it when you die. Each has advantages and disadvantages: some avoid probate court proceedings, save on taxes or allow more flexibility to those who inherit your property. If you don't leave clear instructions, state law determines who inherits your property.

TOPICS
EXECUTORS AND ADMINISTRATORS
GIFT AND ESTATE TAX
INHERITANCE BY A SPOUSE
INHERITANCE BY MINOR CHILDREN
INHERITANCE WHEN THERE'S NO WILL
JOINT TENANCY
LIVING TRUSTS
LONG-TERM TRUSTS
PAY-ON-DEATH ACCOUNTS
PROBATE
WILLS

RELATED TOPICS
SERIOUS ILLNESS
Durable Power of Attorney for Finances
Durable Power of Attorney for Health Care
Living Wills
CHILDREN
Guardianships
RELATIONSHIPS
Community and Separate Property

ADDITIONAL RESOURCES
WillMaker (Nolo Press) (software for Macintosh, Windows or DOS) lets users create a valid will, living will and final arrangements document with a computer.

Nolo's Law Form Kit: Wills (Nolo Press), contains a simple fill-in-the-blanks will.

Nolo's Simple Will Book, by Denis Clifford (Nolo Press), contains a detailed discussion and forms for creating a will.

Plan Your Estate, by Denis Clifford (Nolo Press), is a detailed guide to estate planning.

Make Your Own Living Trust, by Denis Clifford (Nolo Press), explains how a living trust can help you avoid probate fees and lower estate taxes and contains forms showing you how you can prepare your own living trust.

Nolo's Living Trust (software for Macintosh computers) allows users to make a simple revocable probate-avoidance trust on a computer.

How To Probate an Estate, by Julia Nissley (Nolo Press), contains forms and instructions for probating an estate in California.

IRS Instructions for Form 706 (Federal Estate Tax Return).

IRS Publication 448, Federal Estate and Gift Taxes.

EXECUTORS AND ADMINISTRATORS

The executor is the person you name in your will to wind up your affairs after your death. The probate court, which will be in charge of seeing that the terms of your will are carried out, will affirm your choice unless the person you named is clearly not fit. The probate court confirms the authority of the executor by issuing a document called "Letters Testamentary."

If there is no will, or the person appointed in the will cannot serve, the court appoints an "administrator," who has the same duties as an executor. State law determines who is appointed. The surviving spouse is the first choice; if there is none, the deceased person's children are appointed. (Probate Code § 8461.)

The executor or administrator must:

- get certified copies of the death certificate
- locate will beneficiaries
- inventory the deceased person's assets and safe deposit box
- collect the deceased person's mail
- cancel credit cards and subscriptions
- notify Social Security and Medi-Cal, if necessary
- collect death benefits and insurance proceeds
- file the deceased person's final income tax return
- file federal and California estate tax returns, if required
- pay debts
- handle probate, if required
- transfer property that doesn't go through probate, including community property left to the surviving spouse and joint tenancy property.

GIFT AND ESTATE TAX

Federal gift and estate tax is assessed when someone gives away property, either during life or at death. The giver, not the recipient, is taxed. The tax rate is the same whether the property is given before or after death.

Most people pay no federal gift or estate tax, because anyone may give away (during life or at death) at least $600,000 tax-free. Gifts of any amount to a spouse who is a U.S. citizen, to a tax-exempt organization or for medical expenses or school tuition are always exempt from gift/estate tax.

Gift Tax

By taxing property regardless of when it's given, the gift tax is intended to thwart people who try to avoid estate tax by giving property away before they die. Any gift worth more than $10,000 given to one person in one year is subject to the federal gift tax. Each member of a married couple gets this $10,000 exclusion, so together they can give up to $20,000 per recipient per year, without reducing either's $600,000 exemption amount. So in practice, people can give away sizeable amounts of property and avoid the estate tax assessed at death.

EXAMPLE: *Robin gives her son $6,000 in cash and $10,000 in real estate in one calendar year. She must file a gift tax return for the amount over $10,000. She will not have to pay tax but will use part of her $600,000 credit, leaving a $594,000 credit when she dies (assuming she makes no more non-exempt gifts). If Robin waited until next year to give the real estate, both gifts would be entirely exempt.*

If you make non-exempt gifts, you can't pay the tax now and save your $600,000 exemption for property you leave when you die. Because estate and gift tax cannot be figured until you have either died or given away $600,000 in non-exempt gifts, you don't pay taxes on gifts when you make them unless the $600,000 figure has been exceeded. But every non-exempt gift reduces the amount of the $600,000 exemption you have left.

You must file a gift tax return if you give away more than $10,000 to one person (not including a tax-exempt organization), even if you do not, because of the tax credit, have to pay any tax. Gift tax returns must be filed with a regular annual income tax return. They can be tricky; you may need help from a tax preparer or tax attorney.

Estate Tax

A federal estate tax return (IRS Form 706) must be filed within nine months after death for someone whose gross estate (everything owned at the date of death) exceeds $600,000.

The return must be filed even if no tax is due. For example, if someone leaves $1 million to his wife, no tax will be due (because property left to a U.S. citizen spouse is tax-exempt), but an estate tax return must be filed.

California has no state gift or estate tax, but it takes a cut of the federal tax, if any is due. The California estate tax return, a one-page form available from the State Controller's office in your district, is due at the same time as the federal return.

INHERITANCE BY A SPOUSE

Each member of a married couple owns half of the couple's community property, and is free to leave it to whomever he or she pleases. The other spouse has no claim to it. Separate property may also be left to a beneficiary of the owner's choosing.

If a married person dies without a will, however, all community property goes to the surviving spouse. The survivor also inherits some or all of the separately owned property, depending on whether or not the deceased spouse left surviving children or other close relatives.

A Spouse's Right To Inherit

The law also tries to make sure that no one is unintentionally omitted from his or her spouse's will. So if someone marries after making a will and then dies without changing that will to provide for the new spouse (or indicating in the will an intent to disinherit the new spouse), the surviving spouse may have a claim to some of the deceased spouse's property. Specifically, the spouse is entitled to:

- the deceased spouse's half of the couple's community property and quasi-community property
- up to one-half of the deceased spouse's separate property.

This property is called the spouse's "statutory share" of the deceased spouse's estate. (Probate Code §§ 6560-6562.)

Inheritance Without Probate

All property left without restriction to a surviving spouse, regardless of the size of the deceased spouse's estate, may be transferred to the survivor without a full-blown probate court proceeding.

Two different documents are used to transfer ownership to the surviving spouse, depending on the type of property:

- an affidavit (sworn statement) for community property real estate
- a Spousal Property Order, issued by the Superior Court, for other property.

Affidavit for community property real estate. For community property real estate, all the surviving spouse has to do is wait 40 days after the death of the first spouse and then fill out a simple affidavit, describing the property. The affidavit must be signed in front of a notary public and then recorded (put on file) in the County Recorder's office in the county in which the property is located. No court is involved.

Spousal property order. For other kinds of property—for example, real estate owned in the name of the deceased spouse alone, or stocks and bonds—a slightly more involved procedure is required. The surviving spouse must submit a Spousal Property Petition to the local Superior Court (which functions as the probate court).

The petition is a fill-in-the-blanks form provided by the court. The spouse must also mail notice of the petition to people who might be interested—close relatives and the beneficiaries of the spouse's will.

If no one objects, the court issues a Spousal Property Order, officially transferring ownership to the surviving spouse. The entire procedure takes about a month.

INHERITANCE BY MINOR CHILDREN

If a minor (a child under 18) inherits up to $5,000 worth of property, it can simply be given to the minor's parents. (Probate Code § 3401.) But if a minor inherits property worth more than $5,000, a more formal arrangement is required. If the giver did not make other arrangements, a court must appoint and supervise a guardian to manage the property. The court usually appoints one of the child's parents if possible.

Avoiding Guardianship Proceedings

There are several ways to leave money or valuable property to a minor without creating a guardianship:

- **Leave the property to an adult.** Many people don't leave property directly to a child. Instead, they leave it to the child's parent or to the person they expect to have care and custody of the child if neither parent is available. There's no formal legal arrangement, but they trust the adult to use the property for the child's benefit.

- **Name a custodian under the California Uniform Transfers to Minors Act.** You can name a "custodian" to manage property you leave a child until the child reaches an age you choose, from 18 to 25. (Probate Code §§ 3900-3925.) The custodian is responsible for collecting and investing the property and using it for the child's needs. The custodian is not supervised by a court.

- **Create a child's trust.** You can establish a trust for a minor in your will or living trust. You must choose an adult to manage the property and dole it out for the child's education, health and other needs. The trust ends at whatever age you designate, and any remaining property is turned over to the child outright.

CHILDREN WITH SPECIAL NEEDS

These property management options are not designed to provide long-term property management for a child with serious disabilities. See a lawyer and make arrangements geared to your particular situation.

INHERITANCE WHEN THERE'S NO WILL

When someone dies without a will ("intestate"), that person's property goes to his closest relatives, under California's "intestate succession" law. (Probate Code §§ 6400-6414.) Here are the basic rules:

- If a married person dies without a will, the surviving spouse inherits all community property. The surviving spouse also inherits one-third, one-half or all of the separate property, depending on whether or not the decedent is survived by children or other close relatives. The rest of the separate property is divided into shares and distributed to the children, parents, grandparents or siblings of the decedent.

- If an unmarried person dies without a will, his or her children inherit all the property. If there are no surviving children, more distant relatives inherit it.

- If someone dies without a will and leaves only more distant relatives (no spouse, children, grandchildren, great-grandchildren, parents or their issue, or grandparents or their issue), then the property goes to the "next of kin," as defined by Probate Code § 6402.

To inherit property from someone who dies without a will after December 31, 1989, a person must survive the deceased person for at least 120 hours. (Probate Code § 6403.)

These rules apply only to personal property and real estate in California; real estate in another state is passed according to the intestate succession law of the state in which it is located.

Adopted Children

Under the intestate succession law, a child who has been adopted may inherit from a birth parent only if:

- the deceased parent was married to or living with the other natural parent at the time of the child's conception and died before the child was born; and
- the adoption was by the spouse of either of the natural parents or took place after the death of either natural parent.

JOINT TENANCY

Joint tenancy is a way two or more people can hold title to property they own together. The most important feature of joint tenancy is that when one joint owner (called a joint tenant) dies, the surviving owners automatically get complete ownership of the property, without probate. This is called the "right of survivorship." The surviving owners need only fill out some simple paperwork to transfer the property into their names alone.

All joint tenants must own equal shares of the property. A joint tenant cannot leave his or her share to anyone other than the surviving joint tenants. So, for example, if a joint tenant leaves a will giving her share of the property to her son instead of the other joint tenant, the will would have no effect. However, a joint tenant can, while still alive, transfer his or her interest in the property or change the way title is held to get around this rule.

Joint tenancy often works well for unmarried couples who acquire real estate or other valuable property together. If they take title in joint tenancy, probate is avoided when the first owner dies. Married couples are usually better off taking title as community property—a designation that can result in some estate tax advantages.

Creating a Joint Tenancy

To create a joint tenancy, all the co-owners need to do is call themselves joint tenants on the document that shows ownership of property, such as a deed to real estate, a car's title slip or a card establishing a bank account.

Drawbacks of Joint Tenancy

Joint tenancy has some disadvantages that may make it a poor estate planning choice, depending on the circumstances. For example, an older person who, seeking only to avoid probate, puts solely owned property into joint tenancy with someone else, may be surprised to learn that he or she has given up half ownership of the property. The new owner can, for example, sell or mortgage his or her share, or it could be taken by creditors.

Other potential drawbacks of joint tenancy:

- If one joint tenant becomes incapacitated and cannot make decisions, and has not created a durable power of attorney to authorize someone else to act for her, the other owners must get legal authority to sell or mortgage the property. That may mean going to court to get someone (called a conservator) appointed to manage the incapacitated person's affairs.

- If you create a joint tenancy by making another person a co-owner, federal gift tax may be assessed on the transfer. However, if two or more people open a bank account in joint tenancy, but one person puts all or most of the money in, no gift tax is assessed against that person. But tax may be assessed when a joint tenant who has contributed little or nothing to the account withdraws money from it. Also, the recipient loses a future income tax benefit by receiving the property while the giver is alive, rather than at his or her death. Because of IRS "tax basis" rules, the taxable profit will be greater when the property is eventually sold.

- If spouses own property as joint tenants, the surviving spouse could miss out on a big income tax break later, when the property is sold. For property owned in joint tenancy, the surviving spouse gets a stepped-up tax basis only for that half of the property owned by the deceased spouse. (The tax basis is the amount from which taxable profit is figured when property is sold; the basis is "stepped-up" to the value at the time of death.) To get a stepped-up basis on the whole thing, the surviving spouse must prove that the property was actually community property; the IRS presumes that property held in joint tenancy is not community property.

LIVING TRUSTS

A revocable living trust lets your property pass to those you want to inherit it without the supervision of the probate court. Probate is notoriously slow, expensive and, for most people, unnecessary. A living trust performs the same function as a will, but wills are subject to probate.

Creating a Living Trust

A trust, like a corporation, is an entity that exists only on paper but is legally capable of owning property. You can create a trust simply by preparing and signing a document called a Declaration of Trust.

Once the trust has been created, you can transfer property to it. The trust becomes the legal owner. There must, however, be a flesh-and-blood person actually in charge of the property; that person is called the trustee.

How a Living Trust Works

When you create a revocable living trust, you transfer ownership of some or all of your property to the living trust. You also appoint yourself trustee, with full power over trust property. You keep absolute control over the property in your living trust, even though technically it's owned by the living trust. You can revoke (terminate) the trust at any time.

After you die, the person you named in your trust document to be "successor trustee" takes over. He or she is in charge of transferring the trust property to the family, friends or charities you named as the trust beneficiaries. No probate is necessary for property that was transferred to the living trust. In most cases, the whole thing can be handled within a few weeks. When the property has all been transferred to the beneficiaries, the living trust ceases to exist.

If you become incapacitated while serving as trustee, the successor trustee—the person you named in the trust document—is authorized to take over managing the trust property. Your incapacity must be certified in a doctor's written statement.

LONG-TERM TRUSTS

A trust, like a corporation, is an entity that exists only on paper but is legally capable of owning property. You can create a trust by preparing and signing a document called a Declaration of Trust. Once the trust has been created, you can transfer property to it. The trust then becomes the legal owner. A trustee manages the property on behalf of someone else, called the beneficiary.

Different kinds of trusts can be used to provide for children, save on taxes or provide for a disabled adult.

Children's Trusts

It's fairly common, if you want to leave a substantial amount of property to a child under 18, to create a child's trust. For more information, see "Inheritance by Minor Children."

Tax-Saving Trusts

No federal estate tax is assessed on property left to a surviving spouse who is a U.S. citizen; this is called the marital deduction. But this really just postpones estate tax until the second spouse dies and there's no marital deduction. Most elderly couples who have a combined estate of more than $600,000 should avoid leaving large sums to each other.

One way around this trap is for each spouse to put their property in a "marital life estate trust," sometimes called a "spousal trust" or "A-B trust." When one spouse dies, his or her half of the property goes to the children—with the crucial condition that the surviving spouse gets the right to use the deceased spouse's half of the property for life and is entitled to any income it generates. The surviving spouse is usually also given limited power to use up some of the property if it's necessary for medical or other reasons. When the second spouse dies, the property goes to the children outright. Using this kind of trust keeps the second spouse's estate half as small as it would be if the property were left to the spouse.

EXAMPLE: *Thomas and Maria, husband and wife, are in their mid-70s, and each has an estate worth $550,000. They establish a marital life estate trust, with the income to go to the survivor for life and the principal to the children at the survivor's death. When Thomas dies, Maria's estate remains at $550,000, plus any income she receives from the trust property.*

Maria dies in 1994. Because $600,000 can be left to anyone free of estate tax, there is no estate tax liability either from Maria's $550,000, which now goes to the children, or from Thomas's $550,000, which now goes to the children under the terms of the trust. Without the trust, the tax bill would be $155,800.

A marital life estate trust controls what happens to property for years after the first spouse's death. A couple who makes one must be sure that the surviving spouse will be financially and emotionally comfortable receiving only the income from the money or property placed in trust, with the children (or other persons) as the actual owner of the property. Many younger and middle-aged couples find it best to avoid such a trust and simply leave the property to the surviving spouse, who will have the time and opportunity to enjoy it.

Generation-Skipping Trusts

A "generation-skipping" trust won't reduce your own estate tax liability; it can, however, exempt up to $1 million from tax in the next generation.

With this kind of trust, your children are entitled to income from trust property but can't touch the principal. The principal goes to your grandchildren at the death of your children. The property you leave in such a trust is included in your taxable estate when you die. But it's not included in your children's taxable estate when they die.

Spendthrift Trusts

If you want to leave property to an adult who just can't handle money, a "spendthrift trust" is a good idea. A spendthrift trust keeps the money from being squandered by the beneficiary or seized by the beneficiary's creditors.

Trusts for Disabled Persons

A person with a physical or mental disability may not be able to handle property, no matter what his or her age. Often, the solution is to establish a trust with a competent adult as trustee to manage the trust property.

The trust should carefully prepared by an expert familiar with the state law, so that the trust won't jeopardize the beneficiary's eligibility for government benefits.

Flexible Trusts

If you don't want to decide now how your property is spent after your death, you can create a "sprinkling trust." It authorizes the trustee to decide how to spend trust money for the different beneficiaries you name.

PAY-ON-DEATH ACCOUNTS

Setting up a pay-on-death account, also called an informal bank account trust or revocable trust account, is an easy way to transfer cash at your death, quickly and without probate. All you do is designate one or more persons you want to receive the money in the account when you die.

You can use any kind of bank account, including savings, checking or certificate of deposit accounts, by filling out a simple form at your bank. You can also name a beneficiary to receive certain kinds of government securities, including bonds, Treasury Bills and Treasury Notes, at your death.

During your life, the beneficiary has no right to the money in the account. You can withdraw some or all of the money, close the account or change the beneficiary, at any time. When you die, the beneficiary can claim the money by showing the bank the death certificate.

PROBATE

Probate generally refers to the process by which a deceased person's will is proved valid in court, the person's debts and taxes are paid and the remaining property is distributed to inheritors. If there is no will, property must still go through probate unless the deceased person made other arrangements.

The executor named in the will (or, if there is no will, an administrator appointed by the court) is in charge of handling probate paperwork and managing the deceased person's property until it's distributed. In many cases, probate can be handled entirely by mail, without any court appearances.

Cost and Delay

Usually, probate takes seven months to a year, but it can take longer if the estate is complicated. During that time, the beneficiaries get nothing unless the judge allows the decedent's immediate family an allowance.

If an attorney is hired, lawyer, court and other fees can eat up 5% or more of a deceased person's estate (the property left at death). If the estate is complicated, fees can be even larger. State statutes contain a formula for setting lawyer fees, although clients are free to negotiate a different amount. Because the statutory fees are based on the value of the deceased person's property, they often bear no relation to the actual work done. Under the statute, a lawyer may collect:

- 4% of the first $15,000 of the gross value of the probate estate (the property that goes through probate)
- 3% of the next $85,000
- 2% of the next $900,000
- 1% of the next $9 million
- 1/2% of the next $15 million
- a "reasonable amount" (determined by the court) of everything above $25 million. (Probate Code §§ 901, 910.)

That means that if an estate has a gross value of $600,000—even if the deceased person's equity were only $200,000—an attorney could collect $13,150. That figure doesn't include court fees, accountants' and appraisers' bills.

What Property Goes Through Probate

Property left by a will must go through probate before it can be transferred to the beneficiaries. If you don't make a will or some other arrangement (living trust or joint tenancy, for example) to designate who gets your property, the property also goes through probate. It is distributed to your closest relatives according to California's "intestate succession" law.

Several kinds of property can be transferred to beneficiaries without formal probate, including:

- Property left through a living trust
- Property held in joint tenancy
- Funds in a pay-on-death bank account
- Life insurance proceeds
- Funds for which a beneficiary was designated (for example, funds in an Individual Retirement Account)

A streamlined probate court procedure is available for other kinds of property, including:

- Property left to a surviving spouse
- Property in small estates (less than $60,000, not counting property left to a surviving spouse and joint tenancy property).

AVOIDING PROBATE

In most instances, if there are no fears of huge creditors' lawsuits and no fights among relatives, formal probate court proceedings are a waste of time and money. Many people avoid probate by using a living trust or other method that allows property to pass directly to inheritors without probate.

WILLS

A will is a document in which you specify what is to be done with your property when you die. You can also name an executor, who will wind up your affairs after your death, and a guardian to care for your minor children (and their property) in your will.

Writing a Will

Anyone 18 or older who is of sound mind can make a valid will. An entirely handwritten will is valid in California, but it's not recommended; after your death such a will is easier to challenge in court because no witnesses will be available to verify your signature.

The best way to make a will is to type it, then sign and date it in front of at least two witnesses who don't stand to inherit anything under the terms of the will. The witnesses sign a statement under oath that they saw you sign the will; this allows a probate court, after your death, to accept the will as valid.

A very simple, fill-in-the-blanks form will is available from the State Bar of California for $1.

Updating a Will

There are two ways to change a will. You can add a supplement, called a codicil, or just revoke the old one and start fresh. To avoid the possibility of conflicts between the original will and a codicil, it's usually preferable to revoke the old one and prepare a whole new will. It's not much more work, because a codicil must be signed and witnessed just like the original will.

Probate Avoidance

Property left through a will cannot be transferred to the beneficiaries without the approval of the probate court. To avoid probate's expense and delay, many people use probate-avoidance devices, such as living trusts, to leave property. Even if you do this, you should have a will; it's an essential back-up device for property that you don't get around to transferring to your living trust.

LANDLORDS AND TENANTS

State law defines many of the rights and responsibilities of California landlords and tenants. We cover these legal rules here, as well as some practical issues, such as roommates' obligations to each other and rental listing services.

In some cities, municipal rent control ordinances provide much greater protections for tenants than the state requires, and often substantially limit the landlord's ability to evict tenants and raise rents. In addition, many cities have special regulations dealing with motor homes. You must consult current local laws to find out what's required in these areas.

TOPICS

ADDITIONAL RESOURCES
    Tenants' Rights, by Myron Moskovitz and Ralph Warner (Nolo Press), is a detailed discussion of California landlord-tenant law, including how to handle a threatened eviction.

The Landlord's Law Book: Rights and Responsibilities, by David Brown and Ralph Warner (Nolo Press), explains the law (including local rent control rules) California landlords need to know.

The Landlord's Law Book: Evictions, by David Brown (Nolo Press), contains all the forms and instructions for handling an eviction lawsuit without a lawyer.

CONDITION OF RENTED PREMISES
Several state and local laws set housing standards for the physical condition of residential rental property, both when the tenant moves in and during the tenancy.

Habitability Requirements
All rental units in California must:
- be weatherproof, waterproof and rodent proof
- have plumbing in good condition (every unit must have a toilet, wash basin and bathtub or shower)
- have a kitchen with a sink
- provide hot water
- have adequate heat
- have natural light through windows or skylights
- provide electric power if it is available in the area, complete with safe and proper wiring
- have a smoke detector (for multiple unit buildings rented after January 1987) (Health & Safety Code § 13113.7), and
- have adequate garbage storage and removal facilities. (Civ. Code § 1941; Health & Safety Code § 17920.3.)

Your city or county may have other requirements. Check with your local building inspector or health department.

When Premises Are Uninhabitable
If the landlord doesn't meet these minimum requirements, the tenant has several options:
- **Move out.** Even in the middle of a lease (or without the 30 days' notice required under a rental agreement), a tenant can simply move out. (Civ. Code § 1942.) Landlords may be required to pay "relocation benefits" to tenants who must move so repairs can be made. (Health & Safety Code § 17980.7.)
- **Withhold rent.** All leases and rental agreements include an implied promise that the landlord will keep the premises in a habitable condition. (*Green v. Superior Court*, 10 Cal. 3d 616 (1974).) If the landlord is in serious violation of this standard, the tenant may withhold rent until the problem is fixed. The tenant cannot, however, withhold rent or sue the landlord if the violations are minor or the tenant has contributed to the poor condition of the premises. (Civ. Code §§ 1929, 1942 (c).)
- **Call the building inspector.** This local agency—usually part of the Department of Public Works—can order the landlord to make repairs. If the landlord fails to make repairs within 60 days of being ordered to do so, the tenant may sue the landlord and recover any expenses the landlord's actions have cost her, plus an additional $100 to $1,000, plus attorney fees. The court that awards damages for an untenantable building can also order the landlord to repair substandard conditions that significantly affect the occupant's health and safety and can continue to oversee the matter until the repairs are made. (Civ. Code § 1942.4.) The city or county may also bring a lawsuit, or even criminal charges, against a landlord who fails to make repairs demanded by local officials. (Health & Safety Code §§ 17995-17995.5.)
- **Sue the landlord.** A tenant may sue the landlord and receive compensation for discomfort, annoyance and emotional distress. Tenants can even ask the court to appoint a receiver, who would be authorized to collect rents, manage the property and supervise the necessary repairs. (Health & Safety Code § 17980.7.)

Tenant's Right To Repair and Deduct

If a landlord fails to make a repair that is directly related to the health or safety of the tenant, the tenant can make necessary repairs or hire someone to make them, and deduct the cost from the next month's rent. Before having the repairs done, the tenant must give the landlord or manager "reasonable" notice of the problem. The repairs cannot cost more than one month's rent, and the problem must not have been caused by a careless or intentional act of the tenant or a guest. This "repair and deduct" remedy can be used only twice in a 12-month period. (Civ. Code § 1942.)

Landlord's Liability for Injuries

A landlord may be liable to the tenant—or others—for injuries caused by dangerous or defective conditions. For example, if the tenant is hurt falling on a broken stair, the landlord is responsible.

A landlord may be liable for tenant injuries and property damage resulting from the criminal acts of others, but only if the injury was caused by the landlord's unreasonable act—for example, failing to fix a defective lock or install adequate lighting. A landlord can also be liable for damage or injury caused by problem tenants. For example, tenants and others who become victims of the crime that surrounds a drug dealer's home may sue a landlord who does nothing to stop drug dealing on his property.

Disclosure Requirements

Landlords must notify tenants of certain conditions on the property.

- **Asbestos.** If there is asbestos in the materials used to construct the building, and the building has ten or more units and was constructed before 1979, each tenant must be individually notified of the problem. (Health and Safety Code § 25915.)
- **Shared utility arrangements.** If the landlord does not provide separate gas and electric meters for each tenant's unit, the landlord must disclose the situation to all tenants before they sign any rental agreement or lease, and make a written agreement with the tenant as to how utility charges will be divided. (Civ. Code § 1940.9.)

CONDOMINIUM CONVERSION

Where there's a shortage of new homes, many landlords find it profitable to convert their buildings from rental units to owner-occupied condominiums. Instead of paying monthly rent, residents own their apartments and a share of the common space, such as halls and grounds. In many cities, landlords must pay a fee or tax per unit converted.

Before a rental unit is converted to a condominium, each tenant must be given:

- at least 180 days' written notice of intent to convert before their tenancy is terminated. If a tenant's lease has more than 180 days left to run, the tenant can stay as long as the lease specifies.
- the first right to buy the apartment on at least the same terms that the apartment will be offered to the public, with 90 days to decide. (Gov't. Code § 66427.1.)

Many cities and a few counties have stricter rules governing condominium conversions. Check with your local planning commission.

COSIGNING LEASES AND RENTAL AGREEMENTS

Some landlords require that certain tenants (for example, students or persons without steady income) get a parent or friend who is financially secure to cosign the lease or rental agreements. Typically, these contracts require the cosigner to pay for rent or damage to the rental unit if the tenant can't or won't pay.

If a landlord and tenant change the terms of the rental agreement or lease without the approval of the cosigner, the cosigner is no longer liable for unpaid rent or damages. The changed agreement is considered a new contract—one the cosigner didn't agree to. (Civ. Code § 2819; *Wexler v. McLucas,* 48 Cal. App. 3d Supp. 9 (1975).)

DEPOSITS, FEES AND LAST MONTH'S RENT

All deposits and fees required by a landlord, no matter what they are called, are refundable. (Civ. Code § 1950.5.) For example, a so-called nonrefundable move-in, cleaning or pet fee must be refunded if the tenant moves out leaving the premises clean and undamaged.

Limits on Deposits

The amount a landlord can collect as a deposit is limited by state law.

- **Unfurnished units.** The total of all deposits and fees, including last month's rent, may not exceed the amount of two months' rent (two-and-one-half times rent, if the tenant has a waterbed).
- **Furnished units.** The total of all deposits and fees, including last month's rent, may not exceed three months' rent (three-and-one-half times rent, if the tenant has a waterbed). (Civ. Code § 1950.5.)
- **Pet deposits.** A landlord may not charge an extra pet deposit for trained guide dogs, signal dogs or service dogs (Civ. Code § 54.2.)

Increases in Deposits

If the tenant and landlord have signed a written lease, the deposit may not be increased during the terms of a lease unless the lease allows it. If the premises are rented under a month-to-month rental agreement, the landlord may increase the deposit after giving the tenant 30 days' written notice, unless a city rent control ordinance prohibits it.

Interest

California law does not require a landlord to pay interest on deposits. However, ordinances in the cities of Berkeley, Cotati, East Palo Alto, Hayward, Los Angeles, San Francisco, Santa Cruz, Santa Monica, Watsonville and West Hollywood do require it. Check with your city clerk for information about local laws.

Return of Deposits

The landlord has three weeks, after the tenant has vacated the premises, to return the tenant's entire deposit or provide an itemized written statement listing the amount of and reason for any portion of the deposit not returned, together with a check for the balance. (Civ. Code § 1950.5 (f).)

A landlord can withhold only the amount necessary to:

- pay overdue rent
- repair damage caused by the tenant—exclusive of ordinary wear and tear
- clean the premises (only if they need it)
- replace personal property of the landlord—such as furnishings—if the rental agreement or lease allows it.

If a landlord, without a good reason, doesn't refund the tenant's deposit within three weeks, a court may order the landlord to pay the tenant $600 punitive damage, in addition to the amount improperly withheld. (Civ. Code § 1950.5 (k).)

DISCRIMINATION

Discrimination in renting housing is illegal unless it is reasonably related to a legitimate business purpose of the landlord, such as requiring tenants to have a good credit rating. A landlord can adopt income criteria and apply them equally to all tenants, but cannot discriminate based on a group characteristic such as race, religion, ethnic background or national origin, sex, marital status, age, families with children (except in certain designated senior housing), disability, sexual orientation or receipt of public assistance.

Courts can levy substantial fines against landlords who unlawfully discriminate, and can order a landlord to rent to any person discriminated against. (Civ. Code § 51, *Marina Point v. Wolfson*, 30 Cal. 3d 721 (1982).)

EVICTIONS

A landlord must file a lawsuit in Municipal Court to evict a tenant. The case is officially called an unlawful detainer action.

Giving the Tenant Notice

An eviction cannot occur until the tenant gets proper written notice of the landlord's intent to end the tenancy. If the tenant has a month-to-month rental agreement, the tenant's rent is paid up and the tenant is not in violation of any provision in the rental agreement, a landlord must provide 30 days' written notice to end the tenancy. Unless local law requires it, the landlord does not have to give a reason for ending the tenancy. However, in many rent control cities, this notice must state a "just cause" (a legitimate reason, from a list in the ordinance) for eviction, except when the tenant is guilty of serious misconduct. A 30-day notice can be given any time during the month; it need not coincide with the date rent is due. If the tenant doesn't move out after the 30 days, the landlord can file an eviction lawsuit.

However, if the tenant fails to pay rent, violates a lease or rental agreement clause, seriously damages the premises or uses the property for an illegal purpose, only three days' notice is required to terminate the tenancy. If the violation can be corrected (the tenant could pay overdue rent or get rid of a pet that violates the lease, for example), the notice must give the tenant a choice—remedy the problem in three days or move. For very serious problems, such as drug dealing, the three-day notice can simply require the tenant to leave.

The Eviction Process

After an appropriate three-day or 30-day notice to terminate the tenancy has been properly served on (delivered to) the tenant and that time has passed without the tenant moving out or correcting the violation, the landlord can file an eviction (unlawful detainer) lawsuit in Municipal Court. After a summons and complaint are served on the tenant, the tenant has five days to file a written response. A court hearing is then held, usually within 20 days of the landlord's request.

If the court finds in favor of the landlord, it will award the landlord a judgment for possession of the property. A sheriff will then give the tenant a "writ of execution," ordering him or her to leave within five days or be physically removed.

To appeal an eviction order, a tenant must file a notice of appeal within 30 days of receiving notice of the court judgment. To stay in a rental unit pending the outcome of an appeal, the tenant must also be granted a stay of eviction by the Municipal Court. To get a stay of eviction, the tenant must show that:

- the tenant will suffer extreme hardship if he or she is evicted, and
- the landlord will not be hurt by the stay. This usually means that the tenant must pay rent and agree to any other conditions imposed by the judge.

DEFENSES TO AN EVICTION

These are the most common grounds on which tenants fight eviction.

- The landlord's claim that the tenant violated a lease or rental agreement provision is false.
- Rent was withheld because the premises were uninhabitable.
- The landlord is attempting to evict the tenant for exercising a legal right, such as complaining to a city official about substandard conditions.
- The landlord failed to give the tenant proper legal notices to either end the tenancy or initiate the eviction lawsuit.
- The landlord has no just cause to evict, in rent control cities where it is required.

Illegal Evictions

It is illegal for a landlord to evict a tenant by force or threat (Code of Civ. Proc. §§ 1159-1160.) It is also illegal for a landlord to:

- lock the tenant out or change locks
- remove doors or windows
- remove the tenant's furniture or property, or
- shut off any utilities or cause them to be shut off. (Civ. Code § 789.3.)

Any provision in a lease or rental agreement that purports to allow any of these actions is void. In the case of an unlawful lock-out, property removal or utility shutoff, the landlord can be penalized up to $100 per day, with a $250 minimum, and must also reimburse the tenant for actual losses.

Landlords cannot legally terminate a tenancy because of race, religion or other arbitrary reasons or as a means of retaliating against a tenant for exercising any right under the law.

LEASES AND RENTAL AGREEMENTS

Leases and rental agreements are contracts to rent property. They can be oral (as long as the term is less than a year) or written, and usually contain provisions regulating the rent, number of occupants, types and number of pets, amount of deposits, noise, who pays for utilities and the tenant's and landlord's duties to maintain and repair the premises.

Leases

A lease gives a tenant the right to occupy a rental unit at a fixed rent for a certain number of months or years, as long as the tenant pays the rent and complies with other lease provisions. If a tenant moves out before the lease expires, the landlord is owed the remaining rent due under the lease, less the amount the landlord could reasonably recover by finding a new tenant.

At the end of the lease term, the landlord can ask the tenant to leave without stating a reason, except in those cities requiring just cause for eviction. If the tenant stays on, some leases provide for an automatic renewal for the same time period as the original lease. To be legal, this provision must be printed, in at least eight-point boldface type, immediately above the tenant's signature. (Civ. Code § 1945.5.) In the absence of such a renewal provision, the tenant becomes a month-to-month tenant under the terms of the original lease. (Civ. Code § 1945.)

Rental Agreements

Usually, a rental agreement is from month-to-month, but periods as short as seven days are legal. For monthly rentals, the tenant can move or the landlord can raise the rent, change other terms of the rental agreement or order the tenant to move on 30 days' written notice. However, in some cities with rent control ordinances, a landlord must show "just cause" to end the tenancy.

MANAGERS

A landlord must give tenants the name and address of someone authorized to accept legal documents on the landlord's behalf. (Civ. Code § 1962.7.) This can be either the landlord or the manager. This notification must be in writing if the tenant has a written lease or rental agreement, and available on demand if the rental agreement is oral.

Any apartment complex with 16 or more rental units must employ a resident manager. (Cal. Code of Regulations, Title 25, § 42.)

A landlord is legally responsible for the acts of a manager or management company acting within the scope of their duties. For example, if a manager illegally refuses to rent to a couple with children, the landlord will be liable.

If the court finds in favor of the landlord, it will award the landlord a judgment for possession of the property. A sheriff will then give the tenant a "writ of execution," ordering him or her to leave within five days or be physically removed.

To appeal an eviction order, a tenant must file a notice of appeal within 30 days of receiving notice of the court judgment. To stay in a rental unit pending the outcome

of an appeal, the tenant must also be granted a stay of eviction by the Municipal Court. To get a stay of eviction, the tenant must show that:
- the tenant will suffer extreme hardship if he or she is evicted, and
- the landlord will not be hurt by the stay. This usually means that the tenant must pay rent and agree to any other conditions imposed by the judge.

TIPS FOR LANDLORDS

Landlords can avoid being held liable for a manager's acts by:
- limiting, in writing, the authority delegated to a manager
- making sure the manager understands and applies basic landlord/tenant law, especially the duty not to discriminate against prospective tenants or retaliate against tenants who exercise their lawful rights
- buying insurance that covers the illegal acts of managers
- setting up an easy way for tenants to communicate directly with the landlord if they believe the manager is doing a poor job or violating their rights.

PETS

A landlord can restrict or prohibit a tenant's right to keep any pet except properly-trained dogs of the blind, visually handicapped, deaf or physically disabled. (Civ. Code § 54.1.) A landlord may not charge an extra pet deposit for trained guide dogs, signal dogs or service dogs. (Civ. Code § 54.2.)

Tenants in federally subsidized housing are also entitled to keep pets.

PRIVACY AND THE LANDLORD'S RIGHT TO ENTER

Tenants are guaranteed reasonable privacy. (Civ. Code § 1953(a)(1).) This right can't be waived or modified by any lease or rental agreement provision. A landlord, manager or employee may enter the tenant's premises while the tenant is living there only:
- in case of emergency
- to make necessary or agreed-on repairs (or to assess the need for them)
- when the tenant gives permission, or
- to show the property to a prospective tenant or purchaser. (Civ. Code § 1954.)

Except for emergencies and when the tenant gives permission, the landlord, manager, employee or contractor can enter only during "normal business hours," which aren't defined in the statute. The tenant must also receive reasonable notice; 24-hour notice is presumed to be reasonable.

RENT

The landlord and tenant may agree on any dollar amount for rent, except in certain cities covered by rent control.

When Rent Is Due

By custom, almost all leases and rental agreements require rent to be paid monthly, in advance. Often rent is due on the first day of the month. However, it is legal for a landlord to require rent to be paid at different intervals or on a different day of the month.

Rent Increases

If the tenant and landlord have signed a fixed-term lease, the rent can't be raised unless the lease allows it. At the end of a lease, rent may be raised to any amount, except in cities covered by rent control. The landlord is not required to give the tenant written notice of such an increase.

If the tenant is renting under an oral or written month-to-month tenancy, the landlord can increase the rent by any amount if the landlord gives the tenant 30 days' written notice, unless the landlord does so to retaliate against the tenant for exercising a legal right. Local rent control ordinances may limit the increase allowed.

Late Fees

Fees for late payment of rent are legal, as long as they are reasonable. A few rent control cities regulate the amount. Typically, late fees of up to $10 per day, with a $50 limit, are considered reasonable.

RENT CONTROL

No state laws regulate the rent landlords can charge, but several cities have adopted rent control ordinances.

RENT CONTROL CITIES

Berkeley	Los Angeles	San Jose
Beverly Hills	Los Gatos	Santa Monica
Cotati	Oakland	Thousand Oaks
East Palo Alto	Palm Springs	West Hollywood
Hayward	San Francisco	

Rent control ordinances generally control more than how much rent a landlord may charge; they often govern how and under what circumstances a landlord may terminate a tenancy. Rent control laws fall into several broad categories.

Weak Rent Control: Hayward, Los Gatos, Oakland and San Jose

In these cities, landlords can raise rent by a generous annual percentage. Additional rent increases are possible if the tenant doesn't object, and landlords have free rein to raise the rent when a unit is vacated. Landlords need not register units with any government agency. Just cause for eviction is not required except in Hayward.

Moderate Rent Control: Beverly Hills, Los Angeles, Palm Springs, San Francisco and Thousand Oaks

These cities establish a fairly tight limit on annual rent increases. Above that, a landlord must get permission from the rent board on a case-by-case basis, and the tenant has the opportunity to object. In all these cities except Palm Springs, when a tenant moves out, a landlord can raise the rent to any level (called vacancy decontrol).

In all these cities except Palm Springs, a landlord who wants to terminate a tenancy must show "just cause," such as a tenant's failure to pay rent, violating a lease or rental agreement provision, damaging the premises, disturbing other tenants or committing significant illegal activity on the premises (such as selling drugs). A landlord may also evict a tenant to let an immediate family member, or the landlord, move in. For other just cause provisions, check with your city's rent control board.

Strict Rent Control: Berkeley, Cotati, East Palo Alto, Santa Monica and West Hollywood

In these cities, landlords must register rental units with the rent board. Citywide yearly percentage increases tend to be low, and typically it's difficult to get the rent board to approve a bigger increase. In these cities (except West Hollywood), rents remain fixed (are not "decontrolled") when a tenant moves out, and a landlord must show just cause to evict.

RENTAL LISTING SERVICES

Rental listing services charge a fee in exchange for allowing people who are looking for apartments to use their listings. These businesses must be licensed with the California Department of Real Estate, and must offer prospective customers a written contract that spells out all terms of the agreement.

The listing service must offer three available rental units within five days after a customer enters into a contract with the service, or give a full refund. In addition, if the customer finds a rental through another source while using the listing service, the agency must refund all but $25 of the fee, if the customer requests this refund in writing. (Bus. & Prof. Code § 10167 and following.)

RETALIATORY EVICTIONS AND RENT INCREASES

It is illegal for a landlord to evict a tenant, raise the rent or decrease services because a tenant took advantage of any lawful right, such as the right to withhold rent because the premises are uninhabitable or the right to repair a serious defect and deduct the cost from rent payments, or because the tenant organizes or joins a tenants' organization. (Civ. Code § 1942.5.)

If a tenant whose rent is paid up complains to a government agency about defects in the premises, or claims that the rental unit is uninhabitable in a lawsuit or arbitration proceeding, and the landlord subsequently raises the rent, decreases services or evicts the tenant within 180 days, the law presumes that retaliation has occurred. (Civ. Code § 1942.5(a).)

A tenant who asserts a legal right and claims retaliation more than 180 days after complaining to a government agency must prove that the rent increase, tenancy termination or decrease in service is retaliatory.

ROOMMATES

People who share rental premises have legal rights and obligations to each other and to the landlord.

Legal Obligations of Roommates

Tenants who enter into a lease or rental agreement (written or oral) are each obligated to the landlord for all rent and the cost of repairing all damage to the unit. Tenants may agree among themselves—orally or in writing—to split deposits, rent and chores necessary to maintain the premises in any way they wish. Should one tenant fail to pay his or her fair share, the others are still obligated to pay the landlord, but also have the right to sue the other tenant for the agreed-upon amount.

New Roommates, Assignments and Sublets

Many written lease and rental agreements limit the number of people who can live in the unit and state that all tenants must be named on the lease or rental agreement, or specifically prohibit subletting. A tenant may violate this provision by:

- leaving in the middle of a month or lease term and finding someone to take over the lease or rental agreement (this is called assignment of the lease),
- renting the rental property to someone else temporarily—for example, during a vacation (subletting), or

- renting out a room to someone, in violation of the lease or rental agreement.

The landlord may evict a tenant who violates the lease or rental agreement this way. However, if a person moves into a rental unit without permission from the landlord, but the landlord accepts rent from that person and otherwise treats her as a tenant, this creates a month-to-month tenancy.

When Roommates Move Out

In most cities, roommates have an equal right to stay in a unit should each want the other out, unless there is a written agreement to the contrary.

SALE OF RENTED PROPERTY

When a landlord sells a rental house or apartment building, and the new owner steps in as the landlord, the new owner is subject to the terms of the lease or rental agreement the tenants made with the previous owner.

The former landlord must transfer all security deposits, less any legal deduction for damage to the unit, to either the tenants or the new owner. If the seller transfers deposits to the new owner, the seller must give tenants a written notice of the change of ownership, itemizing all deductions (such as back rent) and giving the new owner's name, address and phone number. (Civ. Code § 1950.5(g)(1).) If the former landlord does not transfer the entire deposit, tenants may be required to make up the difference only if they were notified of the deduction and the deposit was legally withheld. (Civ. Code § 1950.5.) If the old owner doesn't give the required notice, the new owner will be responsible for returning the entire original security deposit (less legitimate deductions) when the tenant moves out.

If a landlord is forced to sell rented property because of severe financial problems, tenants' rights are curtailed. A tenant may be evicted even in the middle of a fixed-term lease if the landlord's mortgage has been foreclosed upon and the lender who has foreclosed wants the tenant out in order to sell the property.

REAL ESTATE

People can buy or sell property on their own, without a real estate agent or lawyer; they are bound only by a legal duty to disclose certain problems with the property and not to discriminate against prospective buyers for arbitrary reasons. However, if a real estate agent is involved in the transaction, his or her role is restricted by law.

Here we cover the practical, financial aspects of property ownership, including taxes, taking title and neighborhood disputes.

TOPICS
ADVERSE POSSESSION
BUYING AND SELLING A HOUSE
DEEDS
EARTHQUAKE INSURANCE
EASEMENTS
FENCES
HOMESTEADS
MORTGAGES
NOISE
NUISANCE
PROPERTY TAXES
SOLAR ENERGY
TAXES FROM THE SALE OF A HOUSE
TITLE SEARCHES AND INSURANCE
TITLE TO REAL ESTATE
TREES
VIEWS
ZONING

RELATED TOPICS
CONSUMERS' RIGHTS
    Contractors
DEBTS, LOANS AND CREDIT
    Liens
GOVERNMENT BENEFITS
    Housing
INHERITANCE AND WILLS
    Joint Tenancy
LANDLORD AND TENANTS
RELATIONSHIPS
    Community and Separate Property

ADDITIONAL RESOURCES

How To Buy a House in California, by Ralph Warner, Ira Serkes and George Devine (Nolo Press), explains all the details of the house-buying process and contains tear-out contracts.

Neighbor Law: Fences, Trees, Boundaries and Noise, by Cora Jordan (Nolo Press), explains the laws that affect neighbors and shows how to resolve common disputes without lawsuits.

For Sale By Owner, by George Devine (Nolo Press), takes homeowners through the process of selling a house, with or without a real estate agent.

The Deeds Book, by Mary Randolph (Nolo Press), contains tear-out deed forms and instructions for transferring California real estate.

Homestead Your House, by Ralph Warner, Charles Sherman and Toni Ihara (Nolo Press), contains a tear-out homestead form for California.

Safe Homes, Safe Neighborhoods, by Stephanie Mann and Mary Claire Blakeman (Nolo Press), provides detailed information on how to improve home security and reduce neighborhood crime.

The California Seismic Safety Commission provides seismic hazard disclosure forms and booklets for a small charge. Call or write to the commission at 1900 K St., Suite 100, Sacramento, CA 95814, (916) 322-4917.

ADVERSE POSSESSION

Adverse possession is often confused with an easement (see Easements below.) Easements involve just a portion of property whereas adverse possession involves the entire property. You gain ownership of property by adverse possession when you use someone else's property for five years openly, continuously and exclusively, without their permission and while paying the annual real estate taxes. Property owners may prevent this by recording with the County Recorder or by posting signs stating "permission is granted to use this property but may be revoked at any time."

BUYING AND SELLING A HOUSE

You can legally buy or sell your own California house without a real estate broker or attorney—as long as you (and all other owners) are sane and at least 18 years old.

Real Estate Brokers

With a few exceptions, anyone who represents you in selling a house must have an active real estate broker's license or be a licensed agent supervised by an active licensed broker. If you pay someone who does not have a real estate license to be your broker, you can be fined up to $100. A nonlicensed agent can be fined up to $10,000 and sentenced to six months in county jail. (Bus. & Prof. Code §§ 10138-39.)

A broker can legally represent the buyer, seller or both. Traditionally, all brokers and agents (even those who primarily help the buyer) legally represent and are paid by the seller. However, it is increasingly common for buyers to insist on dual agency, which means the broker legally represents both buyer and seller even though the seller pays the commission. And some buyers hire and pay their own agent.

Payment and Commissions. It is illegal for brokers to get together and establish a statewide or regionwide commission rate. By common practice, however, most real estate brokers set their individual commissions at 6-8% of the sale price of a house, although some discount rates are available. Brokers must tell prospective clients that commissions are negotiable.

Usually, brokers are paid when a house closes escrow. However, if a seller lists a house with a broker under an Exclusive Authorization or Exclusive Agency contract, and the broker brings an offer that meets or exceeds the listing price and terms, the seller owes a commission—whether or not the seller goes through with the sale.

Disclosure

Sellers must give buyers a disclosure form, called a Real Estate Transfer Disclosure Statement. (Civ. Code § 1102.) Sellers are expected to know about and disclose:

- neighborhood nuisances such as noise or traffic
- environmental hazards such as asbestos or lead-based paint
- whether or not any work done on the house was according to local building codes and done with permits
- any restrictions on the use of the property, such as zoning ordinances, planning restrictions and "covenants, conditions and restrictions" (CC&Rs) and homeowners' association dues
- defective conditions such as a leaky roof or problems with electrical or plumbing systems.

Sellers must also tell prospective buyers if the property is in a flood hazard area (42 U.S.C. §§ 4104, 4106), whether or not the property lies within a Special Studies Zone (areas along earthquake faults identified by state geologists) (Pub. Res. Code §§ 2621-25), if the property lies within a Seismic Hazards Zone (Pub. Res. Code §§ 2690-99.6) or if the house has any of seven known seismic deficiencies, such as a foundation or wall made of unreinforced masonry or stone. (Gov't. Code § 8897.) Sellers of property in unincorporated areas (outside city limits) must tell the buyer if the property is located in a state-designated fire hazard area. (Pub. Res. Code § 4136.)

Sellers are responsible only for disclosing information within their personal knowledge. However, they must fill out the form honestly and must take "ordinary care" in obtaining information about the property that they know or, as a reasonable homeowner, should know. If a seller carelessly or intentionally makes an error or omission in the disclosure statement, the sale is still valid, but the seller will be liable for any actual losses the buyer suffers as a result.

A prospective purchaser who doesn't receive a copy of the disclosure statement until after making an offer to buy the house has three days (five days if the statement was mailed, rather than personally delivered) to withdraw the offer.

Discrimination

It's illegal to discriminate in the sale of real property on the basis of race, sex and other group characteristics.

The House Sales Contract

A contract to sell real estate must be in writing to be valid. An oral offer to purchase real estate is legally worthless—meaning a seller can't accept the offer and the resulting contract—if the buyer wants out of the deal. (Civ. Code § 1624(c).)

The asking price listed in a newspaper ad or flyer is just a starting point for negotiations over price and other terms of sale. A seller is not obligated to sell at the advertised price even if someone offers that amount.

Deposits and contingencies. Most sellers require the buyer to put down a deposit when the buyer makes an offer. Most buyers make their offers contingent upon several factors, such as the house passing a physical inspection or the buyer being able to arrange financing. If the deal doesn't go through because a contingency can't be fulfilled, the seller must return the deposit.

If the buyer backs out simply because she changes her mind, or doesn't try in good faith to fulfill a contingency (for instance, the buyer doesn't apply for a loan), this is considered a default, and the seller need not return the deposit. Most house purchase contracts provide a specific amount that the seller can keep if the buyer breaches the contract. California law generally prohibits sellers from keeping more than 3% of the agreed-upon sale price. (Civ. Code § 1675.)

Breach of contract. If the seller backs out of the deal, the prospective buyer can mediate, arbitrate or sue. If it comes to a lawsuit, the buyer will probably ask the court to order the seller to go through with the sale and reimburse her for out-of-pocket losses.

A real estate purchase contract is enforceable even if the buyer or the seller dies, because a deceased person's estate is responsible for fulfilling that person's lawful obligations. If the executors of the deceased person's estate want to get out of the deal, however, they may negotiate a release.

DEEDS

A deed is a document that transfers ownership of real estate.

Kinds of Deeds

In California, the most common kinds of deeds are grant, quitclaim and trust deeds.

- **Grant deed.** The most commonly used type of deed. It guarantees that the land being transferred hasn't already been transferred to someone else or been encumbered, except as specified in the deed. (Civ. Code § 1113.)

- **Quitclaim deed.** A deed that is used to give up one's claims to land. It makes no promises about the title being transferred; the maker of a quitclaim deed simply transfers whatever interest in the land he may have. Quitclaims are often used when couples divorce; one spouse signs a quitclaim deed, giving up any claims he may have to the other's property. The other spouse doesn't have to worry about a claim being made later.
- **Trust deed (deed of trust).** A trust deed is not like other deeds—it's more like a mortgage. It is used when someone pledges real estate as security for a loan, in conjunction with a promissory note (a written promise to pay back the loan). The buyer signs the note and a trust deed, which permits its holder (the trustee) to sell the property and pay off the loan if the buyer defaults. If a homeowner takes out a second loan that is secured by the property, the trust deed is called a "second deed of trust."

Preparing a Deed

Fill-in-the-blank deed forms are available at stationery stores and law libraries. A deed must contain the name of the grantor (person transferring the property), the grantee (the new owner) and a legal description of the property (copied from the old deed). It must be signed in the presence of a notary public, who verifies the signatures.

Recording a Deed

All deeds should be recorded—that is, put on file at the County Recorder's Office. Recording creates a public record of who owns every inch of land in the state. It allows a prospective buyer to look up a parcel of property and find out who owns it, how much it is mortgaged for and whether or not it is subject to any other encumbrances or restrictions—a lien or easement, for example.

To record a deed, take the original signed deed to the local office; the clerk will make a copy and file it in the public records. Recording costs a few dollars per page. You will also have to fill out a change of ownership form, which notifies the county tax assessor that the property has changed hands.

EARTHQUAKE INSURANCE

Whenever an insurance company issues a homeowner's insurance policy, it must offer earthquake insurance. The offered policy must cover loss or damage to the dwelling and its contents and living expenses for the occupants if the house is temporarily uninhabitable. The offer of earthquake coverage must be printed in 10-point bold type. (Ins. Code § 10083.)

If the homeowner decides not to buy earthquake coverage, the insurance company must send the owner written notice that the policy does not include earthquake coverage. The insurance company must continue to offer earthquake insurance every other year, and every policy renewal must include the statement that the policy doesn't contain earthquake coverage. (Ins. Code § 10086.1.)

EASEMENTS

An easement is a legal right to use someone else's land for a particular purpose. The property owner must allow the easement holder to use the property according to the terms of the easement.

Written Easements

Easements are usually in writing and recorded (put on file), like property deeds, at the County Recorder's office. They may also be referred to in property deeds or title insurance reports.

Utility easements are the most common kind. For example, the electric company may have the right to string wires across your property, or the water or gas company may have an easement to run pipes under your land. To find out where utility easements are located on your property, call the company or check the maps at the county planning office or city hall. A survey of the property will also show utility easements.

Property may also be subject to private written easements—easements that allow a neighbor to use a driveway or ensure that a neighbor has sewer or solar access, for example. If your property is subject to private easements, get copies of the easement documents from your neighbor or the County Recorder. If you don't know where the easements are and what uses they allow, you could unknowingly interfere with the easement rights and be liable for the damage.

Easements by Necessity

Even if it isn't written down, a legal easement can exist if it's absolutely necessary to cross someone's land for a legitimate purpose. The law grants people a right of access to their homes, for example. So if the only access to a piece of land is by crossing a neighbor's property, the law recognizes an easement allowing access over the neighbor's land. This is called an "easement by necessity."

Easements Acquired By Use of Property

Someone can acquire an easement over another's land for a particular purpose by using the land without permission, openly and continuously for five years. (Code of Civ. Proc. § 321.) An easement acquired in this way is called a prescriptive easement.

Typically, a prescriptive easement is created when someone uses land for access, such as a driveway or short-cut. But many times, a neighbor simply begins using a part of the adjoining property. He may farm it or even build on it. After five years, he gains a legal right to use the property for that purpose.

PREVENTING PRESCRIPTIVE EASEMENTS

If you don't mind someone using part of your property, the simplest way to prevent a prescriptive easement is to grant the person permission to use the property. Permission of the owner to use property cancels a trespasser's claim to a prescriptive easement. You should put the permission in writing.

If you don't want anyone using your property, tell the person to stop doing so. If the person doesn't stop, you may have to take more drastic measures, such as calling the police or suing for trespassing.

Public Easements

When trespassing is done by the public, a public right to use property can be created. For example, if the owner of beachfront property lets the county pave her private drive, which is used by many people for access to the beach, the public would gain a right to use the drive.

When the public is using a private strip, posting signs granting permission at every entrance and at certain intervals protects you from claims of a prescriptive easement. (Civ. Code § 1008.) If possible, also put the permission in writing and record it (file a copy) at the County Recorder's office. (Civ. Code § 813.)

Terminating an Easement

Easements don't change when the property changes hands. Subsequent owners must continue to let whoever owns the easement use the property. (Civ. Code § 1104.)

A property owner can, however, buy back an easement from the easement's owner. The document should be recorded, like the original easement, at the County Recorder's office. And a prescriptive easement that isn't used for many years may be forfeited because it has been legally abandoned. (Civ. Code § 811.)

FENCES

Local laws often regulate fence height and materials, and sometimes they require a building permit before a fence can be constructed. Fences in front yards are often limited to four feet in height; in backyards, six feet is often the maximum allowed. A row of trees that is used as a fence may also be subject to these laws. These laws are often loosely enforced; if no one complains, most cities ignore violations.

Regulations in planned communities and subdivisions (called Covenants, Conditions and Restrictions, or CC&Rs) may be more detailed.

Cities and homeowners' associations grant exemptions from fence ordinances or rules if the property owner has a good reason—for example, if a tall fence is needed to screen property from a heavily-used street.

Boundary Fences

A boundary fence is a fence that is on the line between two properties and is used by both owners. Neither may remove it without the other's permission, and both are responsible for maintaining it. (Civ. Code § 841.) An owner who makes needed repairs can demand that the other neighbor chip in half the cost.

Spite Fences

A spite fence is any fence that is more than 10 feet high, was built to annoy a neighbor and has no reasonable use for its owner—for example, a 12-foot rough wood fence built a foot from a neighbor's windows. (Civ. Code § 841.4.) The affected neighbor can sue the fence builder and ask a court to order the spite fence removed.

Rural Fences

Most California counties follow the "closed range" rule, which means that livestock owners must fence in their animals or be liable for any damage they cause to others' property. Some counties, however, follow the "open range" rule. In those counties, landowners who don't fence their property can't complain about damage caused by others' animals.

HOMESTEAD

A homestead is not the land a settler could get for free in the 1800s from the federal government. Rather, it refers to the portion of an owner's equity interest in a house, condominium or motor home that is protected from creditors.

There are two kinds of homestead protection. Every owner with equity in residential property that he or she lives in is entitled to automatic homestead protection—that is, he or she can keep a certain amount of the proceeds from a forced sale of the home. To get greater protection, and to discourage creditors from forcing a sale of the home in the first place, some owners file a Declaration of Homestead. (Code of Civ. Proc. § 704.710 and following.)

How a Declaration of Homestead Works

A Declaration of Homestead is a legal document that homeowners can file with the County Recorder in the county where they live. The document protects a specified amount of the owners' equity in their home from a forced sale, just like an automatic homestead. However, a Declaration of Homestead also protects that same amount from creditors if the owners voluntarily sell their home. For six months after the sale, this amount is protected from creditors. If the owners invest the money in a new home and file another Homestead Declaration on that home during the six-month period, the money remains protected.

A creditor can force a sale of a homesteaded home only if there will be sufficient proceeds to:

- pay all existing liens (claims against the property)
- pay off all mortgages and other loans secured by equity in the home, and
- pay the owner the required amount of his or her equity.

The creditor will also want to make sure that there is enough money left over to pay for the costs of selling the house and pay the debt owed by the owner. Many creditors find that it isn't worth the trouble to force a sale.

How Much Equity Is Protected

The amount of equity an owner can keep depends on the owner's circumstances when the home is sold.

- Single owners can exempt $50,000.
- Members of a family (which includes spouses living together and most family members, but does not include unmarried couples) can exempt $75,000.
- Those who are over 55 and whose income is $15,000 or less (single) or $20,000 or less (married) can exempt $100,000.
- Those who are disabled or are over 65 can exempt $100,000.

Debts That Are Unaffected by Homestead

A homestead does not protect the owner's equity in a home against certain kinds of debts. This means that if the creditor wishes, he or she can force a sale of the home despite the homestead, and can take even that portion of equity that the homestead protects. These debts are:

- Child support and spousal support (alimony).
- Mortgage and home equity loans. If you pledge your home as collateral for the loan, the creditor must be able to sell the home to collect on the debt.
- Tax debts.

How To File a Declaration of Homestead

A Declaration of Homestead is a simple one-page form. The owner must fill it out, have it notarized and send it in to the County Recorder in the county where he or she resides. There is a small filing fee.

MORTGAGES

In California, when someone borrows money from a lender to finance the purchase of a house, the document recorded at the County Recorder's Office is called a deed of trust. The process of transferring ownership or "closing escrow" occurs when the seller is paid and the deed transferring the property to the buyer is recorded at the County Recorder's Office.

When the borrower signs a deed of trust, he gives a trustee (often a title company) the right to sell his property (foreclose), with no court approval, if he fails to pay the lender on time. In other words, if the buyer defaults, the lender can request that the trustee sell the house and pay the lender from the proceeds. The foreclosure process usually takes six to 18 months, and the borrower has several chances to make up missed payments.

Deducting Mortgage Interest Payments

With certain restrictions, the mortgage interest paid on a home is deductible from state and federal income taxes. For mortgages taken out before October 1987, there is no limit on the amount of interest you can deduct. For mortgages taken out after October 1987, the IRS limits how much interest you can deduct annually to:

- $1,000,000 for mortgages to buy, build or improve a home
- $100,000 for mortgages used for other purposes (for example, a home equity loan to finance a car.)

NOISE

Almost every community has an ordinance prohibiting excessive and unreasonable noise. Police enforce these laws, and it's up to the investigating officer to decide what is unreasonable under the circumstances.

Many municipal ordinances forbid:

- loud noise during "quiet hours," such as after 11 p.m. or before 8 a.m.
- noise that exceeds certain decibel limits, or
- specific kinds of noise, such as continually barking dogs or loud motorcycles.

If a neighbor's noise is excessive and deliberate, it may also violate state law against disturbing the peace. (Pen. Code § 415.)

NUISANCE

If your neighbor is doing something that is indecent, offensive or unsafe and prevents you from enjoying your property, that is a nuisance. (Civ. Code § 3479.) Some common examples include making excessive noise, producing offensive fumes or drug dealing.

Even if there's not a specific law banning the activity, you can sue your neighbor to have it stopped. (Civ. Code § 3501.) A lawsuit is rarely necessary, however; disputes can usually be resolved with help from a neighborhood mediation service. If you can't work things out short of legal action, Small Claims Court is usually the best choice.

The law also allows someone affected by a nuisance to remove or destroy the thing that constitutes the nuisance, as long as he or she gives notice to the neighbor first and doesn't commit a "breach of the peace" or cause unnecessary injury. (Civ. Code § 3495.)

PROPERTY TAXES

California has a unique system of taxing real estate. It's the result of Proposition 13, a ballot measure passed in 1979 that amended the state constitution.

All property tax assessments are based on the value of the property in the 1975-

76 tax year. As long as the property doesn't change hands, the assessment can increase only 2% each year from that base figure, unless local voters approve a larger increase—for example, to fund local schools.

However, the assessment is raised to the current market value of the property when ownership of the property is transferred (except in certain intra-family transfers, such as between spouses or from parent to child.) That virtually always means a big tax increase for a new owner. Improvements that increase the value of the house can also increase the tax assessment. Property taxes are 1% to 1.25% (depending on the county) annually of the assessed value of the house.

Assessment Exception for Homeowners Over 55

Homeowners over age 55 (only one spouse of a married couple need qualify) who sell one house and purchase another of equal or lesser value within two years in the same county (or in a county that participates in a statewide transfer system) may transfer their old tax assessment rate to the new house.

Deducting Property Taxes

Payments made for property taxes are fully deductible from state and federal income taxes.

Transfers to Living Trusts

When real estate is transferred to a revocable living trust, and the owner of the real estate is the trustee of the trust, the property is not reassessed for property tax purposes. (Rev. & Tax. Code § 62(d).)

SOLAR ENERGY

Solar Energy Systems

There may be no prohibition of the use or installation of a solar energy system under any deed, contract, covenant, condition, restriction or other instrument for the transfer or sale of real property or which affects any interest in real property. However, reasonable restrictions on the use of solar energy systems are permitted, especially by homeowners' associations. (Civ. Code §§ 714, 714.1.) A violation of this Section by anyone other than a public entity is punishable by a civil penalty of up to $1,000.

Solar Easements

California law specifically recognizes solar easements—easements that give a property owner the right to receive sunlight to power a solar energy system. The document creating the easement must describe the dimensions of the easement, the restrictions on vegetation or structures that would block sunlight and the conditions under which the easement can be revised or terminated. (Civ. Code § 801.5.)

TAXES FROM THE SALE OF A HOUSE

The IRS gives homeowners two ways to avoid paying a hefty tax on the profit made by selling a home.

Rolling Over Profits

If you sell an owner-occupied house at a profit and buy and occupy a more expensive house, you pay no federal or California tax on the profit now, if the sale of the first home and the purchase of the second occur within 24 months of each other. (I.R.C. § 1034.) You'll eventually owe the tax when you sell a house and don't buy one of equal or greater value.

Capital Gains Exclusion for Sellers Over 55

If you (or your spouse, if you are married) are over 55, and you sell one home and buy another of lesser value, federal tax law lets you exclude from profit (capital gains) up to $125,000 if:

- you lived in the house as your principal residence for any three of the past five years, and
- you (or your spouse) haven't used the exclusion before, even as a single person or in a prior marriage (I.R.C. § 121.)

TITLE SEARCHES AND INSURANCE

Title insurance guarantees that someone who's selling a piece of real estate has the legal right to sell it, and that no one else has ownership rights that could surface later and cause problems for the new owner.

Title Searches

A title search is a search of all public records relating to a certain parcel of property. It's routine when real estate is sold; the goal is to find out if there are any problems (unpaid property taxes, for example) that will interfere with the transfer.

A title search costs about $150 to $250 and is usually done by a title insurance company. A title search tells you if:

- the property has been pledged as security for a loan (mortgaged)
- a written easement has been granted
- certain liens (legal claims) have been placed on the property
- the property taxes haven't been paid
- a lawsuit has been filed contesting ownership of the property, or
- a prior deed was invalid.

Unrecorded transfers, of course, don't show up in a title search. Also, easements that haven't been written and recorded, and community property interests, won't be uncovered in a title search—even if the deed to a house is in one spouse's name alone, it may legally belong to both. Similarly, an unmarried live-in lover may have property rights based on an implied contract that won't be apparent to the title insurance company.

Title Insurance

Title companies guarantee the results of their searches by issuing title insurance policies. Title insurance protects a buyer (or a lender who finances the purchase of the property) against claims that the search overlooked. A typical title insurance policy would cover an owner's losses if, for example, any of the transfer documents are fraudulent or forged, or there is a lien or easement on the property that the title company didn't find when it searched the records.

Separate policies protect the buyer and the lender. The buyer's policy is for the amount of the purchase price. If someone (including the seller) is lending money to the buyer, and the loan is secured by a deed of trust on the property, the lender usually buys a policy for the amount of the loan.

The price of insurance depends on the value of the property; expect to pay $1,000 to $1,500 for property worth $100,000.

TITLE TO REAL ESTATE

Someone who owns property is said to have title to it. If more than one person owns a piece of property, title can be held in different ways. Here are the main features of the different ways to hold title.

Tenancy in Common

To create a tenancy in common, the deed must transfer property to two or more persons either "as tenants in common" or without specifying how title is to be held. Shares of co-owners are presumed to be equal unless unequal shares are specified on the deed. Any co-owner may transfer his or her interest or ask a court to order the property sold and the proceeds divided among the co-owners. (This is called a partition order.) Co-owners can create a joint tenancy (or community property ownership, if they're married) by signing a new deed. When a co-owner dies, his or her interest passes to the heirs under state law or beneficiaries named in a will or living trust.

Joint Tenancy

To create a joint tenancy, the deed must transfer property to two or more persons "as joint tenants" or "with right of survivorship." All joint tenants must own equal shares of the property. A joint tenant may end the joint tenancy by transferring his interest to himself or someone else as tenants in common, or may get a partition order from the court. (Civ. Code § 683.2.) A deceased joint tenant's share automatically goes to the surviving joint tenants without probate proceedings, even if the deceased owner's will leaves his share of the property to someone else.

Community Property

Community property is created when a deed transfers property to a married couple "as community property" or "as husband and wife." Each spouse owns a one-half interest in the property. Community property ownership ends when the property is transferred to someone outside the marriage or the spouses transfer the property to another form of ownership (such as to themselves as tenants in common, for example.) However, both spouses must approve transfers of community real estate. A spouse can leave his or her half of the property to anyone, but if the deceased spouse's will says nothing to the contrary, it goes to the surviving spouse.

Partnership

Partnership property is created when a deed transfers property to the partnership by name or partnership money is used to buy the property. (Civ. Code § 684.) The share of each co-owner and the conditions under which the partnership can sell or give away the property are determined by the partnership agreement or the Uniform Partnership Act. (Corp. Code §§ 15001 and following.) When one partner dies, his or her interest in the property usually goes to the partner's heirs under state law or the beneficiaries named in the will, but the partnership agreement may limit who can inherit the property.

TREES

A number of state laws affect trees, recognizing their special place in the hearts of those who own them.

Ownership

The location of the trunk determines who owns a tree. If the trunk is entirely on one person's land, that person owns the tree, even though the roots may grow into the other's land. If the trunk is on a boundary line, it belongs to both (or all) landowners. (Civ. Code § 833.)

The owners of a boundary tree are responsible for its care and maintenance. Neither owner may harm or remove a healthy boundary tree without the other's permission. (A court might make an exception to this rule if removing the tree were absolutely necessary for one owner to make reasonable use of his or her property.) If the tree is dangerous because it is diseased or dead, either owner may (and should) remove it.

Damage to a Tree

Generally, someone who wrongfully damages or removes a tree is liable to the owner for three times the amount of the actual monetary loss. If, however, the damage was unintentional or the person reasonably believed the tree was on his land, the amount owed is only twice the amount of the actual loss. (Civ. Code § 3346.) If the damage or removal was intentional or malicious, a court might also make the wrongdoer pay an additional amount (called punitive damages) as punishment.

Intentionally harming someone's tree is also a crime—a misdemeanor, punishable by a fine of up to $1,000, up to six months in the county jail or both. (Pen. Code § 384(a).)

Encroaching Branches and Roots

Property owners have the right to cut off branches and roots that stray onto their property. But the owner may not:
- trim past the property line
- enter the neighbor's property without permission unless the limbs threaten imminent, grave harm
- cut down the tree itself
- destroy the tree by the trimming.

A city permit may be required for any significant trimming or for pruning certain species of tree; check with the city clerk's office.

A landowner seriously inconvenienced by the encroaching branches or roots of a neighbor's tree can also sue the neighbor for nuisance.

Dangerous or Diseased Trees

Some cities remove dangerous trees from private property themselves. Others order the owner to do it, pronto; if the owner doesn't do it, the city steps in, takes out the tree and bills the owner.

A tree owner in a town or city who knows, or should know, that a tree is obviously unsound and likely to cause damage must correct the problem or be liable for any injury or property damage that does occur. In rural areas, owners may not be held liable if they didn't know the tree was dangerous.

Protected and Forbidden Trees

It's increasingly common for cities to restrict removal of certain valuable native species of trees, such as redwoods or certain pine trees. Other species may be designated a nuisance or a danger, and their planting may be prohibited.

VIEWS

Most California landowners have no legal right to an unobstructed view from their property. Neighbors are free to block the view by letting their trees grow or by building useful structures.

Dozens of cities, however, have passed ordinances that give owners the right to sue neighbors whose growing trees have blocked the view they had when they moved in or on a certain date. These laws usually require the person who sues to pay for the tree trimming. Some exempt certain kinds of trees; Oakland, for example, doesn't allow a neighbor to force the cutting of a redwood, live oak, box elder, bigleaf maple and other species.

Subdivision restrictions may also protect residents' views. Check your rules, usually called Covenants, Conditions and Restrictions (CC&Rs).

ZONING

Zoning ordinances regulate how landowners can use their property. A primary goal is to separate incompatible uses, such as residences and industries.

Zoning Ordinances

City and county zoning laws divide an area into districts, which are set aside for particular uses. Usually, there are districts for single-family homes and other districts for apartments or mixed uses. Other zones are earmarked for different types of commercial usage. Usually some part of town is reserved for light and heavy manufacturing. Outside of cities, laws allow various types of agriculture.

Within zoning districts, more detailed rules apply. In most places, dwellings must be set back from the street a minimum distance, and only a certain percentage of the lot may be covered by structures and driveways. In most places, however, zoning officials don't go looking for violations; they take their cues from neighbors' complaints.

To check on zoning laws for your city or county, call the local planning or zoning department or read the ordinances themselves at the public or law library.

Exceptions to Zoning Laws

Cities and counties sometimes give permission to use land in a way that isn't allowed by the zoning ordinance. These exceptions are called variances or conditional use permits.

GETTING AN EXCEPTION TO A ZONING ORDINANCE

To get an exception, first outline your plans to someone in the Zoning or Planning Department and get some feedback. The staff should be able to refer you to the local ordinance that sets out criteria for granting exceptions.

You'll have to make a formal written request, and the zoning department will probably hold public hearings to give neighbors a chance to object. Get neighbors to speak in your behalf or to write letters or sign a supportive petition. You're very unlikely to get a variance if the neighborhood is against you. If you're turned down, most places have a planning or zoning board you can appeal to. If you lose again, you can probably appeal to a second board, often the city council. If this doesn't work, consider trying to get your property rezoned or even getting the zoning ordinance itself amended. You may also be able to challenge the ordinance, or the city's enforcement practices, in court.

RELATIONSHIPS

Federal and state laws enter into even our most private relationships. This section discusses the legalities or marriage and divorce, as well as gay and lesbian relationships and unmarried couples who live together.

The section also covers federal and state regulations regarding birth control and abortion. Be aware that the law in these areas is volatile and changes with the political climate.

TOPICS
- **ABORTION**
- **ADULTERY**
- **ANNULMENT**
- **BIGAMY**
- **BIRTH CONTROL**
- **COMMON LAW MARRIAGE**
- **COMMUNITY AND SEPARATE PROPERTY**
- **DIVORCE**
- **DOMESTIC PARTNERS**
- **DOMESTIC VIOLENCE**
- **GAY AND LESBIAN COUPLES**
- **LIVING TOGETHER**
- **MARITAL DEBTS**
- **MARRIAGE**
- **SEPARATION**
- **SPOUSAL SUPPORT (ALIMONY)**

RELATED TOPICS
- **CHILDREN**
    - Adoption
    - Artificial Insemination
    - Child Support
    - Children Born to Unmarried Parents
    - Custody
    - Gay and Lesbian Parents
    - Visitation
- **LANDLORDS AND TENANTS**
    - Discrimination
    - Roommates
- **REAL ESTATE**
    - Title to Real Estate

ADDITIONAL RESOURCES

California Marriage and Divorce Law, by Ralph Warner, Toni Ihara and Stephen Elias (Nolo Press), explains state laws about marriage, divorce and child custody and support.

Divorce and Money: How to Make the Best Financial Decisions During Divorce, by Violet Woodhouse and Victoria Felton-Collins, with M.C. Blakeman (Nolo Press), explains the financial aspects of divorce and how to divide property fairly.

How to Raise and Lower Child Support in California, by Roderic Duncan and Warren Siegel (Nolo Press), contains forms and instructions.

The Living Together Kit, by Toni Ihara and Ralph Warner (Nolo Press), explains the legal rules that apply to unmarried couples and includes sample contracts governing jointly-owned property.

A Legal Guide for Lesbian and Gay Couples, by Hayden Curry, Denis Clifford and Robin Leonard (Nolo Press), sets out the law and contains sample agreements for couples.

Nolo's Pocket Guide to Family Law, by Robin Leonard and Stephen Elias (Nolo Press), explains legal concepts you may run across if you're involved in a divorce, adoption or other family law matter.

How To Do Your Own Divorce in California, by Charles Sherman (Nolo Press), contains step-by-step instructions on obtaining a divorce without a lawyer.

Annulment: Your Chance To Remarry Within the Catholic Church, by Joseph P. Zwack (Harper & Row), explains how to get a religious annulment.

California Divorce Helpline, (800) 359-7004, provides legal information about divorce, over the phone, for $10 per call and $2.50 a minute.

Planned Parenthood Regional Office, 333 Broadway, 3rd Floor, San Francisco, CA 94133, (415) 956-8856, gives information about abortion and birth control.

ABORTION

As the law stands today, women in California 18 or older have a broad legal right to an abortion. Women under 18 have the right to an abortion once their parents are notified, although exceptions are routinely made by doctors and by courts. However, the issue is complicated and changing.

Abortion law is determined both by the state and the federal governments. States are free to allow abortions in any circumstances they choose, but cannot restrict abortions in ways that the U.S. Supreme Court determines would violate the federal constitution. Under the U.S. Supreme Court's 1973 ruling in *Roe v. Wade*, states may not restrict a woman's right to an abortion during the first trimester of pregnancy. After the first trimester, a woman's right to choose an abortion must be balanced with the state's right to protect a fetus.

In 1992, the Supreme Court cut back on abortion rights, ruling that although states may not ban all abortions, they are free to place severe limits on them—including an "informed consent" provision that requires doctors to provide a woman with information designed to discourage her from getting an abortion 24 hours before the procedure. (*Planned Parenthood of Southeastern Pennsylvania v. Casey.*)

California Abortion Law

Proposed restrictions on abortions in California must be interpreted according to the state constitution, which, unlike the federal constitution, includes an explicit right to privacy that is usually interpreted to include a woman's right to choose abortion. Because of this broad constitutional protection, many legal scholars say that the only way severe restrictions on abortions could be passed in California would be if the U.S. Supreme Court first ruled that a fetus is a person entitled to privacy protection under the state constitution. The Supreme Court may soon consider cases that ask it to decide that issue.

ADULTERY

Adultery is sexual intercourse between a married person and someone other than his or her spouse. Adultery is not a crime in California. And because California has a no-fault divorce law, adultery is not relevant in obtaining a divorce or dividing marital property.

ANNULMENT

An annulment is a legal proceeding to end a marriage and treat it as though it never happened. In California, a marriage may be annulled if:

- A person under age 18 marries without parental or court permission. The annulment must take place before the minor reaches 18.
- A person has remarried, but her first spouse shows up after being missing or believed dead for at least five years. The second marriage may be annulled.
- A person of "unsound mind" (not capable of consenting to marry) enters into a marriage. A person who comes to reason and remains in the marriage, however, is not entitled to an annulment.
- A person enters into a marriage after being defrauded by the other spouse. A misled spouse who learns the truth and stays in the marriage, however, can't get an annulment.
- A person agrees to marry after being forced to do so by the other spouse. Again, a person who freely lives with the other after the marriage begins won't be granted an annulment.
- A person was, at the time the marriage began, incapable of having children and such incapacity continues and appears to be incurable. (Fam. Code §§ 2201, 2210.)

To file for an annulment, spouses use the same forms they would use if they were filing for divorce. If a marriage is annulled, the couple's property is divided as though they had been married. If one spouse defrauded or forced the other into the marriage, the "non-innocent" spouse may be awarded less than 50% of the accumulated property. Children of an annulled marriage are treated like children in divorce—that is, custody and child support will have to be determined.

Religious Annulments

There are different requirements to obtain a religious annulment. Within the Roman Catholic church, a couple may obtain a religious annulment after obtaining a civil divorce. Many people do this so they can remarry within the Church.

BIGAMY

Bigamy is the crime committed when a married person knowingly marries again. However, someone who remarries after his or her spouse has been missing or believed dead for at least five years is not guilty of bigamy if the first spouse turns up. Prosecution for bigamy is rare, unless the bigamist defrauds one of his spouses financially—for example, by spending the second spouse's income on the first spouse.

Bigamy is punishable by a fine of up to $10,000 or imprisonment for up to one year. A "spouse" who marries a person known to already be married may be punished by a fine of at least $5,000 or a term of imprisonment (no length specified). (Pen. Code §§ 281-284.)

BIRTH CONTROL

The right to decide whether or not to use contraception is an individual privacy right guaranteed by the California and U.S. constitutions. Although the right to privacy has been under recent attack in federal court decisions involving abortion, the right to use contraception is not currently at risk.

The Rights of Minors

Federal law requires that public health facilities provide family planning services to all women of childbearing age. However, private doctors and church-affiliated hospitals may refuse to provide these services to minor or unmarried patients.

California law does not require parental notification or consent before a person under 18 can receive contraceptive services from a doctor or health service agency. In addition, no one is legally prevented, because of age, from buying non-prescription contraceptives, such as condoms and spermicidal foam.

BIRTH CONTROL AVAILABILITY

The right to use birth control and access to birth control are two different things. Availability of birth control often depends more on its cost, and whether or not it requires a doctor's prescription, than on the legal status of contraceptive rights.

The federal Food and Drug Administration is often instrumental in determining whether or not a particular contraceptive can be marketed in the U.S. Because it is responsible for determining the safety and value of products sold in the U.S., the FDA can speed or slow access to new contraceptive technologies.

COMMON LAW MARRIAGE

In some states, couples can become legally married by living together for a long period of time, holding themselves out to others as husband and wife and intending to be married. These are called common law marriages. Contrary to popular belief, a common law marriage is not obtained simply by living together for a long time, even in the states with common law marriages. The couple must intend to be married.

A common law marriage cannot be established in California; a couple must obtain a marriage license and have a ceremony to get married in this state. If a couple moves to this state after having formed a common law marriage in one of the states listed below, however, California will treat the marriage as valid.

If either party to a common law marriage denies that it exists, the other may file an action in the Superior Court to have the validity of the marriage determined. (Civ. Code § 4212.) To end a common law marriage, a couple must obtain a divorce or annulment.

STATES THAT ALLOW COMMON LAW MARRIAGES

Alabama	Kansas	Rhode Island
Colorado	Montana	South Carolina
Georgia	Ohio	Texas
Idaho	Oklahoma	Utah
Iowa	Pennsylvania	Washington, D.C.

COMMUNITY AND SEPARATE PROPERTY

In California, property owned by a married person is classified either as community property or separate property. Community property belongs equally to both spouses; separate property legally belongs to just one spouse. Whether property is community or separate depends on when it was acquired, what kind of property it is and how it has been used.

Classifying Property

Here are the general rules on classifying property that belongs to a married person.

Property Acquired Before Marriage. All property that one spouse owned before marriage is that spouse's separate property.

Property Acquired During Marriage. Generally, all property acquired by either spouse during marriage is community property, except for gifts and inheritances, which remain the separate property of the recipient. (Civ. Code § 5110.) Also, any property purchased during marriage entirely with money acquired before marriage is separate property, as is property acquired during marriage with the proceeds of or income from separate property. (Civ. Code § 5107.) Here are the specific rules:

- **Wages, salaries and tips** earned during marriage are community property, unless they are deposited into a separate account, entirely under the control of the spouse who earned them, and are not combined with any community funds, in which case they are the separate property of the earner spouse.
- **Pensions.** The portion of a pension earned during the marriage is community property; the remainder is the separate property of the pension earner.
- **Social Security benefits** are the separate property of the earning spouse.
- **Employment benefits** (such as stock options or profit-sharing plans) are

155

community property if they are based on the spouse's work during the marriage, even if they will not be distributed until after the marriage has ended. Benefits based on the spouse's work before marriage or after separation are separate property, even if they are distributed during the marriage.

- **Copyrights, patents, artwork and royalties** are community property if they are created, invented or generated during marriage. If created before marriage or after separation, they are separate property, even if they are sold during the marriage.

- **Personal injury recoveries** that either spouse receives during marriage from a third party are community property during the marriage. At divorce, however, these funds become the separate property of the injured spouse, unless the money has been combined with community property. (Civ. Code §§ 4800(b)(4), 5126.)

- **Businesses** existing before marriage are the separate property of the owner spouse, but if either spouse contributes community money or expends efforts to run or improve the business during the marriage, the value of this contribution is community property. Businesses created during marriage are community property, unless they are created entirely from separate property.

- **Property held in joint title** (joint tenancy, tenancy in common, community property, husband and wife) is presumed to be community property.

- **Revenues and profits** (such as rent or interest) earned on community property are community property. Similarly, profits from separate property are the separate property of the owner spouse. And if a particular item is purchased with community property money (for example, from the sale of real estate bought with the couples' wages), that item is community property. The same rule applies for separate property: if one spouse uses his or her own separate property to buy something, the item purchased is separate property. (This is referred to as the "source rule.")

Property Acquired After Separation. If the separation is permanent—that is, the couple intends to divorce—all property acquired afterward is separate property. If it is a trial separation, and they may reunite, all property acquired is community property. (Civ. Code § 5118.)

Property Acquired Outside California. If a couple acquires property when living outside of California that would have been community property if the couple had been living in California, that property is treated as community property when the couple moves to California. It is referred to as quasi-community property. (Civ. Code § 4803.)

Making Your Own Decisions About Property

These legal rules are only presumptions. If you and your spouse decide, for example, that your pension will be entirely your own separate property, you need only sign an agreement to that effect. Similarly, you may make a gift of your separate property to the community if you wish; the property then becomes community property.

Beware, however, of unintended transfers. When separate and community property are combined in a bank account, the resulting mixture is presumed to be community property. The only way a spouse can claim that a particular item purchased with the combined money is really that spouse's separate property is to trace all deposits and withdrawals. When spouses combine community and separate property to make a purchase such as a house or car, the property is considered community. However, if the couple splits up, each spouse will be entitled to be reimbursed for the separate property contributions. Similarly, if one spouse spends separate property on a community property asset or on a separate property asset of the other spouse, the spouse will be entitled to a reimbursement at divorce. Only a written agreement expressly changing separate property to community or community property to separate can change the characterization of marital property.

Dividing Property at Divorce

Spouses can divide their property at divorce any way they like. If they cannot reach an agreement and take their dispute to court, however, the judge will generally award all separate property to the owner-spouse and divide the community property equally.

DIVORCE

Technically called "dissolution of a marriage," divorce is the legal procedure necessary to end a marriage. A divorce may be granted based on irreconcilable differences between the spouses or incurable insanity of one spouse. There is no need to allege fault on the part of either spouse; if one spouse wants a divorce, there is nothing the other one can do, legally, to block it.

California Residency Requirement

One spouse must reside in California for at least six months, and in the county where the case is filed for three months, immediately before filing for divorce. As long as this residency requirement is met, it makes no difference where the marriage occurred. Once the case is filed, it doesn't matter if one or both spouses move out of state; the California court still has authority to grant the divorce.

Divorce Proceedings

There are two ways to get a divorce in California. A *summary dissolution* requires very little paperwork and no court appearance. It is limited to couples who:
- have been married less than five years
- have no children, and the wife is not currently pregnant
- own no real estate
- have less than $5,000 in community debts (not counting car loans)
- own less than $25,000 in community property (not counting cars), and
- have less than $25,000 in separate property (not counting cars) each.

Both spouses must sign a property agreement (unless there is no property) when the divorce is filed. The divorce becomes final six months after filing. During this period, either spouse can revoke the summary dissolution and insist on a regular dissolution.

Couples who don't meet the requirements for a summary dissolution must get a *regular dissolution*. A regular dissolution can be handled by mail in some cases, but sometimes requires a court appearance and extensive paperwork. The divorce will not be final until at least six months from the date one spouse was served with the summons and other legal papers.

Restraining Orders

Certain restraining orders are automatic in every divorce. Neither spouse can:
- take the couple's children out of state without prior written permission from the other spouse and the court
- borrow against, transfer or sell any property except in the normal course of business or with the written consent of the other party or a court order
- cash in, borrow against or cancel any insurance policy (health, auto, life, disability) held for the benefit of the divorcing couple or their minor children.

A spouse who needs a restraining order for physical protection from the other spouse must request it from the court. (See "Domestic Violence.")

DOMESTIC PARTNERS

A few California cities—Berkeley, Laguna Beach, Los Angeles, Sacramento, San Francisco, Santa Cruz and West Hollywood—offer "domestic partner" benefits to unmarried (gay, lesbian and heterosexual) city employees and, in a few instances, allow all unmarried adult couples who are city residents to register with the city. Contact the City Attorney's office for details.

In Laguna Beach, Sacramento, San Francisco and West Hollywood, registered couples are entitled to certain public benefits, such as family health benefits, family leave, and hospital and jail visiting privileges normally reserved for married couples.

DOMESTIC VIOLENCE

There is illegal domestic violence in well over half of all California households, according to several surveys by women's organizations. Those who are abused range in age from children to the elderly, from all backgrounds and income levels. The majority of domestic violence victims are women abused by men, but women also abuse other women, men abuse men and women abuse men.

Many forms of abuse are considered domestic violence, including:

- physical behavior such as slapping, punching, pulling hair or shoving
- unconsented-to sexual acts or behavior such as unwanted fondling or intercourse, jokes and insults aimed at sexuality
- threats of abuse—threatening to hit, harm or use a weapon on another, or to tell others confidential information
- psychological abuse—attacks on self-esteem, controlling or limiting another's behavior, repeated insults and interrogation. (Civ. Code § 4354.)

Typically, many kinds of abuse go on at the same time in a household.

Temporary Restraining Orders

The most powerful legal tool to stop domestic violence is a temporary restraining order—a decree from the court, tailored to the particular circumstances of the relationship, requiring that the batterer stop the abuse. To get a restraining order, an abused person must testify about or show a court evidence of the abuse (hospital or police records, for example). Police are also authorized to issue restraining orders under some circumstances, but they rarely do so.

Typical restraining orders require that the batterer must:

- stop the striking, bothering, molesting, telephoning, sexually assaulting or other harassment
- stay a certain distance away from the person who was being abused, the family, household or any other specific places such as work, school or a residence
- leave a residence he or she was living in
- not take or sell any of the property of the person he or she was harassing or any of their community property if there is a marriage
- not take a minor child out of California or a local area without written permission from the harassed parent
- not use any of the property jointly owned with the harassed person, and
- adhere to a specific visitation schedule for minor children.

A person who is being abused can get a restraining order against a:

- spouse or former spouse
- cohabitant or former cohabitant
- adult blood relative, or
- person with whom he or she has had a dating or engagement relationship.

Depending on the relationship between the abused person and the abuser, restraining orders may be obtained under one of three California laws: the Domestic Violence Protection Act (Civ. Code § 435), Family Law Act (Civ. Code § 4000) or the Uniform Parentage Act (Fam. Code § 7600).

Once a restraining order is in effect, police must arrest a harasser who violates it—and in many cases, criminal charges can be pressed.

GETTING HELP

The most important step you can take if you have experienced domestic violence is to find out what your options are. A number of groups provide counseling, transportation, shelter, interpreting services, legal help and referrals. Look in the telephone book under Crisis Intervention Service or Women's Organizations.

GAY AND LESBIAN COUPLES

Homosexual sex (legally referred to as sodomy) is no longer illegal in California, although it remains a crime in some states. Because lesbian and gay couples cannot legally marry, they are not entitled to any of the benefits that government and private institutions offer to married couples. (A case pending in Hawaii may, however, ultimately authorize same-sex marriages.) For example, gay and lesbian couples cannot file joint tax returns, receive Social Security or veteran's benefits if their lover dies, or obtain residency status for a non-citizen lover to avoid deportation. They may not be eligible to visit each other in a hospital, obtain family discounts on auto insurance or obtain employment benefits for each other.

Some of these restrictions can be minimized by using durable powers of attorney, writing a will or other estate planning tools, and creating living together contracts to spell out property ownership.

LIVING TOGETHER

Unmarried couples can live together (cohabit) legally in California. It is illegal for someone selling a house or condominium to discriminate against unmarried couples, but a landlord may be able to avoid renting to unmarried couples if doing so would violate his religious beliefs.

Contracts

Contracts between unmarried couples to share income, purchase property and provide for support are legal as long as they are not based on the performance of sexual services. (*Marvin v. Marvin*, 18 Cal. 3d 660 (1976).) In theory, oral and implied contracts are just as valid as contracts in writing; in practice, however, it is difficult to get a court to enforce any contract not in writing.

Inheritance

Unlike married couples, unmarried couples do not automatically inherit from each other if there is no will. You can, however, leave property to anyone you choose by will or living trust. Or you can own property in joint tenancy with your partner, which gives the survivor an automatic right to inherit the deceased person's share.

Credit Discrimination

The federal Equal Credit Opportunity Act forbids discrimination on the basis of marital status and requires creditors to treat unmarried and married couples equally. (15 U.S.C. § 1691.)

Employment Discrimination

No clear statewide law protects unmarried couples from being discriminated against based on their marital status. Some city ordinances, however, do provide this protection, so check your local laws.

MARITAL DEBTS

For a married or divorced couple, responsibility for paying a debt depends on when the debt was incurred, who incurred it and what it was for. A debt is treated like a form of property for legal purposes: it can be a separate debt of only one spouse or a community debt owed by both spouses. Most debts incurred during marriage are community debts. Generally, only the spouse who incurred a separate debt is legally responsible for repaying it, but both spouses are liable for repayment of a community debt.

Debts Incurred Before Marriage

Generally, a spouse is not responsible for repaying the debts his or her mate incurred before marriage. (Civ. Code § 5120.130.) Creditors, however, are entitled to seize the debtor spouse's half of the couple's community property, as well as the debtor spouse's separate property, to repay the debt.

Debts Incurred During Marriage

Both spouses are generally liable for all debts incurred during marriage, with the following exceptions:
- If the creditor was looking to only one spouse and that spouse's separate property for repayment (because, for example, the spouse listed only her own credit information and separate property accounts on the application), only that spouse is responsible for paying the debt.
- If the debt is of no benefit to the marriage (rent payments for an apartment one spouse keeps for meeting his or her lover, for example), the spouse who benefits by the debt is solely responsible for paying it. (Civ. Code § 4800(d).)
- If a spouse agrees to pay certain community debts as part of a divorce settlement, this agreement is binding only on the two spouses. The creditors can still seek repayment from both spouses. (Civ. Code §§ 4800.6, 5120.160.)

If one spouse incurred debts during marriage that are considered separate under these rules, the separate property of the other spouse can be taken by creditors to pay the debt only if it is for the "necessaries of life" (food, clothing or medical care) and the debtor spouse has no separate or community property left to pay the creditor. (Fam. Code §§ 2623, 914.)

Educational Debts

After divorce, debts for education must be paid by the spouse who incurred them. The theory is that it is unfair to penalize the spouse who not only didn't receive the benefit of the education, but more than likely supported the other during the schooling. (Fam. Code § 2641.)

Tax Debts

If a spouse enters the marriage owing taxes, all of that spouse's separate property and all of the couple's community property can be taken to satisfy the IRS. If a spouse owes back taxes for a year after marriage and the couple filed jointly, both spouses are liable for repaying the debt, even if the bill comes after the divorce is final. The innocent spouse's liability may be reduced if:

- the bill is for unreported income more than 25% over the amount originally reported, she didn't know or had no reason to know of the underreporting, and she did not significantly benefit from the omitted income; or
- the bill is for omitted income or an illegal deduction, he didn't know or had no reason to know that there was an understatement of his tax liability, and it would be unfair to hold him liable for the taxes owed.

Debts Incurred Between Separation and Divorce

Debts incurred after permanent separation and before divorce are jointly owed by both spouses only if they are for necessaries of life (food, shelter and clothing) for a spouse or children, and the debt has not been assigned to only one spouse under the provisions of a child support order. A creditor may obtain payment from either spouse. (Fam. Code § 2623.)

A spouse, however, is generally not liable for other debts incurred by his or her mate after permanent separation. (Fam. Code § 913.)

MARRIAGE

California requires that people who want to marry be:

- of the **opposite sex**. Some lesbian and gay couples go through religious marriage or commitment ceremonies, but the resulting relationship is not recognized by the state, even if the marriage was performed in a country where same-sex marriage is legal (such as Denmark or Norway).
- at least **18 years old**. People under 18 need the consent of a parent or guardian and of a Superior Court judge, who probably will require marriage counseling. (Fam. Code §§ 200, 212, 301-304.)
- sufficiently **unrelated** to each other. Parents and children, grandparents and grandchildren, brothers and sisters (including half siblings), and uncles and nieces or aunts and nephews cannot marry each other. (Fam. Code § 2200.) First cousins can marry each other in California, although these marriages are banned in many states.
- **sane** and mentally capable of consent. Insane and severely mentally retarded persons can't marry. Because it is difficult to tell when someone is or isn't insane, a person experiencing a lucid interval between periods of insanity can legally marry. That a person has been mentally ill in the past is no bar to marriage.
- **sober**. The county clerk can deny a marriage license to a person who has been drinking or is obviously under the influence of a drug. (Fam. Code §§ 350-355.)
- physically **able to consummate the marriage**. In theory, each party to a marriage must have the physical ability to have sexual intercourse, even if the

woman is past child-bearing age. (This requirement is not enforced.)

- **unmarried**. You can be married to only one person at a time. (Civ. Code § 4100.)

  To get married, you must have the following:

- a **license**. Both spouses must visit the county clerk's office to buy a license before marrying. You must give the clerk a physician's statement, no more than 30 days old, saying that neither has communicable syphilis, and that both have been offered an HIV test. Also, the woman, unless she is over 50 or surgically sterilized, must present a doctor's note stating whether or not she is immune to German measles (rubella).

- a **ceremony**. You must participate in some form of ceremony, performed by an active or retired judge, commissioner or assistant commissioner, or by a priest, minister or rabbi of any religion.

- a **witness**. You need one witness other than the person conducting the ceremony.

Confidential Marriages

Couples who wish to avoid the licensing and blood test requirements may choose a confidential marriage (Civ. Code § 4213.) To be eligible, a couple must have lived together for a period of time established by the county, and must both be 18 or older. You can get a confidential marriage from the county clerk or from a notary public who is licensed to perform such marriages. In either case, you must pay a fee and file a marriage certificate. Ask the county clerk for details.

SEPARATION

Separation can be formal (legal) or informal.

Formal separation is a substitute for divorce. The couple divides their property and debts, decides custody and visitation, and arranges child and spousal support, just as in a divorce. Legal separation often occurs when a couple will not divorce for religious reasons, or if a dependent spouse needs medical care and cannot afford it alone.

Informal separation can be either:

- trial separation—living apart for a test period to decide whether to go separate ways or to get back together, or

- permanent separation, in which the couple has decided to split up for good.

Assets received and debts incurred by the spouses during a trial separation are considered community property—that is, the spouses are entitled to equal shares of the property and are equally obligated to pay the debts.

Assets received and debts incurred after permanent separation are the separate property or responsibility of the spouse obtaining or incurring them. A court, however, can order that debts for necessities (food, clothing and shelter) incurred after permanent separation for the benefit of either spouse or the minor children be paid by the spouse who was better able to pay the debt when it was incurred. (Fam. Code § 2623.)

SPOUSAL SUPPORT (ALIMONY)

Spousal support (also referred to as alimony) is a series of payments made to one spouse by the other for a specified period of time after divorce. It is granted in fewer than 20% of divorce cases. When deciding whether or not to award support, the court must consider these factors:

- the age and health of each spouse
- whether the earning capacity of each spouse is sufficient to maintain the standard of living established during the marriage
- the supported spouse's marketable skills
- the degree to which one spouse contributed to the education, training or career of the other
- the needs of each spouse
- the obligations and assets of each party (including separate property)
- the duration of the marriage—there is a presumption that spousal support is appropriate in marriages that lasted more than 10 years
- the ability of the supported spouse to work without an adverse effect on the children
- the time required for the supported spouse to become retrained and self-supporting
- the standard of living established during the marriage
- any limitations on the supported spouse's employability due to periods of unemployment to take care of the children or house
- the ability of the supporting spouse to pay
- the tax consequences to each party. (Fam. Code §§ 3651, 3653, 3654, 4320, 4330-4337, 4339.)

In addition, many judges now consider whether and how much child support the paying spouse is obligated to pay. As a general rule, if child support obligations are large, spousal support will be granted in a reduced amount.

Tax Rules

Spousal support payments made under the terms of a written court order or separation agreement are tax deductible to the person paying. They are taxable income to the recipient.

Modifying Spousal Support

Unless a court order expressly prohibits it, a court can change the terms of a spousal support order—both amount and duration of support—as long as the order is in effect. In marriages lasting more than ten years, the court retains the power to modify spousal support indefinitely, unless both spouses sign a written waiver.

To modify spousal support, a spouse must file papers with the court that granted the divorce. The spouse must show that there has been a material change of circumstances since the last spousal support order.

Spousal support may be reduced if the payor can show inability to pay or that the recipient's need for support has decreased. The court will presume that the recipient's need for support has diminished if he or she is living with someone of the opposite sex, but this presumption can be rebutted by evidence that need has not changed.

Spousal support may be increased if the recipient can show needs that are not being met by the original court order, decreased income or an increase in the payor's income. The court will also consider the effects of inflation since the previous court order.

Ending Spousal Support

Unless otherwise agreed by the parties, spousal support ends:

- when the recipient remarries or dies, or
- after the period of time established in the court order has passed. (Fam. Code §§ 3651, 3653, 3654, 4320, 4330-4337, 4339, 4323.)

Serious Illness

Many of us are concerned about what will happen to us if a serious accident or illness strikes and we are unable to make our own medical and financial decisions. This section covers the legal options we have if we become incapacitated, as well as some other legal issues raised by serious illness.

TOPICS

> CONSERVATORSHIPS
> DURABLE POWER OF ATTORNEY FOR FINANCES
> DURABLE POWER OF ATTORNEY FOR HEALTHCARE
> EMERGENCY MEDICAL TREATMENT
> MEDICAL DIRECTIVES (LIVING WILLS AND POWERS
>   OF ATTORNEY)
> ORGAN AND BODY DONATION

RELATED TOPICS

> GOVERNMENT BENEFITS
>> Disability Insurance
>> Medi-Cal
>> Medicare
> INHERITANCE AND WILLS

ADDITIONAL RESOURCES

> *WillMaker*, (Nolo Press) (software for Macintosh, Windows or DOS), lets users create a valid will, living will, and final arrangements document with a computer.

> *The Conservatorship Book*, by Lisa Goldoftas and Carolyn Farren (Nolo Press), contains forms and instructions for getting a conservator appointed, without a lawyer.

> *Handbook for Conservators* (California Judicial Council), available through the Probate Division of the Superior Court, outlines procedures for California conservators.

> *Who Will Handle Your Finances If You Can't?*, by Denis Clifford and Mary Randolph (Nolo Press), contains information and forms for preparing a durable power of attorney for finances.

> *Beat the Nursing Home Trap: A Consumer's Guide to Choosing and Financing Long-Term Care*, by Joseph Matthews (Nolo Press), explains options for people who must find long-term care for themselves or a family member.

CONSERVATORSHIPS

A conservatorship is a legal arrangement in which an adult appointed by a court oversees the personal care or property of another adult considered incapable of managing alone. The person who takes over is the "conservator." The incapacitated person is the "conservatee." Often conservatees suffer from advanced stages of Alzheimer's disease, are in comas or have other serious illnesses.

Depending on the circumstances, the conservatee might not be permitted to make decisions about how his or her money is managed or spent. The conservatee could be denied the right to make his or her own medical decisions, vote or have access to a car.

A conservatorship lasts until the conservatee dies or the conservatee can resume caring for himself or herself or his or her finances. The court will monitor a conservatorship to ensure that it remains necessary and that the conservator is doing a good job. A conservator who is harming the conservatee or taking unauthorized actions regarding the conservatee's property can be removed from his job. A court must approve the ending of a conservatorship.

Types of Conservatorships

There are several kinds of conservatorships:

- **Conservator of the person.** The conservator is responsible for attending to the conservatee's personal needs. Depending on the court's findings, the conservator may need to make important medical choices. Before permanently moving the conservatee out of California, a conservator first must obtain a court order. (Probate Code § 2352.)

- **Conservator of the estate.** The conservator uses the conservatee's money and other assets to support and educate the conservatee and any dependents (Probate Code § 2420), invests and handles the conservatee's funds carefully and obtains court approval before undertaking any risky transactions, and prepares periodic accounting reports for the court.

- **Conservator of the person and estate.** The conservator takes care of the conservatee's personal needs and manages the conservatee's assets.

- **Limited conservatorship for developmentally disabled adult**. Specially tailored to encourage developmentally disabled adults to be self-reliant and independent. Examples of developmental disabilities include mental retardation, cerebral palsy, epilepsy and autism.

- **Mental health (LPS) conservatorship**. May be established to provide individualized mental health treatment and services for someone who has a mental disorder or is impaired by chronic alcoholism and is a danger to himself or others or is "gravely disabled"—unable to take care of basic personal needs such as food, shelter and clothing. (Welf. & Inst. Code §§ 5000-5550.) LPS conservatees, either adults or minors, are sometimes hospitalized in mental health treatment facilities or placed in board and care homes. LPS conservatorships are initiated by professionals in mental health facilities.

How To Create a Conservatorship

To set up a conservatorship, an adult must file documents with a court and have copies given to the proposed conservatee and mailed to the proposed conservatee's close relatives. A court investigator talks to the proposed conservatee and others who are familiar with the situation. A hearing date is set up, and the judge decides whether or not to appoint a conservator.

DURABLE POWER OF ATTORNEY FOR FINANCES

When you create and sign a document called a power of attorney, you give another person legal authority to act on your behalf. The person who is given this authority is called your "attorney-in-fact." (The word "attorney" means anyone authorized to act for another; it's not restricted to lawyers.)

A "durable" power of attorney stays valid even if you become physically or mentally incapacitated. With it, you can arrange for someone to handle your property and finances if you become unable to do so. You can give your attorney-in-fact authority to pay your bills, make bank deposits, deal with the paperwork of collecting insurance and government benefits and handle other aspects of your financial affairs.

You can make the durable power of attorney effective as soon as you sign it. Or you can specify that it will take effect only if you become incapacitated, as stated in writing, by a physician of your choice. If you are older or face an upcoming operation or life-threatening illness, preparing a durable power of attorney is a simple, very inexpensive and reliable way to ensure that your finances stay in the hands of someone you trust.

Creating a Durable Power of Attorney

It's easy to create a durable power of attorney for finances. California has a statutory fill-in-the-blanks form, which you must complete and sign in front of a notary public. It doesn't need to be filed with a court or government agency. This form is contained in *Who Will Handle Your Finances If You Can't?*, by Denis Clifford and Mary Randolph (Nolo Press).

If You Don't Make a Durable Power of Attorney

If you don't prepare a durable power of attorney for finances, and then become unable to handle your financial affairs, a court will probably have to hold a hearing and appoint someone, called a conservator, to manage your affairs.

DURABLE POWER OF ATTORNEY FOR HEALTHCARE

A durable power of attorney for healthcare is a document that authorizes another person to make medical decisions for you if you are unable to do so. Usually, it takes effect only if you become incapacitated and unable to consent to or refuse medical treatment. Many people prepare these documents to make sure that they won't be kept alive by artificial means.

Although doctors will usually follow the wishes of family members—particularly a parent or spouse—regarding a patient's care, a durable power of attorney allows the patient to state who, legally, may speak for him or her. This is particularly important if family members disagree about proper medical treatment, or if the patient wants someone who is not legally considered a family member—a gay or lesbian lover, for example—to make his or her medical decisions.

The Attorney-In-Fact

The person designated to make medical decisions is called the attorney-in-fact. The attorney-in-fact cannot be your treating healthcare provider or your provider's employee, or the operator or employee of either a community or residential care facility. (Civ. Code § 2432.)

The attorney-in-fact can consent to or refuse or withdraw any medical care, treatment, service or procedure to maintain, diagnose or treat a physical or mental condition. In the durable power of attorney document, the patient can put any limitations on care that he or she desires, and can specifically authorize or refuse specific procedures and treatments.

The powers of the attorney-in-fact, unless otherwise limited by the patient, include the rights to:

- give, withhold or withdraw consent to surgical or medical procedures
- hire, fire and grant releases to medical personnel
- have access to medical records and other personal information
- get court authorization required to obtain or withhold medical treatment, or
- spend or withhold money necessary to carry out medical treatment.

Unless directed otherwise by the durable power of attorney document, the attorney-in-fact has the authority to take these actions after the patient dies:

- authorize an autopsy
- donate the body for scientific study or the body parts for transplant, and
- direct disposition of the remains. (Civ. Code § 2434.)

A durable power of attorney for healthcare must be signed by two witnesses who are 18 or older. Like the attorney-in-fact, they cannot be involved in treating the patient. Any durable power of attorney for healthcare that you draw up and have witnessed exists indefinitely, unless you specify that it expires after a certain period of time.

EMERGENCY MEDICAL TREATMENT

Hospitals routinely provide necessary emergency care, even if the patient is unconscious and unable to consent to treatment. Although hospitals prefer to have at least the consent of a family member (a parent or spouse, for example), emergency treatment can be provided without this consent.

MEDICAL DIRECTIVES (LIVING WILLS AND POWERS OF ATTORNEY)

The right to die with dignity, and without the tremendous agony and expense for both patient and family caused by prolonging lives artificially, has been addressed now by the U.S. Supreme Court, the federal government and the state legislature.

This individual right also protects someone who wants more extensive care than doctors wish to provide. For example, a doctor may be unwilling to try experimental treatments or maintain long-term treatments on a patient who he or she feels has slim chances of recovering.

California was the first state to pass laws authorizing individuals to create simple documents that set out their wishes concerning life-prolonging medical care. The documents are called a Declaration—formerly known as a Living Will—and a Durable Power of Attorney for Healthcare. It is important to note that these medical directives take effect only when a patient is diagnosed to have a terminal condition or to be in a permanent coma and cannot communicate with medical personnel.

The basic difference between the two documents is simple. The Declaration is a statement made by you directly to medical personnel. It spells out the medical care you do or do not wish to receive if you become terminally ill and incapacitated. A Declaration is presented to your doctor and the hospital or other medical provider and becomes a part of your official medical record, legally binding the doctor or hospital to follow your wishes. It acts as a contract with the treating doctor, who must either honor the wishes that you have expressed or transfer you to another doctor or facility that will honor them.

In a Durable Power of Attorney for Healthcare, you can appoint someone else to oversee your doctors to make sure they provide you with the kind of medical care you want. The person you appoint is called an attorney-in-fact. Your attorney-in-fact has the power to ensure that doctors and hospitals follow your wishes. It is a good idea to appoint a second person as a backup or replacement attorney-in-fact to act if your first choice is unable or unwilling to serve.

To make an informed decision about which procedures you do and do not want it may be a good idea to discuss your medical directive with your physician. He or she can explain the medical procedures more fully and can discuss the options with you. You will also find out whether your doctor has any medical or moral objections to following your wishes. If he or she will not agree to follow your wishes, you may want to consider changing doctors.

In most instances, you do not need to consult a lawyer to prepare a Declaration or Power of Attorney for Healthcare. The forms are usually quite simple and can be obtained, free or for a nominal fee, from a number of sources.

- Contact a local hospital. Most will give you the forms free and many have Patient Representatives on staff who will help you in filling them out.
- Nolo Press has developed an easy-to-use software program, WillMaker, that helps you prepare and update a medical directive for any state. It comes with a manual providing necessary background information and leads you step-by-step through the process.
- The white pages in most telephone directories have a listing for Senior Referral & Information. You can get referrals to agencies, groups and other sources of assistance for seniors, including where to get medical directive forms and help in filling them out.
- The national nonprofit organization Choice in Dying (formerly the Society for the Right to Die) is one of the nation's oldest patients' advocacy groups. It welcomes donations, but will provide free information on current laws on medical directives and can provide forms. Send a stamped, self-addressed envelope, along with your request for information on California's medical directive laws to:

Choice in Dying
200 Varick Street
New York, NY 10014-4810
(212) 366-5540

ORGAN AND BODY DONATION

A body donation and an organ donation are two different things. You may donate particular organs for transplant, donate all organs and tissues or give your entire body to a medical school to aid in research and education. To prevent potential abuses in selling bodies and body parts, the family or estate of the donor cannot receive money for the donation.

Organ Donation

Many California hospitals perform organ transplants. Most people who are not afflicted with cancer, AIDS, hepatitis, venereal, heart and bone disease or other infectious diseases are eligible to donate organs. Age limits for acceptable donors vary, depending on whether the organ is to be used for research or for transplant. And time limits on when the transplant must be performed also vary tremendously— from six months in the case of a liver for transplant, to no limit in the case of an eye, eye parts or the middle ear given for research. Organs will be removed only from a body that is medically deemed to be brain-dead—and two physicians must certify that this is so.

State laws require that hospital staff ask the family of a dying patient whether they would be willing to donate the organs and tissues of the deceased, but these laws are often ignored. The best way to indicate your preference that your organs be donated is to obtain an Organ Donor Card or Uniform Donor Card, identifying you as a willing potential donor. It grants permission and instructs doctors and other medical personnel to regard you as a potential organ donor when you die. You can obtain the proper document from organ donor agencies in your community. You can also arrange to be identified as a potential donor by affixing a designation to your driver's license; contact your local Department of Motor Vehicles.

You should make sure your family knows that you want to be a donor. Regardless of the steps you have taken, no medical facility or doctor will accept an organ for donation if family members object.

Body Donation

There is no age limit for body donations. To be accepted, a body must not be embalmed or autopsied, and the person must not have died of a contagious disease.

As with organ donations, your family can object to a body donation, so you should make sure they know what you want.

If you wish to donate your body, you must contact the institution that will be receiving it. The institution will provide you with its own form that you must sign and have witnessed. Remains will be cremated and scattered or buried by the institution; they will not be returned to your family.

You can find out more about body donation options from the National Anatomical service, which operates a 24-hour phone service at (800) 727-0700.

SMALL BUSINESSES

This section covers basic material for business people, including legal rules for forming different kinds of businesses and choosing a business name.

Many laws that affect businesses are made on a local level. We do not cover these laws—including license and permit requirements and specific zoning regulations—here. Check local ordinances for more information.

TOPICS
- CORPORATIONS
- FICTITIOUS BUSINESS NAMES
- NONPROFIT CORPORATIONS
- PARTNERSHIPS
- PROFESSIONAL CORPORATIONS
- RESPONSIBILITY TO EMPLOYEES
- SOLE PROPRIETORSHIPS
- TRADEMARKS AND SERVICE MARKS
- TRADE SECRETS

RELATED TOPICS
- CONSUMERS' RIGHTS
  - Sales Tax
- COPYRIGHTS AND PATENTS
- EMPLOYEES' RIGHTS
- LANDLORDS AND TENANTS
  - Leases and Rental Agreements

ADDITIONAL RESOURCES

How to Write a Business Plan, by Mike McKeever (Nolo Press) shows new business owners how to write a business plan and secure financing.

The Legal Guide to Starting and Running a Small Business, by Fred S. Steingold (Nolo Press) is a complete legal guide for small businesses.

Trademark: How to Name Your Business and Product, by Kate McGrath and Stephen Elias (Nolo Press) tells small business owners how to choose a name that competitors can't use.

The Partnership Book, by Denis Clifford and Ralph Warner (Nolo Press) shows, step by step, how to write a partnership agreement that will prevent problems later.

Nolo's Partnership Maker (Nolo Press), is a software program that helps you prepare a partnership agreement with your IBM-compatible computer.

The California Nonprofit Corporation Handbook, by Anthony Mancuso (Nolo Press), shows how to form a nonprofit corporation and includes all necessary forms.

The California Professional Corporation Handbook, by Anthony Mancuso (Nolo Press), contains forms and instructions for creating a professional corporation.

How To Form Your Own California Corporation, by Anthony Mancuso (Nolo Press) is the definitive guide to incorporating a California business without a lawyer.

California Incorporator, by Anthony Mancuso (Nolo Press) is software for IBM-compatible computers that lets users prepare all the paperwork for incorporation.

Questions and Answers About Trademarks is a free pamphlet available from the U.S. Patent and Trademark Office, Washington, DC 20231.

CORPORATIONS

Unlike a sole proprietorship or a partnership, a corporation is a legal entity separate from its creators and owners. The corporation itself can own property, owe money and pay taxes. Doing business as a corporation offers distinct advantages, particularly limitation of the business owners' (shareholders') liability for normal corporate debts, and sometimes tax savings. However, for many new small businesses, the expense and paperwork required to incorporate outweigh the possible benefits, at least until the business is more established.

Limited Liability

One of the main advantages of incorporating is that, in most cases, it limits the personal liability of the people who own the business. If the corporation loses a lawsuit, for example, the owners' personal property cannot be seized to pay the judgment. They stand to lose only the money that they have invested in the corporation. However, an owner who personally guarantees business loans or contracts loses this limited liability.

To preserve limited liability, the business owners must keep their finances and the corporation's finances separate. If a court concludes that they have mingled personal and corporate funds to the extent that the corporation isn't really a separate entity, or that the owners have significantly underfunded the corporation, the court might hold them personally liable for the corporation's debts, especially if they engaged in fraud.

Taxes

A corporation is a separate, tax-paying entity. The primary tax advantage of incorporating is the ability to split business income between yourself and your business to take advantage of lower corporate tax rates on business income. For example, the first $50,000 of taxable corporate income is taxed at 15%, significantly less than the maximum 39% plus marginal (top) tax rate that can apply to individual income. Additional amounts of corporate taxable income are taxed at the next higher corporate tax rate tiers of 25%, 34% and 36%, each still below the top individual tax rate. The real trick to making incorporation work for you is finding the right mix of personal and business income that lowers your overall tax bill yet still channels enough cash to you personally and to your business to keep both comfortable.

Income splitting is not possible in a sole proprietorship or a partnership, in which each owner must report the income of the business on her personal income tax return in the the year in which the money was made, regardless of whether or not he or she actually takes the money out of the business in that year. Salaries, payments for benefits, bonuses and so on are all deductible expenses for the corporation. Employees who receive this money must report it on their personal income tax returns (except for benefits, which are not reported or taxed), but the corporation pays taxes only on the income left after deducting all expenses of doing business, including an owner's salary as an employee.

The IRS allows a corporation to retain a significant amount of earnings (for most businesses, a minimum of $250,000), without paying it to the shareholders as dividends, which are taxable at both the corporate and individual level. Additional earnings can be kept in the corporation without penalty to meet the legitimate future needs of the business.

In California, a corporation must pay an annual corporate franchise tax, based on its net income in the previous year. The tax rate is 9.3% of annual taxable corporate income, with a minimum of $800 per year.

How To Incorporate

Here are the steps to incorporate a small, privately held corporation (that is, a corporation in which stock will not be sold publicly, but will instead be held by a small group of people who know each other) in California:

- Choose a president, secretary and treasurer. One person can hold all of these positions, as well as being the entire board of directors and the sole stockholder. In other words, in California, you can form a one-person corporation.

- Choose a name for your corporation that is not the same or confusingly similar to that of an existing California corporation. If you choose a name that is already on the books, the Secretary of State will reject your Articles of Incorporation.

- File the Articles of Incorporation, the document that creates and describes the corporation, with the California Secretary of State's office. In this document, you must give your corporate name, along with the names of the corporate directors or incorporators and the number of shares in your company. After these are filed with the Secretary of State, you should write bylaws. These specify the dates for corporate meetings and restate the most significant provisions of state law that will apply to your corporation.

- Pay a filing fee of $100, as well as the minimum annual franchise tax payment of $800.

- Comply with California's securities laws. For most small business corporations, this simply means filing a one-page form with the Department of Corporations and paying a $25 fee. Publicly held corporations are subject to more complicated stock issuance regulations promulgated by the U.S. Securities and Exchange Commission.

S Corporations

"S Corporation" status is a special corporate tax election that provides the legal benefits of a corporation (limited personal liability) and the tax status of a partnership. All income of the corporation is reported on the owners' tax returns, in the year that the corporation earned it (even if this is not the year in which the money was taken out of the corporation). S corporation status can be useful in the early years of an unprofitable corporation, because corporate losses can usually be used to offset income from other sources on an owner's personal tax return. It also may be useful for profitable corporations in the event that corporate tax rates are higher than the individual rates of the shareholders—by passing profits to the shareholders to be taxed on their individual income tax returns, corporate taxation of business income is avoided.

FICTITIOUS BUSINESS NAMES

Most businesses use a name—Speedy Printers, King Street Market—that the owners made up. A fictitious business name is any name that is different than the name of the individual, partnership or corporate name of the business owners. Any business name that includes the name of the business owner and suggests the existence of additional owners (for example, Smith & Company, Jones & Sons) is also a fictitious business name.

A business using a fictitious business name must register the name within 40 days of starting to regularly transact business in California. A business that doesn't register its fictitious name cannot use the courts to bring a lawsuit. Also, banks usually won't open an account in the name of the business without proof of registration.

Nonprofit corporations and real estate investment trusts are not required by law to register their fictitious business names.

How To File a Fictitious Business Name Statement

Fictitious business name statements are filed with the clerk of the county of the business' principal place of business in California. Businesses that have no place of business in the state, or that do business in many counties, can file with the clerk's office in Sacramento County.

The clerk can provide a blank form for the statement, or owners can make their own. The statement must include:

- the fictitious business name
- the street address of the primary place of business, in or out of state
- the names of the business owners, partnership, or corporation using the name, and what form of business it is (for example, limited partnership or sole proprietorship)
- the date the business began doing business using the name
- the signatures of the business owners.

Within 30 days of filing the statement, the business owners must publish it in a newspaper of general circulation in the California county that is the principal place of business, or in Sacramento County if there is no place of business in California. The statement must run at least once a week for four successive weeks. Within 30 days of completing publication, the owners must file an affidavit (a sworn statement that the business statement was published), including the publication itself, with the county clerk.

A fictitious business name statement expires after five years and must be filed again at expiration. In addition, a new statement must be filed within 40 days after any required information in the old statement changes, or that statement expires. (Bus. & Prof. Code § 17900 and following.)

NONPROFIT CORPORATIONS

Certain types of organizations can become nonprofit corporations. Most non-profit groups elect nonprofit corporate status primarily to attract tax-exempt and tax-deductible support for worthy causes. Nonprofit corporations get the benefits granted to all corporations, such as limited personal liability for shareholders.

Requirements

In California, a nonprofit corporation must fit into one of these three categories:

- **Public benefit corporation.** A business formed for a public or charitable purpose, such as building a local library or raising money to help AIDS patients.
- **Religious corporation.** A business formed for religious purposes. This can include an organized religion, a group formed to promote the study of a certain religion, or even a group to promote better understanding between people of different religions.
- **Mutual benefit corporation.** A business formed to benefit its own members, such as a trade association, rotary club or automobile association. Because mutual benefit corporations are regulated under separate rules, they are not covered here.

The Articles of Incorporation (the papers filed with the California Secretary of State to create the corporation) must state which type of nonprofit is being formed. They must also state that the corporation is not organized for any person's private gain (unless it is a mutual benefit corporation).

Tax-Exempt Status

Unlike regular corporations, nonprofit corporations can apply for tax-exempt status and avoid paying federal income taxes altogether. The rules for tax-exempt status can be found in Section 501(c)(3) of the Internal Revenue Code; because of this, tax-exempt corporations are often called 501(c)(3) corporations. Tax-exempt status is not an automatic benefit of organizing as a nonprofit corporation; you must apply for tax exemption separately.

To qualify for tax-exempt status, a nonprofit corporation:

- must be organized and operated exclusively for charitable, religious, scientific, literary and/or educational purposes
- cannot substantially engage in activities that are unrelated to the group's tax-exempt purpose. For example, a corporation formed to promote literacy should not spend too much time running a for-profit book sales operation.
- cannot be organized to benefit individuals associated with the corporation. No corporate earnings can be distributed to the individuals who run the corporation, except for salaries paid to staff workers. Any corporate profits must be used to benefit the public interest, and any corporate assets remaining when the corporation liquidates must be given to another tax-exempt nonprofit.
- are forbidden from participating in political campaigns involving candidates for public office and cannot substantially engage in other political activities, such as attempting to influence the outcome of legislation.

If a corporation qualifies as tax-exempt under one of these federal tests, it will also qualify as tax-exempt in California, because California's tax-exempt statutes mirror the IRS rules. This means that the corporation does not have to pay an annual franchise tax to the state as regular corporations do.

Unrelated Business Tax. Nonprofit corporations must pay tax on money made from activities unrelated to their tax-exempt purposes. The first $1,000 of unrelated business income is not taxed, but normal corporate tax rate applies to any income beyond that. This is true both for federal and state taxes.

California Welfare Exemption. Nonprofit corporations that own or lease property to use for their tax-exempt purpose can avoid paying property taxes by qualifying for this exemption. Other state property exemptions exist for nonprofit corporations as well. Contact your County Tax Assessor for an application and information.

Public Charity or Private Foundation?

There are two types of 501(c)(3) tax-exempt nonprofit corporations: public charities and private foundations. The IRS presumes that a corporation is a private foundation unless it meets the requirements to be classified as a public charity. Some of these rules are very technical; we only summarize them here.

Most 501(c)(3) nonprofits formed in California qualify as public charities. Public charity status is extremely valuable. Private foundations are burdened by numerous operating restrictions, including limitations on holdings in private businesses and the requirement that the corporation annually distribute its net income for charitable purposes; public charities are not similarly limited. In addition, those who contribute to private foundations can deduct only up to 30% of their adjusted gross income, but contributors to public charities can deduct up to 50% of their adjusted gross income.

To qualify as a public charity, a corporation must meet one of the following tests:

- **Automatic qualification.** Some types of corporations automatically qualify as public charities: churches, schools, hospitals and medical research organizations, public safety organizations (generally, groups that test products to determine whether or not they are fit for use by consumers), and government organizations. In addition, any corporation operated solely in connection with one of these groups qualifies automatically.
- **Public support.** Corporations can qualify under this heading if they regularly solicit funds from the general public and normally receive money from government agencies and a number of different private contributors and agencies. A

corporation that relies primarily on a few large grants or donors will probably not qualify as a publicly supported charity.

Two tests are used by the IRS to determine if a corporation receives enough public support to qualify:

— if it receives at least one-third of its total support from government sources, contributions made by the general public or other publicly supported organizations, it will qualify.

— if it receives at least one-tenth of its total support from the sources listed above, AND attracts public support using a program to continuously solicit funds from the public, it will qualify.

Note that these one-third and one-tenth calculations are made based on the cumulative figures from the four prior tax years. Every year does not have to meet this standard; if average public support over the four years is one-third or one-tenth of total support, that is sufficient.

- **Gross receipts support test.** Groups that plan to generate income from performing tax-exempt services may qualify under this test. The corporation must:

   — Receive more that one-third of its total support from gifts, grants, contributions or membership fees, and gross receipts from admissions, selling merchandise, performing services, or providing facilities in an activity related to the group's tax-exempt purpose. For example, a dance theater could count money made from ticket and t-shirt sales.

   — Not make more than one-third of its annual support from businesses or investment income unrelated to its tax-exempt purpose. For example, if a corporation formed to run a school also owned property, the money made by renting out that property would count as unrelated investment income.

Tax Deductions for Donors

Individuals may deduct up to 50% of their adjusted gross income for contributions to tax-exempt public charities. Corporations may deduct charitable contributions up to 10% of their annual taxable income. Contributions that can be deducted include donations of cash or property. The deductibility rules are the same for federal and state income tax.

PARTNERSHIPS

A partnership consists of two or more people doing business together, sharing duties, expenses and profits in a manner they've agreed on. It is relatively easy to set up, and partners can tailor their arrangements to meet their needs with a written partnership agreement.

Creating a Partnership

No special legal paperwork is necessary to create a partnership. However, the partnership must complete the paperwork required of any California business, such as registering a fictitious business name and getting necessary permits and licenses.

If you don't make a written partnership agreement, many aspects of your partnership will be determined by a law called the Uniform Partnership Act, a national law that has been adopted by California. (Corp. Code § 15001 and following.) By writing an agreement, the partners can fashion many details of their partnership to meet their specific needs. For example, partners can agree to own unequal shares of the business, or agree to particular buy-out procedures, or agree that one partner will be in charge of day-to-day management of the business. Written partnership agreements are private and don't have to be filed with any state agency.

Liability

Any partner can obligate the partnership—for example, take out a debt, sign a contract or enter a business agreement for the partnership. In addition, unlike a corporation, partners are personally liable for partnership debts. If the partnership loses a lawsuit, the judgment can be collected not only from the property of the partnership, but also from the personal property of all the partners. However, most sensible businesses purchase insurance to guard against this risk.

Taxes

Partnerships, unlike corporations, are not a separate entity for tax purposes. Partners pay taxes on their share of partnership profits on their personal income tax returns, in the year in which the partnership made the money. This means that partners can use partnership losses to offset profits made from other sources in the same tax year.

Limited Partnerships

A limited partnership is a hybrid business form that combines aspects of both corporations and partnerships. A limited partnership must have at least one general partner, who is responsible for running the business and is personally liable for partnership debts, as explained above. The general partner can be either a person or a corporation. In addition, the business has limited partners, passive investors who do not actually participate in running the partnership business. The liability of limited partners for partnership debts is limited to the amount that they invested. Limited partnerships are often created to invest in real estate or when other types of partnership businesses need capital but don't want to take on new general partners or incorporate.

Limited partnerships are more heavily regulated than general partnerships. A limited partnership must register with the California Secretary of State. (Corp. Code § 15621.) It must also comply with complicated federal securities regulations, unless the limited partnerships are all sold in one state or are sold privately to a few people (often 35 or less) who have close business or personal ties or are sophisticated investors.

PROFESSIONAL CORPORATIONS

Traditionally, professionals such as physicians, lawyers and veterinarians were not allowed to incorporate, because it was thought that incorporation would distance the usually close relationship between professionals and their clients. Today, professionals are allowed to incorporate, but in many cases must form a professional corporation, with different (and in many cases, more stringent) rules than regular corporations. In addition to the general principles stated here, each profession has its own regulations and requirements; consult the agency that oversees your profession for more details.

Who Must Form Professional Corporations

Members of the following professions must incorporate as professional corporations if they choose to incorporate:

- accountants
- acupuncturists
- attorneys
- chiropractors
- clinical social workers (licensed)
- dentists
- doctors
- marriage, family and child counselors
- nurses
- optometrists
- osteopaths
- pharmacists
- physical therapists
- physicians' assistants
- podiatrists
- psychologists
- shorthand reporters
- speech pathologists and audiologists. (Moscone-Knox Professional Corporations Act, Corp. Code § 13400 and following.)

Architects and veterinarians have a choice of incorporating as professional corporations or regular corporations.

Limited Liability

Professional corporations don't provide the same measure of protection against personal liability as regular corporations do. Employees of a regular corporation are not personally liable for the corporation's debts. However, in a professional corporation, a professional employee is always personally liable for his or her own malpractice or the malpractice of those under his or her supervision or control. However, the professional is insulated from personal liability for the malpractice of other professionals in the corporation. The professionals in the corporation must carry the minimum insurance set out in the regulations for that profession.

Just like employees of a regular corporation, professionals are not personally liable for non-malpractice work incidents, business claims against the corporation or other corporate debts.

Taxes

Professional corporations must pay the California corporate franchise tax, just like a regular corporation. This tax is 9.3% of the corporation's annual taxable income, with a minimum of $800.

Professional corporations also must pay federal income tax. A professional corporation must pay the regular corporate tax rate unless it qualifies as a professional service corporations in which:

- all stock in the corporation is held by employees performing professional services for the corporation, and
- all activities of the corporation involve performing services in the field of health, law, engineering, architecture, accounting, actuarial science, performing arts or consulting.

These professional service corporations must pay a 34% flat federal corporate tax rate on all taxable income.

Requirements for Incorporation

In addition to the requirements to form a regular corporation, and the requirements specific to the profession, professional corporations:

- must be licensed by the appropriate state board
- must choose a proper name. Some are required to indicate that they are a professional corporation. In addition, some professions may not use fictitious business names, but must use the names of one or more shareholders as their corporate name
- may only have shareholders, directors and officers who are licensed in that profession. Some professions allow people who are licensed in specified related professions to hold these positions
- may be required to get a minimum amount of liability insurance
- may be required to file annual reports with the agency that oversees that profession.

RESPONSIBILITY TO EMPLOYEES

Employers must know and respect the legal rights of their employees. These rights, protected by both federal and California law, include:

- the right not to be discriminated against or harassed because of race, sex, age, religion or other protected characteristics
- the right to reasonable privacy in interviews and on the job
- the right to a safe workplace, as determined by both the federal and California Occupational Safety and Health Agencies
- the right to a certain amount of income security, in the form of workers' compensation, unemployment benefits and minimum wage protections.

All of these subjects are covered, from the employee's perspective, in Employees' Rights.

Taxes and Withholding

Employers are responsible for withholding a certain percentage of their employees' paychecks for federal and California income tax and another portion for Social Security tax and state disability insurance. In addition, the employer must pay a share of Social Security tax and federal unemployment tax for each employee.

SOLE PROPRIETORSHIPS

If you own your business as a sole proprietor, legally speaking, you and your business are treated the same. You have unlimited personal liability for business debts and other legal obligations of your business (lawsuits over negligence or breach of warranty, for example). If your business can't meet its financial obligations, creditors can come after your non-business property.

For income tax purposes, you and your business are also a single entity. You report business profits and losses on your personal income tax return. This means that you can offset business losses with income from other sources. The income of your business is taxed to you in the year that the business receives it, whether or not you remove the money from the business.

To begin a business as a sole proprietor, all you are required to do is file a fictitious name certificate with your county, get a sales tax permit if you plan to sell things to customers and get any licenses and permits necessary to do business in your chosen field and region.

TRADEMARKS AND SERVICE MARKS

A trademark is a word, phrase, logo or other graphic used by a business to distinguish its products from those of its competitors. If a business uses the name or logo to identify a service (providing fast food, for example), it is called a service mark. In practice, legal protections for trademarks and service marks are identical; we refer to both as trademarks.

The value of a trademark lies in its ability to distinguish the products of the company, and so to attract customers. As a general rule, the first business to use a protectable mark has the exclusive right to continue using it. That business can sue others to prevent them from using it, or any name or graphic that is similar enough to cause customer confusion.

What Trademarks Can Be Protected

Not all names are entitled to trademark protection. Ordinary words used in their usual context, called "weak" marks, are not normally protectable, because no single company is allowed to monopolize their use. Examples include descriptive terms, such as "dependable" or "tasty," personal or place names, such as "Bob's Barber Shop" or "Downtown Cleaners," and words that praise the product, such as "Blue Ribbon" or "Tip-Top." However, names using ordinary words may become protectable if, through long use and extensive public familiarity, they become associated exclusively with one company. "McDonald's" and "Best Foods" are well-known examples.

Strong trademarks can be exclusively used by the company that created them. A strong mark could be a name made up by the company, such as "Exxon" or "Reebok." Ordinary words used in arbitrary or surprising ways, such as Apple computers or Penguin books, are also strong marks. Finally, names that are creatively suggestive of the product's qualities, without being merely descriptive, are also strong marks. Examples include the "Roach Motel" and "Chicken of the Sea" tuna.

Trademark Searches

Once a business chooses a trademark, it should conduct a search to be sure no other business is already using it. If the mark is already in use, using it means risking a lawsuit. Businesses can conduct trademark searches themselves, either manually or by using trademark search software, or hire a search firm.

Registration

Once a mark is in use in California, it can be registered with the California Secretary of State. (Bus. & Prof. Code § 14200 and following.) The Secretary of State provides the application form and charges $50. Registration lasts for ten years; when it expires, it can be renewed for another ten.

If a mark is used across state, territorial or national lines, or will be in the near future, it can be registered with the U.S. Patent and Trademark Office.

Registration is not required to get the protection of trademark laws. Registration, however, gives notice to all would-be copiers that the trademark is in use. Also, those who own registered trademarks are entitled to higher money awards if a dispute over the trademark ends up in court. (15 U.S.C. § 1050 and following.)

Infringement

In California, if someone uses a trademark without permission, the business that owns the trademark can sue for a court order stopping the use. If the trademark is very distinctive, it isn't necessary to show that customers are confused by the similarity; it is enough that the distinctiveness of the mark is "diluted" by its unauthorized use. The use of a trademark can also be stopped without a showing of customer confusion if the use would tend to damage the trademark owner's business reputation.

If the mark is registered in California, and another business uses it to advertise or sell counterfeit goods or services, the business can sue for a court order seizing the counterfeit goods. The infringing business may also have to pay up to three times the loss caused by the counterfeiting.

TRADE SECRETS

A trade secret is any information that gives a business a competitive advantage and that the business tries to keep confidential. A trade secret can be a formula, process, device or even a unique compilation of information that is widely available in other forms, such as a marketing list.

A business must take reasonable precautions to protect the confidentiality of its trade secrets in order to be assured of help from the courts. If a business doesn't try to keep its restricted information confidential, the court won't treat the information as a trade secret, and will not step in to prevent others from using the information. Reasonable precautions include:

- restricting access to the secrets, through the use of passwords, codes and restricted locations
- posting warnings and telling all employees that the information is considered a trade secret and must be kept confidential
- using non-disclosure agreements, which require persons to whom trade secrets must be disclosed for business purposes to get proper authorization before disclosing the trade secret
- using confidentiality agreements, by which employees agree not to disclose trade secrets
- using covenants not to compete, by which an employee who leaves the company, or former employees of a company that is sold, agrees not to use the information.

If a trade secret is stolen or used by another, the business can sue both the thief and the ultimate user of the information—usually a new employer—for trade secret infringement. The business can ask the court to issue an injunction (court order) preventing use of the trade secret, and in some cases to award money to compensate for profits improperly made by use of the protected information, money lost as a result of the theft or royalty payments. If the theft is willful and malicious, the court may double the monetary award. (Civ. Code §§ 3426.1-3426.10.)

TRAFFIC AND VEHICLE LAWS

Although traffic offenses are technically criminal violations, we have included them in this book because they are part of our everyday dealings with the law. Here, you will find explanations of the most common offenses and the penalties for committing them, as well as the basic laws that govern driving and registering your vehicle.

TOPICS
ALCOHOL AND DRUG RELATED OFFENSES
CAR INSURANCE REQUIREMENTS
EQUIPMENT, LICENSE AND REGISTRATION VIOLATIONS
LICENSE SUSPENSION AND REVOCATION
MOVING VIOLATIONS
PARKING TICKETS
REGISTRATION AND SMOG CHECKS
SEAT BELTS AND CHILD RESTRAINT REQUIREMENTS

RELATED TOPICS
CONSUMERS' RIGHTS
Car Rentals
Car Repairs
Car Sales

ADDITIONAL RESOURCES
Fight Your Ticket, by Dave Brown (Nolo Press), shows how to contest a parking or traffic ticket in California.

Bureau of Automotive Repair, (800) 952-5210, provides information about compliance with emission laws.

ALCOHOL AND DRUG RELATED OFFENSES

Several traffic violations involve alcohol or drugs, but are not as serious as drunk driving. Most are infractions, which means the driver will get a ticket and will have to send in the fine or appear in court.

- **Open container on person of driver.** You can be cited for this offense if, while driving a car, you had an open (unsealed) container holding any amount of alcohol on your person (that is, in your hand, in your pocket or in your purse). If the container was not on your person, but rather was in the car or on a passenger, you have not committed this offense. (Veh. Code § 23222(a).)
- **Open container kept in vehicle by driver or owner.** You can be cited for this offense if you are in a car or own it, and there is an open container holding any amount of alcohol someplace in the car, other than the trunk or the living quarters of a camper. You do not have to be driving the car to commit this offense; if the car is parked and you are in it, that is sufficient. (Veh. Code § 23225.)
- **Driver drinking in vehicle.** An officer who sees you drink alcohol while driving will cite you for this offense. (Veh. Code § 23220.)
- **Marijuana in vehicle.** You can be cited for a misdemeanor if you are driving with up to one ounce of marijuana in your car. (Veh. Code § 23222(b).) An officer who pulls you over and smells marijuana is entitled to search your entire car.

Drunk Driving

These offenses are all misdemeanors, and carry fairly stiff penalties.

- **Driving under the influence.** It's illegal to drive while your ability to drive safely is significantly affected by alcohol or drugs. Your blood alcohol level is immaterial: if alcohol or drugs are impairing your driving, you have committed this offense. (Veh. Code § 23152(a).)
- **Driving with blood alcohol of 0.08% or more.** It's also illegal to drive when the concentration of alcohol in your blood is 0.08% or greater. (Veh. Code § 23152(b).) If an officer wants to test your blood alcohol level, you must be given a choice of blood, breath or urine tests. If you do not submit to a test, your license can be suspended. (Veh. Code § 13353.)
- **Attempted drunk driving.** If you are drunk and attempt to start or drive a vehicle, you can be cited. The penalties are half those for driving under the influence. (Pen. Code § 664.)

  If you kill or injure someone while drunk driving, you can be charged with a felony. (Veh. Code §§ 23153, 23180, 23185, 23190.)
- **Young Drivers.** The police may seize the driver's license of a driver under the age of 21 on the spot if they suspect the young motorist of drinking and the youth fails to pass a breath test. (Veh. Code § 23136.) The law limits blood alcohol levels for drivers under 21 to 0.01%, which means that any amount of alcohol in a young driver's blood is illegal.

  Drivers who refuse to take the breath test can still lose their license for one year after the officer submits a sworn statement to the DMV reporting, among other facts, the officer's grounds for believing the driver violated Veh. Code § 23136. Drivers can appeal the action within 10 days of receiving the notice of the order of suspension or revocation or ask the DMV for a restricted license if there is a critical need to drive. When the license is reinstated, the driver pays an additional $100 to cover the expense of implementing the law.

Penalties

For a first conviction of driving under the influence or with a blood alcohol level of 0.08% or more, you must be fined a minimum of $390, and you may spend up to 96 hours in jail if probation is not granted. The maximum penalty is a $1,000 fine and six months in jail. Penalties for subsequent convictions are much more severe; you may sentenced to up to a year in jail, and your license may be revoked. For a fourth offense, you can be sent to state prison for up to three years.

CAR INSURANCE REQUIREMENTS

All California drivers are required to have insurance that covers damage caused by a car that they own or drive. The minimum coverage allowed is:

- bodily injury: $15,000 per person/$30,000 per accident
- property damage: $5,000 per accident.

Drivers must also carry liability insurance to protect against the following risks:

- injuries the driver causes to someone else while operating a motor vehicle
- damage the driver causes to someone else's property, including another car, a street light, telephone pole or building, while operating a motor vehicle.

The police cannot stop cars merely to enforce insurance laws. There are only two instances when the police can ask for proof of insurance: when you are involved in an accident, and when you are cited for a moving violation. (Veh. Code § 16028.)

If the police ask you for proof of insurance, you must give the name and number of your insurance policy. A very few drivers are "self-insurers"; this means that they keep a sum of money sufficient to cover the minimum insurance requirement on deposit with the state. These people must provide their deposit number. If the vehicle you are driving is owned by the United States government, you need only show proof of its ownership, not proof of insurance.

The penalty for a first offense of driving without proper insurance is a $95 fine, plus $25 in penalty assessments. The penalties are much higher—a $200 fine plus $60 in assessments—if you receive the ticket in conjunction with a drunk driving arrest for which you are later convicted.

Insurance Policies and Rates

A company can change the rate within 60 days of verifying the rate and underwriting (determining the risk of) a new policy. After that time it cannot change the premium during the policy period. A company that originally insured you may reject your application for coverage within the first 60 days, but it must give you at least 10 days' notice. After 60 days, an insurance company can cancel your policy only if:

- you fail to pay premiums
- you gave false information on your application or otherwise commit fraud, or
- there is a major change in your risk to the insurance company after your policy is issued—for example, your driver's license is suspended or revoked.

The company must mail you a notice of cancellation at least 20 days before cancelling. Only 10 days' notice of cancellation is required if you didn't pay the premium.

At renewal time, an insurance company will examine your claims record. If you have made too many claims or have been cited for one or more moving violations, your premium probably will be increased. If your driving record has deteriorated, the company may choose not to renew your policy. Your premiums cannot be increased, however, due to an accident in which you were not at fault. (Ins. Code § 491.)

EQUIPMENT, LICENSE AND REGISTRATION VIOLATIONS

These violations are correctable. If you fix the condition for which you got the ticket, you are entitled to have the violation erased, and it won't go on your record.

Equipment Violations

If your car has a minor problem, such as a broken tail light or missing mirror, you can be cited for an equipment violation. You should be given a chance to correct the problem and have the charges against you dismissed, unless the problem:

- was caused by persistent neglect (bald tires, for example)
- shows evidence of fraud (such as a forged registration sticker), or
- is an immediate safety hazard (such as a broken windshield).

After you repair the condition for which you were ticketed, you can get any highway patrolman or any police officer to certify that you have made the correction. (Call the sheriff or police department to arrange an appointment.) This can be done on the back of the ticket. Then, send the signed ticket to the traffic court, along with a $10 administrative fee, and the charges will be dismissed. (Veh. Code § 40610.)

License and Registration Violations

You are legally required to have your driver's license and proof of valid registration with you when driving. If you don't, an officer will usually cite you with a correctable violation. You can have any highway patrolman, police officer, or DMV employee certify (on the back of the citation) that you have a valid current license or registration. Send this certification and a $10 fee to the traffic court, and the violation will be dismissed.

If your license is not current or your vehicle is unregistered when you are stopped, you have committed a different offense. This is not correctable, since you cannot show proof that you were properly licensed or registered. You must get a license or proper registration and pay a substantial fine.

LICENSE SUSPENSIONS AND REVOCATIONS

The California Department of Motor Vehicles (DMV) is authorized to take away your driver's license under certain circumstances. If your license is taken for up to three years, this is considered a suspension. A revocation lasts more than three years. During the time your license is suspended or revoked, you are not legally allowed to drive a vehicle.

Suspension or Revocation Following a Hearing

If you commit any of the following acts, the DMV will hold a hearing to determine if your license should be suspended:

- **Negligent driving.** The DMV uses a point system to identify negligent drivers. A moving violation or accident that is your fault, as reported by an officer, counts as one point. Serious violations, such as reckless driving, hit-and-run, driving over 100 mph and driving under the influence of alcohol or drugs, count as two points. If you accumulate four points over any 12-month period, six points in a 24-month period, or eight points in a 36-month period, you are considered a negligent driver, and your license can be taken away.

  Even if your point count isn't high enough to be considered negligent under this formula, your license can be taken away if you:

  — are involved in an accident involving death, injury or serious damage to property (Veh. Code § 13800)

  — are involved in three or more accidents in a 12-month period (Veh. Code § 13800)

  — are convicted of reckless driving two or more times (Veh. Code § 13361)

  — are convicted of hit-and-run driving (Veh. Code § 13361)

  — are convicted of vehicular manslaughter (Veh. Code § 13800)

  — violate driving restrictions imposed on your license (Veh. Code § 13800)

- **Driving under the influence.** Your license can be suspended for four months for driving with a blood alcohol level of 0.08% or above. The DMV can impose a 1 year or 16 month license suspension for a second or third offense, respectively.
- **Refusing to take a blood, breath or urine test.** If you are stopped by an officer who suspects you of driving under the influence, you must submit to a test or lose your license for a year. You are entitled to a choice of tests, and the officer must inform you that your failure to take any test will result in a license suspension. If you have already had a suspension or conviction for driving under the influence, your license can be suspended for an additional two years. (Veh. Code § 13353.)

The DMV Hearing

The DMV will notify you of your right to a hearing before your license is suspended. If you don't request such a hearing, in writing, within 10 days from the date this notice was sent to you, you lose your right to dispute the suspension.

DEFENDING YOURSELF AT A DMV HEARING

You may bring witnesses and other evidence to the hearing if you wish. The referee will let you tell your side of the story, and will probably ask some questions about the violations. You will need to convince the referee that there are good reasons why your license should not be suspended. Evidence you should consider presenting includes:

- anything about the violations that is in your favor
- proof that an accident was not your fault
- testimony that you were not offered a choice of blood alcohol tests, or that the officer did not have reasonable cause to believe you were driving under the influence
- proof that you drive many miles a year
- evidence that your livelihood depends on your ability to drive
- statements by witnesses that you are a careful and good driver
- physician's reports of your physical condition and ability to drive
- evidence that you have recently completed a driver's training class.

The hearing will be conducted by a DMV "referee," who acts as a judge. The referee can suspend or revoke your license or put you on probation. The terms of probation may include a restricted license (one that allows you to drive only to work, for example) or a requirement that you take a driving class. You can appeal the referee's decision within 15 days to a DMV appeals board; you will receive information on how to appeal when you are sent the referee's decision.

Automatic Suspensions

The DMV will take away your license without a hearing if you are convicted of the following:

- a felony in which a vehicle was used (Veh. Code § 13350(c))
- causing injury or death while driving under the influence (Veh. Code § 13352)
- misdemeanor driving under the influence (Veh. Code § 13352)

- reckless driving, hit-and-run involving bodily injury or three convictions of hit-and-run or reckless driving within one year. (Veh. Code §§ 13350, 13351, 13355.)

MOVING VIOLATIONS

Many traffic offenses are infractions, which means that you cannot be sentenced to jail if you are convicted. The maximum fine for a first offense is $290. Most of these offenses are reported to the DMV, and go on your driving record; this may affect your insurance rates. Your license may also be suspended if you get numerous violations.

Speeding

It is always illegal to exceed 55 mph, unless you are on a freeway where the posted speed limit is 65 mph. (Veh. Code §§ 22349, 22356.)

A speeding citation can also be given if you exceed a safe speed. This is called the basic speed law. The basic speed law prohibits driving faster than is reasonable or prudent, considering conditions such as weather, visibility, traffic and the condition and size of the roadway, or driving at a speed that endangers people or property. Surprisingly, under the basic speed law, it is not necessarily illegal to exceed the posted limit on a street. The posted limit is presumed to be the fastest speed at which you can drive safely, but if the conditions merit, you may be speeding while driving beneath the posted limit, or driving safely above the limit. (Veh. Code §§ 22350, 22351.)

Not Stopping

You can be cited if you fail to come to a complete stop at a stop sign. You must stop at the limit line, crosswalk or the entrance to the intersection. You can also be cited for failure to stop if you enter an intersection while a stop light is red. (But as long as your front bumper enters the intersection while the light is yellow, you have not committed this offense.) (Veh. Code §§ 22450, 21453.)

Blocking the Box

It is illegal to enter an intersection unless there is enough room to get across without blocking traffic from either side. This is known as the Anti-Gridlock act. It is most often enforced when traffic is heavy or stopped, and vehicles are stuck in the intersection after the light changes. (Veh. Code § 22526.)

Improper Turning

Several offenses are related to turning. (Veh. Code §§ 22100-22106.)

- **Staying to the right or left edge of the road.** You must stay as close as practicable to the right or left edge of the street (in the lane that is travelling in your direction) when turning right or left.
- **Prohibited U-turns.** You may not make a U-turn if a sign prohibits it. In a business district, you can make a U-turn only at an intersection or opening in a divided highway. In a residential district, you can make a U-turn at any intersection that has a stop sign or light, or anywhere else as long as no car is approaching within 200 feet.
- **Unsafe turning and lane changes.** You must pull out and back up from a stopped position safely. You must signal turns for 100 feet before turning, and you must signal lane changes similarly if there is anyone behind you in any lane traveling in your direction.

Failure to Yield to Pedestrians

Drivers must yield the right-of-way to pedestrians who are crossing the street in a marked crosswalk or who are crossing at an intersection in an unmarked crosswalk. An unmarked crosswalk is the part of the street that would connect sidewalks on either side of an intersection. (Veh. Code § 21950(a).)

Miscellaneous Violations

A number of moving violations can be fairly lumped together under the category of rudeness. These include failure to yield the right of way, driving too slowly, blocking traffic, tailgating, driving improperly in a car-pool lane and improper passing.

Dealing with an Infraction Citation

You have several options for dealing with infraction citations. You can:
- pay the fine
- go to traffic school and pay the fine (if you do this, the offense won't go on your record)
- plead "guilty with an explanation" at an informal hearing or arraignment and hope that the judge will give you a smaller fine, or
- plead not guilty and fight the ticket.

If you decide to fight the ticket, you will appear before a judge at a trial. You may bring witnesses or evidence if you wish, and you will have the opportunity to cross-examine the officer who cited you. If the officer does not show up, you will be found innocent: the law requires that you be proven guilty, and only the officer's testimony can do that. (This may change, however, as some courts allow the officer's notes to be introduced at trial, even if the officer isn't present.)

PARKING TICKETS

Parking tickets are big business for the cities and towns that issue them—San Francisco, for example, took in $44 million on parking citations in fiscal year 1992.

If You Don't Pay

Parking tickets won't affect your driving record, as long as you take care of them by either paying the fine or fighting the ticket. But if you accumulate too many parking tickets or wait too long to pay them, the penalties can be severe. The city or county will notify the DMV, which will refuse to renew your registration until you have paid your fines plus an administrative fee. If you get five or more parking tickets in a five-day period, or if your car has no valid license plates, your car can be immobilized (using a Denver Boot) or towed and stored until you pay the fines. (Veh. Code § 22651, 22651.7.)

How To Fight a Parking Ticket

Parking tickets are no longer processed by the courts (except for appeals). Instead, they are handled by the city or county that issued the ticket, or by a private business which handles tickets for the city or county. To contest a parking ticket, you must contact the office listed on the ticket and explain why you don't think you should have to pay. The office will investigate your citation and will mail you the results of the investigation. The office will either cancel your parking ticket (and you are home free) or it will refuse to dismiss the ticket. If the office won't dismiss the ticket, then you will have to request a hearing within 15 days of the mailing of the written denial by mailing the fine with a letter requesting a hearing as soon as possible. You will then be notified by mail of a hearing date. If you win, the fine is refunded to you. (Veh. Code § 40215.)

REGISTRATION AND SMOG TESTS

Every year, you must renew the registration on your car. (Veh. Code § 4600.) If you bring a car here from another state, you must register it within 20 days. (Veh. Code § 4152.5.)

The state may require your car to pass a smog test before you can renew your registration. If your car doesn't pass on the first try, there is a cap on the amount you must spend to bring it into compliance, depending on the car's year:

Model Year	Allowed Charge
1966-71	$50
1972-74	$90
1975-79	$125
1980-89	$175
1990 and newer	$300

If your emissions control equipment (smog equipment) has been removed, modified or disconnected, the cost limits do not apply—you must pay whatever it takes to get your car to comply.

If your vehicle cannot be brought into compliance within the cost limit, call the Bureau of Automotive Repair at (800) 952-5210. BAR may refer you to a Referee Station to issue you a waiver.

- **New cars.** If your car is still under warranty, you are entitled to have defects that cause it to fail a smog test corrected for free by the dealer.
- **Used cars.** The seller is required to give the buyer an original smog certificate, not more than 90 days old. If the vehicle is being transferred to a person's grandparent, parent, spouse, child or grandchild, the old owner does not have to supply a smog certificate.
- **Diesel vehicles.** Diesel vehicles are exempt from smog checks. Owners can fill out the back of their auto renewal registration exempting themselves if the vehicle registration indicates the vehicle is a diesel. If the registration says "gasoline fueled," the owner must have the car examined by a BAR referee station to get an exemption.

SEAT BELT AND CHILD RESTRAINT REQUIREMENTS

California requires all passengers to wear a seat belt or other safety restraint.

Seat Belts

Every passenger over the age of four must wear a seat belt, unless a disability prevents it. If any passenger is not wearing a seat belt when the car is pulled over, the driver may get a ticket. In addition, any passenger over the age of 16 who is not wearing a seat belt may be personally cited. The fine for a first offense is $20.

The owner of a vehicle is personally responsible for maintaining seat belts in working order. If a car is pulled over and the seat belts are not in usable condition, the owner may be cited, even if she is not in the car at the time.

People riding in the back of open pickup or flatbed trucks must wear safety belts. This restriction does not apply on farms or if the back of the truck is enclosed. (Veh. Code § 23116.)

The law used to prohibit officers from stopping cars only for suspected seat belt violations; only if the driver was pulled over for another suspected offense could the officer issue a seat belt citation. However, police and highway patrolmen are now allowed to stop drivers for seat belt violations alone. (Veh. Code § 27315.)

Car Seats for Children

Every child under the age of four or weighing less than 40 pounds must be in a "child passenger restraint system"—a government-approved child car seat, usually with a harness, that fits into a passenger seat—while riding in a vehicle. The person who gets the ticket is the child's parent or, if no parent is in the car, the driver. The fine for a first offense is $100.

The police can stop a car if they suspect that a child in the car is not in a proper car seat. (Veh. Code §§ 27360, 27361.)

INDEX

...more books from Nolo Press

ESTATE PLANNING & PROBATE

Make Your Own Living Trust, *Clifford*	1st Ed	$19.95	LITR
Plan Your Estate With a Living Trust, *Clifford*	2nd Ed	$19.95	NEST
Nolo's Simple Will Book, *Clifford*	2nd Ed	$17.95	SWIL
Who Will Handle Your Finances If You Can't?, *Clifford & Randolph*	1st Ed	$19.95	FINA
The Conservatorship Book, *Goldoftas & Farren*	1st Ed	$24.95	CNSV
How to Probate an Estate, *Nissley*	7th Ed	$34.95	PAE
Nolo's Law Form Kit: Wills, *Clifford & Goldoftas*	1st Ed	$14.95	KWL
Write Your Will (audio cassette), *Warner & Greene*	1st Ed	$14.95	TWYW
5 Ways to Avoid Probate (audio cassette), *Warner & Greene*	1st Ed	$14.95	TPRO

GOING TO COURT

Represent Yourself in Court, *Bergman & Berman-Barrett*	1st Ed	$29.95	RYC
Everybody's Guide to Municipal Court, *Duncan*	1st Ed	$29.95	MUNI
Everybody's Guide to Small Claims Court, *Warner*	11th Ed	$16.95	CSCC
Fight Your Ticket, *Brown*	5th Ed	$18.95	FYT
Collect Your Court Judgment, *Scott, Elias & Goldoftas*	2nd Ed	$19.95	JUDG
How to Change Your Name, *Loeb & Brown*	5th Ed	$19.95	NAME
The Criminal Records Book, *Siegel*	3rd Ed	$19.95	CRIM
Winning in Small Claims Court, *Warner & Greene* (audio cassette)	1st Ed	$14.95	TWIN

LEGAL REFORM

Legal Breakdown: 40 Ways to Fix Our Legal System, *Nolo Press*	1st Ed	$8.95	LEG

BUSINESS & WORKPLACE

💾 Software Development: A Legal Guide, *Fishman*	1st Ed	$44.95	SFT
The Legal Guide for Starting & Running a Small Business, *Steingold*	1st Ed	$22.95	RUNS
Sexual Harassment on the Job, *Petrocelli & Repa*	1st Ed	$14.95	HARS
Your Rights in the Workplace, *Repa*	2nd Ed	$15.95	YRW
How to Write a Business Plan, *McKeever*	4th Ed	$19.95	SBS
Marketing Without Advertising, *Phillips & Rasberry*	1st Ed	$14.00	MWAD
The Partnership Book, *Clifford & Warner*	4th Ed	$24.95	PART`
The California Nonprofit Corporation Handbook, *Mancuso*	6th Ed	$29.95	NON
💾 The California Nonprofit Corporation Handbook, *Mancuso*	DOS	$39.95	NPI
	MAC	$39.95	NPM
How to Form Your Own California Corporation, *Mancuso*	7th Ed	$29.95	CCOR
The California Professional Corporation Handbook, *Mancuso*	5th Ed	$34.95	PROF
The Independent Paralegal's Handbook, *Warner*	2nd Ed	$24.95	PARA
Getting Started as an Independent Paralegal, *Warner* (audio cassette)	2nd Ed	$44.95	GSIP
How To Start Your Own Business:			
Small Business Law, *Warner & Greene* (audio cassette)	1st Ed	$14.95	TBUS

💾 = Books With Disk

THE NEIGHBORHOOD

Neighbor Law: Fences, Trees, Boundaries & Noise, *Jordan*	1st Ed	$14.95	NEI
Safe Home, Safe Neighborhoods: Stopping Crime Where You Live,			
Mann & Blakeman	1st Ed	$14.95	SAFE
Dog Law, *Randolph*	2nd Ed	$12.95	DOG

MONEY MATTERS

Stand Up to the IRS, *Daily*	2nd Ed	$21.95	SIRS
Money Troubles: Legal Strategies to Cope With Your Debts, *Leonard*	2nd Ed	$16.95	MT
How to File for Bankruptcy, *Elias, Renauer & Leonard*	4th Ed	$25.95	HFB
Simple Contracts for Personal Use, *Elias & Stewart*	2nd Ed	$16.95	CONT
Nolo's Law Form Kit: Power of Attorney,*Clifford, Randolph & Goldoftas*	1st Ed	$14.95	KPA
Nolo's Law Form Kit: Personal Bankruptcy,			
Elias, Renauer, Leonard & Goldoftas	1st Ed	$14.95	KBNK
Nolo's Law Form Kit: Rebuild Your Credit, *Leonard & Goldoftas*	1st Ed	$14.95	KCRD
Nolo's Law Form Kit: Loan Agreements, *Stewart & Goldoftas*	1st Ed	$14.95	KLOAN
Nolo's Law Form Kit: Buy & Sell Contracts, *Elias, Stewart & Goldoftas*	1st Ed	$9.95	KCONT

FAMILY MATTERS

How To Raise Or Lower Child Support In California, *Duncan & Siegal*	2nd Ed	$17.95	CHLD
Divorce & Money, *Woodhouse & Felton-Collins with Blakeman*	2nd Ed	$21.95	DIMO
The Living Together Kit, *Ihara & Warner*	6th Ed	$17.95	LTK
The Guardianship Book, *Goldoftas & Brown*	1st Ed	$19.95	GB
A Legal Guide for Lesbian and Gay Couples, *Curry & Clifford*	7th Ed	$21.95	LG
How to Do Your Own Divorce, *Sherman*	19th Ed	$21.95	CDIV
Practical Divorce Solutions, *Sherman*	1st Ed	$14.95	PDS
California Marriage & Divorce Law, *Warner, Ihara & Elias*	11th Ed	$19.95	MARR
How to Adopt Your Stepchild in California, *Zagone & Randolph*	4th Ed	$22.95	ADOP
Nolo's Pocket Guide to Family Law, *Leonard & Elias*	3rd Ed	$14.95	FLD

JUST FOR FUN

29 Reasons Not to Go to Law School, *Warner & Ihara*	3rd Ed	$9.95	29R
Devil's Advocates, *Roth & Roth*	1st Ed	$12.95	DA
Poetic Justice, *Roth & Roth*	1st Ed	$8.95	PJ

PATENT, COPYRIGHT & TRADEMARK

Trademark: How To Name Your Business & Product,			
McGrath & Elias, with Shena	1st Ed	$29.95	TRD
Patent It Yourself, *Pressman*	3rd Ed	$36.95	PAT
The Inventor's Notebook, *Grissom & Pressman*	1st Ed	$19.95	INOT
The Copyright Handbook, *Fishman*	1st Ed	$24.95	COHA

LANDLORDS & TENANTS

The Landlord's Law Book, Vol. 1: Rights & Responsibilities,			
Brown & Warner	4th Ed	$32.95	LBRT
The Landlord's Law Book, Vol. 2: Evictions, *Brown*	4th Ed	$32.95	LBEV
Tenants' Rights, *Moskovitz & Warner*	11th Ed	$15.95	CTEN
Nolo's Law Form Kit: Leases & Rental Agreements, *Warner & Stewart*	1st Ed	$14.95	KLEAS

HOMEOWNERS

How to Buy a House in California, *Warner, Serkes & Devine*	2nd Ed	$19.95	BHCA
For Sale By Owner, *Devine*	2nd Ed	$24.95	FSBO
Homestead Your House, *Warner, Sherman & Ihara*	8th Ed	$9.95	HOME
The Deeds Book, *Randolph*	2nd Ed	$15.95	DEED

OLDER AMERICANS

Beat the Nursing Home Trap: A Consumer's Guide to Choosing & Financing Long Term Care, *Matthews*	2nd Ed	$18.95	ELD
Social Security, Medicare & Pensions, *Matthews with Berman*	5th Ed	$15.95	SOA

RESEARCH/REFERENCE

Legal Research, *Elias & Levinkind*	3rd Ed	$19.95	LRES
Legal Research Made Easy: A Roadmap Through the Law Library Maze (2-1/2 hr videotape & manual), *Nolo & Legal Star*	1st Ed	$89.95	LRME

CONSUMER

How To Get A Green Card: Legal Ways To Stay In The U.S.A., *Nicolas Lewis*	1st Ed	$19.95	GRN
How to Win Your Personal Injury Claim, *Matthews*	1st Ed	$24.95	PICL
Nolo's Pocket Guide to California Law, *Guerin & Nolo Press Editors*	2nd Ed	$10.95	CLAW
Nolo's Pocket Guide to California Law on Disk,	DOS	$24.95	CLI
Guerin & Nolo Press Editors	MAC	$24.95	CLM
Nolo's Law Form Kit: Hiring Child Care & Household Help, *Repa & Goldoftas*	1st Ed	$14.95	KCHLD
Nolo's Pocket Guide to Consumer Rights, *Kaufman*	2nd Ed	$12.95	CAG

SOFTWARE

WillMaker 5.0, *Nolo Press*	Windows	$69.95	WI5
	DOS	$69.95	WI5
	MAC	$69.95	WM5
Nolo's Personal RecordKeeper 3.0, *Pladsen & Warner*	DOS	$49.95	FRI3
	MAC	$49.95	FRM3
Nolo's Living Trust 1.0, *Randolph*	MAC	$79.95	LTM1
Nolo's Partnership Maker 1.0, *Mancuso & Radtke*	DOS	$129.95	PAGI1
California Incorporator 1.0, *Mancuso*	DOS	$129.00	INCI

RECYCLE YOUR OUT-OF-DATE BOOKS AND GET 25% OFF YOUR NEXT PURCHASE
It's important to have the most current legal information. Because laws and legal procedures change often, we update our books regularly. To help keep you up-to-date we are extending this special offer. Cut out and mail the title portion of the cover of any old Nolo book with your next order and we'll give you a 25% discount off the retail price of ANY new Nolo book you purchase directly from us. For current prices and editions call us at 1 (800) 992-6656.

This offer is to individuals only. Prices subject to change.

ORDER FORM

Code	Quantity	Title	Unit price	Total

	Subtotal	
	California residents add Sales Tax	
Shipping & Handling ($4 for 1st item; $1 each additional)		
2nd day UPS (additional $5; $8 in Alaska and Hawaii)		
	TOTAL	

Name

Address

(UPS to street address, Priority Mail to P.O. boxes)

FOR FASTER SERVICE, USE YOUR CREDIT CARD AND OUR TOLL-FREE NUMBERS

Monday-Friday, 7 a.m. to 6 p.m. Pacific Time

Order Line	1 (800) 992-6656 (in the 510 area code, call 549-1976)
General Information	1 (510) 549-1976
Fax your order	1 (800) 645-0895 (in the 510 area code, call 548-5902)

METHOD OF PAYMENT

☐ Check enclosed

☐ VISA ☐ Mastercard ☐ Discover Card ☐ American Express

Account #   **Expiration Date**

Authorizing Signature

Daytime Phone

Allow 2-3 weeks for delivery.
Prices subject to change.

SEND TO: Nolo Press, 950 Parker Street, Berkeley, CA 94710

free nolo news subscription

Register and get our quarterly newspaper, the *Nolo News*, free for two years (U.S. addresses only.) Here's what you'll get in every issue:

Informative articles on such topics as: family law, wills, debts, consumer rights, and much more.

Update Service to keep you informed of changes in the laws that affect Nolo books and software.

Reviews of good consumer and legal books and software from other publishers.

Answers to your legal questions.

Complete catalog of Nolo books and software.

Our famous Lawyer Joke column.

We promise never to give your name and address to any other organization.

NOLO'S POCKET GUIDE TO CALIFORNIA LAW

REGISTRATION CARD

We'd like to know what you think! Please take a moment to fill out and return this postage-paid card for a free two-year subscription to the *Nolo News*. If you already receive the *Nolo News*, we'll extend your subscription.

Name _____ Phone _____

Address _____

City _____ State _____ Zip _____

Where did you hear about this book? _____

For what purpose did you use this book? _____

Comments: _____

_____

_____

_____

_____

Thank You

CLAW 2.0

BUSINESS REPLY MAIL
FIRST CLASS MAIL PERMIT NO. 3283 BERKELEY CA

POSTAGE WILL BE PAID BY ADDRESSEE

NOLO PRESS
950 PARKER STREET
BERKELEY CA 94710-9867